JESUS · A NEW BIOGRAPHY

JESUS

A NEW BIOGRAPHY

By SHIRLEY JACKSON CASE

GREENWOOD PRESS, PUBLISHERS
NEW YORK

PREFACE

THE following pages have been written with a single purpose in mind. They seek to depict Jesus as he actually appeared to the men of his own time in Palestine nineteen hundred years ago. Today portraits of him, whether products of brush or pen, are legion. Their variety grows constantly more perplexing, even though they often show Jesus in poses and colors highly pleasing to the eye of the present-day observer. But the inquirer asks, "Is the picture true to life?"

To answer this question is the duty of historical research. Scholars have worked long and laboriously at the task of recovering the story of Jesus' career. Their energies have centered especially upon a critical examination of the gospels, where they have been so successful in separating later from earlier strata that their conclusions regarding the date and character of one or another of the several documents have become virtually canonical. Today it is common practice to trust mainly "Q" and Mark for historical matters, while John and tradition peculiar to Matthew or Luke become a sort of new apocry-

PREFACE

pha. In the more primitive documents the Jesus of history is thought to be correctly portrayed.

The foregoing procedure is not exactly the method of the present book. While literary criticism has not been ignored, more attention has been given to social orientation. By a too mechanical application of critical technique, "documentarianism," like any other "ism," may ultimately prove subversive of historical truth. One too easily forgets that the picture in the oldest of the documents is also an artist's creation. As history, it has two inevitable defects. It contains too much and too little. It has to be reduced, on the one side, by removing features that owe their presence to the creative impulses of the author and his Christian associates at the moment when the document was written. On the other hand, it has to be supplemented by information, wherever the data may be found, that had escaped the writer's notice. Especially is it necessary to enlarge his horizon by a more complete integration of Jesus within the distinctively Jewish setting where he had actually lived. The present volume has been written with more than usual emphasis upon the social point of view, both in handling the early Christian literature and in reproducing the story of Jesus' life and religion.

PREFACE

This book may be read as a sequel to the earlier volume, *The Historicity of Jesus*, in which the contentions of those who deny his existence were subjected to careful examination.

SHIRLEY JACKSON CASE

UNIVERSITY OF CHICAGO
February 15, 1927

TABLE OF CONTENTS

INTRODUCTION

SOME nineteen centuries ago Jews of Galilee living in and about the city of Capernaum heard it reported that a certain Joshua from Nazareth had appeared in their midst in the rôle of itinerant prophet. At the outset his activity may have occasioned no unusual comment, for the religious agitator was a familiar figure among the Jews. In the course of time this new preacher created a stir among the people, but he never became generally popular throughout Palestine. Most of his followers deserted him toward the close of his career, and even his most faithful disciples were sadly disappointed by his tragic death.

The rejected prophet will soon have been forgotten even by those Jews of Jerusalem who knew of his crucifixion. For them he was only one among hundreds of others executed from time to time by the Romans as part of their policy to stay by violence the rising tide of Jewish revolution. But presently both Jews and Romans learned that the friends of the martyred Nazarene had acquired a fresh confidence in their deceased leader and were conducting in his honor a vigorous missionary enterprise. At a comparatively early date the new movement spread from its original Palestinian home to distant gentile lands. Before the close of a century it was represented by groups of adherents in all important centers of population about the Mediterranean and had produced a literature in which its founder was unequivocally declared to be the Messiah (Christ) whose coming had been foretold in the ancient scriptures, the Lord of the universe with a dignity and authority second only to that of God, and the one all-sufficient savior of mankind.

During the lifetime of Jesus not even his most ardent admirers seem ever to have realized how great were to be his honors as the Lord Jesus Christ of future Christendom. Their tardiness in ascribing to him unexampled dignity while on earth contrasts sharply with that heightening of appreciation which followed so quickly upon his death. This circumstance has bequeathed to Christianity a multiple portrait of its founder.

In one picture Jesus is the persecuted Galilean, living devoutly among his fellow-Jews, persuading a few of his contemporaries to join him in the struggle to attain his ideals of righteousness, and arousing in others a strong feeling of antagonism. Sometimes he exults in the joyous consciousness of communion with his heavenly Father, again he wrestles in prayer when faced by overwhelming difficulties, and finally he exclaims in agony on the cross "My God, my God, why hast thou forsaken me!" (Mark 15:34). Over this portrait might fittingly be inscribed the simple title "The Earthly Jesus."

In a second picture one beholds the form of a glorified being exalted to a position of power at God's right hand in the heavens. The lowly crucified one of earthly memory has now been "made both Lord and Christ" (Acts 2:36). His chief significance no longer lies in his own personal religious living, but in his right to be central in the religion of his followers, who revere and even worship him side by side with God. Eternal destinies are now to be determined by attitudes taken toward this heavenly Lord. Those who confess their faith in him as the Christ promised in ancient prophecy are believed to enjoy the full favor of heaven, while those who refuse him this honor rest under the condemnation of divine displeasure. As here portrayed, Jesus is the founder of a new religion through his triumph over death and his elevation to dignity in heaven, where he has become a worthy object of trust and adoration on the part of his devotees. As thus portrayed, he is distinctively "the heaven-exalted Christ."

The status of Jesus prior to his career on earth is the theme of still a third portrait. Here he is shown pre-existing in heaven and possessing a divine authority which he voluntarily relinquishes to take upon himself human shape and live in servant-like fashion on earth (Phil. 2:5–8). He is the divine Logos (Word), the only begotten Son of God, come down from heaven (John 1:1–18). While the main outlines of this picture are sketched in a few bold strokes, the details for the most part remain obscure. Evidently it was thought sufficient to make plain that the earthly Jesus had heavenly antecedents befitting one who after death was to be elevated to the dignity of the glorified Messiah. A suitable title for the figure here portrayed is "The Preexistent Logos."

These three types of representation were all present in early Christianity. Indeed, often they were freely and variously blended to produce such composite pictures as were needed from time to time to meet the requirements of the new religion. Its first preachers were under constant pressure to emphasize the figure of the heavenly Christ and to overlay the story of his earthly career with colors appropriate to both his pre-existent and his post-resurrection dignity. One of the most urgent demands made upon the Christian missionary was to show that the life of the Galilean carpenter, when reviewed in the light of subsequent events, exhibited clear indications both of the future honors awaiting him as risen Lord and of that afterglow of divine glory which would inevitably adhere to the human form of one who had previously dwelt with God in heaven.

Thus interest in the earthly Jesus was gradually overshadowed by Christendom's concern with its heaven-exalted Christ and its pre-existent Son of God. This state of affairs was already well advanced in the second half of the first century, when the New Testament books came into existence. Again, in the so-called "Apostles' Creed," that earliest formulated declaration of belief that has survived from the ancient church, Christian thinking leaped directly from "born of the Virgin Mary" to "suffered under Pontius Pilate." Henceforth attention centered on Christ as Lord and Savior, while the features of the lowly Jesus of Nazareth gradually faded out of

[5]

the picture. To deny the reality of his earthly career was, indeed, an unpardonable offense, but to interest one's self chiefly in the human side of his living likewise involved sure condemnation for heresy.

In more recent times, however, there has been a vigorous growth of interest in a return to the earthly Jesus. To reconstruct, from Christianity's composite portrait of its Lord Jesus Christ, a reliable account of his career on earth has been the ambition of an increasing number of scholars since the early part of the last century. This quest grows ever more insistent from year to year. We of today would see Jesus, the real Jesus of history, exactly as he lived in Palestine among his contemporaries nineteen hundred years ago.

CHAPTER I
ANCIENT BIOGRAPHIES
OF JESUS

WHERE is an accurate portrait of the real Jesus of history to be found? Although he had lived in Palestine, there is no mention of him in the few brief Palestinian Jewish writings that have survived from the first half of the first century A.D. Outside of the narrow circle of his personal friends he figured inconspicuously in Jewish history. His disciples alone preserved his memory. Although he had left no autobiography, his picturesque career early made a strong appeal to the narrative impulses of those devoted followers whose fidelity withstood the shock of the crucifixion.

At first the story of Jesus' life and teaching was a subject of informal conversation among his surviving friends. In the course of time portions of this early oral tradition were written down to be read for edification in the absence of a preacher whose memory could be drawn upon for this information. As the number of the disciples multiplied, there was a growing demand for suitable materials to use in the meetings of the congregations. In the meantime the ranks of the relatively small group that could personally recall memories of Jesus were destined to diminish, while the need for written records rapidly increased. At least one formal biography had taken shape about the year 70 A.D., and before the close of the century several others had appeared.

Four of these books proved especially popular. They were read not only by individuals in private but also at the gatherings of Christian communities, where ultimately they were given an honored place in public worship side by side with the ancient Jewish scriptures. By the close of the second century their prestige had become so great as to result in a general belief that no other "Life" of Jesus—there now were several others in circulation—could be read in the services of the Christian congregations. Henceforth they alone were to rank as "canonical" gospels, while their competitors were destined to be styled "apocryphal."

In the absence of copyright laws to protect their integrity, even the canonical gospels—Matthew, Mark, Luke, and John—soon suffered

severely at the hands of abbreviators and har-
monizers who had little or no regard for the proprietary rights of the several authors. For more
than seventeen centuries it has been the custom
to dismember, mutilate, and rearrange the contents of these books in order to force from them a
single composite narrative called a "harmony"
or "synopsis." Tatian, about 175 A.D., seems
to have been the first to accomplish this feat.
His *Diatessaron*, as it is commonly called, opens
with the first five verses of John, then follows a
stringing together in succession of Luke 1:5–80;
Matt. 1:18–25; Luke 2:1–39; Matt. 2:1–23; and
so forth to the end of the composite gospel story.
Tatian has had a long line of successors, extend-
ing down even to the present day.

Indiscriminate blending of the gospels results
in a conglomerate account of Jesus' career that
would have caused excruciating agony to any
one of the original evangelists had it come under
his eye. Here he would have observed the con-
tinuity of his own narrative often interrupted
by paragraphs inserted from another book. He
would have noted, on occasion, violent distor-
tions due to the forcing of his materials into a different framework. And he would have had to lament the complete wreck of the specific unity of

[9]

impression and distinctive purpose that his book had aimed to accomplish. But so popular has the harmonizing method proved, as used in modern books on Jesus, in Sunday-school helps, and the like, that ability to read the gospels separately and appreciate the genius of each has to-day become for many persons a lost art.

Until this lost art is recovered, the earthly career of Jesus may remain more veiled than revealed in the gospels. To ignore the originality of each writer, to miss his peculiar point of view, and to remain unaware of the specific interests he designed his work to serve, will inevitably result in great confusion for one who seeks from these documents simply to recover the life-story of the earthly Jesus. We have here to do with separate "Lives" of Jesus each marked by an individuality as pronounced as that which might characterize any similar, number of books written today on the same theme. Each gospel presents a distinctive portrait of its subject.

I

The Marcan description of Jesus places much emphasis on his deeds. It is true that on the first day of his public activity he is said to have arrested the attention of people in the synagogue at

Capernaum by his words. They were all so amazed that "they questioned among themselves saying, What is this? It is a new teaching!" This astonishment had resulted, however, not from any extended discourse of Jesus on moral and spiritual ideals, but from the miracle-working power of his utterances: "With authority he commands even the unclean spirits and they obey him."

Mark contains little or nothing corresponding to those familiar and now highly prized teachings of Jesus found in such narratives as Matthew's Sermon on the Mount, or Luke's Sermon on the Plain, or the remarkable discourse on comfort and promise recorded in chapters 14–17 of the Gospel of John. In Mark, Jesus is conspicuously a performer of mighty deeds. His fiat is instantly effective for the expulsion of demons, the cleansing of lepers, and the revitalizing of palsied limbs. He has authority to overrule the sacred institution of the Sabbath, to forgive men's sins or to withhold forgiveness, to declare the power of Satan broken, to calm a tempestuous sea, to raise the dead, to transform a few loaves and fishes into abundant provisions for a large multitude, to open blind eyes, to make deaf people hear, to loose the tongue of the dumb, to restore the epileptic to health, and to forecast his own triumph over death.

While in Mark Jesus is pre-eminently a figure in action, at the same time he is the bringer of a very definite message, the truth of which he both demonstrates in his conduct and inculcates by his words. He opens his ministry with a prophetic announcement that the time is fulfilled for the Kingdom of God to be established. Right to membership in this new régime is conditioned upon repentance and belief in the good news, of which Jesus is both the herald and the occasion. He formally proclaims the imminence of the Kingdom and exhibits in his own powerful deeds the anticipated blessings of this new order. With the beginning of his public ministry the new age casts its shadow before, and its benefits are already available for such as respond to his summons. But his earthly activity is only preparatory to that impending climactic event "when the Son of Man comes in the glory of his Father with the holy angels" (8:38). This display of heavenly power, to constitute the final scene in the establishment of the Kingdom, will not occur until after the death of Jesus. Yet it is so near at hand and so closely linked with his life-work that certain of his personal companions are expected to live to see its consummation (9:1; 13:30). The forecast of unusual incidents immediately to precede its advent constitutes one of the most lengthy discourses of Jesus reported in Mark (chap. 13).

In the Marcan picture Jesus is also the author of the present Christian society which has been intrusted with the task of perpetuating the new cause during the interim between his death and his early triumphal return from heaven. The first readers of this book must have derived from it much encouragement, as they learned of the wonderful dynamic that had come into their demon-oppressed world through the activity of the founder of the new religion. They would also find much here to assure them of his definite provision for the unhappy conditions by which they themselves were now surrounded. From its pages they would learn that early in his career Jesus had officially designated those leaders to whom the new movement looked for guidance in the crucial period following the crucifixion. These "Twelve," like their master, had power over evil spirits and were commissioned to reiterate his summons to repentance (3:14–19; 6:7–13). Also the rites of the new cult, particularly baptism and the Lord's Supper, were seen to derive their authority from his words and deeds. The missionary enterprise that had now been pushed even beyond Palestine among gentile peoples at large, in the hope of bringing about an early realization of the Kingdom of God, likewise found its sanction in the example and teachings of Jesus. It had been his aim to train disciples for just this sort of activity, and he had extensively anticipated the difficulties and discouragements which they were now encountering.

At first, even on gentile soil, the greatest hostility to the new religion came naturally from Judaism, with which Christianity had most in common. Accordingly, in Mark there is a lively interest in portraying the opposition between Jesus and his Jewish contemporaries. As the official representative of the new Kingdom, he had been superior even to Mosaic ordinances and much more to rabbinic traditions. In fact he possessed a new esoteric wisdom, the "mystery of the Kingdom of God," to be freely revealed only to the inner circle of disciples. Publicly it was preached only in parables in order that the few who had "ears to hear" might enter into the secret, while the veiled form of presentation would hide it from the Jewish multitudes and thus prevent their wholesale appropriation of its benefits (4:2–34). If Jesus had taken such precautions against the entrance of his Jewish kinsmen into the Kingdom, how fitting that his disciples should find the breach widening between themselves and the Jews, while new converts were being secured in larger and larger numbers from among Gentiles! Thus the exigency that had forced the new religion out of its native habitat and compelled it to seek a new home among strangers was discovered in reality to have been strictly in accord with its founder's own designs.

Christians who now saw in Jesus' own procedure a deliberate effort to conceal his unique character and purposes from his Jewish contemporaries could escape the stigma that otherwise might have attached to his failure and theirs to win a substantial following among Jews. If the new religion could not succeed in its original home, should it be thought worthy of attention by Gentiles? In the Marcan story, Jesus himself very effectively answers this question even before it is definitely formulated as a problem of the missionary enterprise. Not because his message was lacking in power of appeal did it fail among those to whom it was first addressed. On the contrary, divine intervention was necessary to prevent its being an inevitable success from the start. Eyes were blinded and hearts hardened and parables used to veil the truth in order that the successful period of the new religion's history might be reserved for the hopes of those who were laboring in the gentile field at the time the Gospel of Mark was composed.

An early Christian missionary had many obstacles to encounter, whether in a Jewish or a gentile environment. As yet there had been no abatement of those typical forces of opposition listed by Paul in a memorable paragraph: "Of the Jews five times received I forty stripes save one. Thrice was I beaten with rods, once was I stoned, thrice I suffered shipwreck, a night and a day have I been in the deep; in journeyings often, in perils of rivers, in perils of robbers, in perils from my countrymen, in perils from the Gentiles, in perils in the city, in perils in the wilderness, in perils in the sea, in perils among false brethren; in labor and travail, in watchings often, in hunger and thirst, in fastings often, in cold and nakedness" (II Cor. 11:24–27; cf. I Cor. 4:9–13). To these inconveniences presently were to be added new troubles caused by the Roman authorities, following the notorious example of Nero who in 64 A.D. made the social un-popularity of Christians the basis for criminal accusation and persecution. At the time Mark was written, martyrdom, as a menace and as an ideal, had already loomed conspicuously on the Christian horizon. It is no accident that almost half of this book is given over to the record of the last week of Jesus' life, when the combined hostility of Jews and Gentiles furnishes the background against which to display Jesus' own glorification of the martyr-ideal.

Throughout the Gospel of Mark, Jesus figures conspicuously as the official founder of a new religion. He had been the authentic herald and preliminary inaugurator of the Kingdom of God foretold by the prophets. At baptism he had received the Holy Spirit and was thus supernaturally qualified to lead in the combat against the forces of evil headed by Satan. The demons were filled with alarm the moment Jesus appeared in their vicinity. Ordinary people might see nothing unusual about his personality; but evil spirits, since they also belonged to the supernatural world, were aware of the victory that Jesus had won when tempted by Satan, the prince of demons. Having this knowledge, they trembled in terror before the superior force which he embodied in his person as a result of his unique possession of the Holy Spirit (1:24; 5:7).

This same official equipment marked him as the worthy object of men's faith. Failure to recognize in him the presence of supernatural power deprived one of the benefits of his miracle-working activity, as when the people of Nazareth through their lack of confidence missed the opportunity to profit by his presence (6:5 f.). Unbelief was cause for astonishment, if not indeed for condemnation; and to deny that the superior dynamic of his personality was due to the presence in him of the Holy Spirit was the one unpardonable sin (3:29 f.).

Unquestionably, the author of Mark was greatly concerned to make plain that Jesus was Christianity's heaven-appointed founder who had been fully worthy of his contemporaries' admiration and reverence. In all of this he was distinctly and pre-eminently the Christ of faith. Yet the signal failure of his immediate associates to perceive his real dignity and to appreciate his unique personality also remained for this evangelist an impressive fact.

In their failure to appraise Jesus correctly, his enemies had been hardly more obtuse than his most intimate friends. Early in his public activity the members of his own family, including even his mother, on learning of his unusual doings and of the stir he was creating, concluded that he had become mentally unbalanced; and they would have taken him home by force (3:21, 31). The especially chosen disciples, although daily in the company of their master, had been scarcely more discerning. On different occasions they had been slow to perceive the meaning of his teaching and had quite failed to comprehend the fulness of his power. During a storm at sea they had been distracted with fear even though he was present with them in the boat. When he had calmed the storm and reproved their tardy confidence in his ability, they were filled with fear, but they still lacked a genuine understanding of what manner of person he actually was (4:35–41). Numerous similar displays of his might did not prevent them from mildly chiding him for asking a seemingly unnecessary question about who had touched him on a particular occasion when they were moving along with a great crowd of people (5:31). Still later when in a desert place with only five loaves and two fishes, apparently they never anticipated that he by blessing their meager supply of food would be able to make it sufficient for the needs of a company of five thousand (6:35–44; cf. 8:1–9). With this incident still fresh in memory they were nevertheless "amazed" that he should be able to walk on the water and again to calm a storm (6:51 f.).

It is reported in Mark that Peter ultimately ascribed to Jesus the honor of messiahship. But this remarkable recognition of dignity was not so penetrating as to prevent an almost immediate protest from Peter against Jesus' own forecast of coming events (8:27–33). His talk about a triumph through martyrdom had seemed to his companions incomprehensible, while they were holding in store for him a more tangible victory that would yield them positions of honor in his cabinet and a substantial remuneration for their fidelity (9:31–34; 10:28–31, 35–45). When the opposition to Jesus neared a climax they lost even such confidence in his prestige as they had earlier entertained. On his entry into Jerusalem they had hailed him as the restorer of David's kingdom (11:8–10), but presently they found him admitting the propriety of paying tribute to Caesar, who was now the hated possessor of David's domain (12:13–17). With the unfavorable turn of events, even the Twelve were overtaken by forebodings of disaster. The confidence of Judas was so badly shaken that he forsook the company altogether, and although the others continued with Jesus they found themselves enveloped by an increasing darkness of fear and perplexity. Instead of holding royal offices in Jerusalem under a new triumphant king of the Davidic line, they found themselves hiding in a garden with one who seemed to be only the helpless prey of scheming opponents. When their master's arrest, trial, and condemnation followed in rapid succession, the disillusionment became complete.

Taken as a whole, the Marcan interest in Jesus must be pronounced dominantly interpretative in character. Even in those sections of the book that portray most vividly the humble and unofficial side of Jesus' career there is a pervasive apologetic atmosphere. Only on the assumption that Jesus had deliberately concealed from the public his real dignity is the evangelist able to account for the failure of his contemporaries to render him the full honors now believed to be his due. Even his disciples had been strangely stupid; their eyes had been blinded, and their hearts hardened. Had he been fully understood, surely everybody would have assumed toward him an attitude of unyielding allegiance. In that event the fact of appreciation would have been the dominant, indeed perhaps the exclusive, feature to be noted in the story of his career. But this ideal is conceded to have been only very imperfectly realized during Jesus' own lifetime. The less spectacular features of his career were still too well remembered to permit of an absolutely free idealization of the past. Although the evangelist had only a secondary interest in the personal religious living of his incomparable hero, the colors appropriate to the Christ of his faith were not spread so thickly upon the canvas as to obscure completely the earlier outlines of an earthly Jesus.

II

No essential characteristic of the Marcan representation of Jesus is lacking in either Matthew or Luke. It is true that at some points these later artists deviate from their model, but in general their copy is very faithfully done. In particular they are at pains to preserve, and occasionally to heighten, those features in the picture that made Jesus the worthy object of religious reverence—his endowment by the Holy Spirit, his official inauguration of the new age, his miracles, his superiority over Judaism, his founding of the Christian society, his triumphant martyrdom, and his prophesied return "in the glory of his Father" (Mark 8:38; Matt. 16:27; Luke 9: 26). They, too, recognize that appreciation of Jesus during his lifetime had remained on a relatively low plane. Although they are able to relieve somewhat the Marcan restraint, nevertheless they also allow that Jesus had been largely misunderstood by his contemporaries.

One will not read far in either Matthew or Luke without discovering that these evangelists have made notable additions to Mark. Each of them renders a new service to the memory of Jesus. As Christians increased in numbers and the movement became more complex in character, there was a growing demand for new types of "Life of Jesus." These needed to be more comprehensive than earlier books had been, to cover a wider range of interests and to furnish more adequate assurances of the divine origin of Christianity. A specific instance of this dissatisfaction with previous writings is definitely affirmed in the Gospel of Luke, where the author states his purpose to be the composition of a narrative that will leave his "most excellent Theophilus" in no possible doubt as to the certainty of events bearing witness to the validity of the new religion. Although there is no similarly explicit definition of purpose in Matthew, on almost every page its presence is easily legible between the lines.

An arresting supplement to the story of Jesus' life appears at the very beginning of both Matthew and Luke. The birth and childhood of Christianity's founder had been passed over without a single notice by the author of Mark. Apparently it had not occurred to him to seek in history credentials for Jesus previous to his contact with John the Baptist. It had seemed a sufficient introduction to cite John's prophetic words about the "mightier one," and to record the descent of the Holy Spirit, when a voice from heaven had designated Jesus the beloved and well-pleasing Son of God. But the authors of Matthew and Luke, working quite independently of one another, penetrated more remotely into the past and put on record accounts of phenomenal occurrences connected with the birth and early youth of their hero.

Matthew opens with a genealogical table tracing Jesus' ancestry from Abraham through David to Joseph "the husband of Mary." Yet this venerable lineage proves to be only a superficial and formal credential, since Jesus is not in truth the son of Joseph but is of divine parentage. His mother, Mary, while still in her virginity "was found with child of the Holy Spirit," and thus there was brought to fulfilment the prophetic announcement regarding a divine redeemer worthy to bear the significant name "Immanuel," meaning "God with us." Even in infancy the child was the savior-king sent by heaven to redeem the chosen people. Wise men from the East, having learned of his birth, had journeyed to Palestine to render him worship, while the reigning Jewish king vainly endeavored to thwart the will of heaven. Both sacred scripture and present revelation were made to converge in their testimony to the Christ-child. To insure his safety, the wise men had been warned in a dream not to return to Herod; and on several occasions Joseph had been similarly instructed with reference to his own movements. In the birth of Jesus at Bethlehem, in the visit of his parents to Egypt, in Herod's vain attempt to destroy Mary's son, and in the later residence at Nazareth the evangelist saw significant fulfilments of ancient prophecy.

The Lucan story of Jesus' career begins with an independent and more lengthy account of his infancy. Heaven intervenes to bring into existence John the Baptist, who "is to make ready for the Lord a prepared people." Six months later the angelic messenger announces to Mary of Nazareth that in consequence of the Holy Spirit's coming upon her she shall bear a son. He shall be called "the Son of the Most High; and the Lord shall give unto him the throne of his father David . . . . the holy thing which is begotten shall be called the Son of God." By the time Theophilus had read a dozen columns from this new book he would have learned that the founder of the new religion, even before he had been conceived in his mother's womb, had been set apart by God for the high and holy office of Divine Savior. While still a babe in arms, he was "Christ the Lord." As a mere child he possessed in unusual measure the wisdom and favor of God. When only twelve years of age he amazed the learned men of Jerusalem by his knowledge and reproved his parents for their failure to perceive that his chief concern was properly with the affairs of God his Father. During his youth he remained subject to Joseph and Mary, but not of necessity. Eighteen years were yet to elapse before the time would be ripe for him to act.

By far the most distinctive feature added to the Marcan picture is Matthew's and Luke's new delineation of Jesus as teacher. In Mark, it is true, one frequently reads that Jesus preached and taught, delivering discourses in the synagogues or addressing audiences in the open. But if Christendom were dependent upon Mark alone, it would be left entirely ignorant of many items in the present tradition of its founder's teaching. Without the additional information in Matthew and Luke there would be no gospel record of the beatitudes, no admonition to forgive and love one's enemies, no Golden Rule, no Lord's Prayer, no parable of the prodigal son, no story of the good Samaritan and no report of many other statements of Jesus commonly regarded nowadays as most truly representative of him and his religion.

When he arrived at the point in Mark's story where it was recorded that people were astonished at Jesus' teaching, the writer of Matthew temporarily halted his copying of Mark. This document seemed to him to offer an entirely inadequate explanation of the arresting character of Jesus' message. In Mark it was the bold and successful command to the demons that stood out so uniquely as to call forth expressions of astonishment at the power of Jesus' words. While the Gospel of Matthew certainly is not

lacking in appreciation of Jesus' authority over
demons, his distinction as a teacher is thought
to have been disclosed more properly in the area
of moral and spiritual precepts given to guide
the disciples in their own living in relation to
God and to their fellow men. Consequently the
author of Matthew at this point inserts into his
narrative an extended account, by way of example, of a discourse delivered by Jesus to the
disciples, the well-known Sermon on the Mount
(Matt., chaps. 5–7). At the close of the Sermon,
when readers have been made familiar with this
new phase of Jesus' work, the language of Mark
is resumed: "The multitudes were astonished at
his teaching, for he taught them as one having
authority and not as their scribes" (Matt. 7:28
f.; Mark 1:22).

A similar dissatisfaction with Mark's too
meager delineation of the content of Jesus'
teaching is felt by the author of Luke. He con-
cedes that the great teacher's commands were
instantly heeded by unclean spirits, but there
was something unusually arresting in his message even when no demons were present to display obedience. Theophilus might be mystified,
if not indeed misled, by Mark's comments on the
astonishing character of Jesus' teaching, unless

previously given a specific illustration of its real content. Hence in Luke at this point Jesus is introduced in the rôle of synagogue preacher at Nazareth, where he causes his hearers to wonder, not on account of his power over demons, but because of "the words of grace which proceeded out of his mouth" (4:22). He took for his text the striking passage from Isaiah, "The spirit of the Lord is upon me, because he anointed me to preach good news to the poor. He has sent me to proclaim relief to the captives, the recovery of sight to the blind, and to set at liberty them that are bruised, to proclaim the acceptable year of the Lord." Thus in Luke as in Matthew, Mark's defect was remedied by recording a typical sermon at the opening of Jesus' ministry. But, as in their narratives of the infancy, each of the later evangelists went his own way and chose for his illustrative purpose entirely different discourses of Jesus.

For the authors of Matthew and Luke, Jesus is always the official founder of a new order, whose validity is supernaturally guaranteed even more conspicuously than in Mark. Yet much of the teaching of Jesus reported in these later gospels belongs to another area of interest. In addition to the Marcan emphasis on Jesus as a performer of wonderful works who displays his authoritative words by driving off demons and effecting numerous marvels, who announces the imminent approach of the Kingdom of God and discourses on the mysteries and signs of its consummation, Matthew and Luke take their readers into regions where they breathe a quite different atmosphere.

It will suffice for purposes of illustration to take the Matthean Sermon on the Mount, with the parallel passages in Luke, as an indication of the new type of tradition here used .to illustrate the character of Jesus' teaching. He pronounces blessings on those who live a life of self-denial for the sake of their religion (5:1-16; Luke 6:20-23). One is advised to effect an agreement with an adversary and avoid the law courts (5:25 f.; Luke 12:58 f.). The truly religious man will love his enemies, even as God shows kindness toward both sinners and righteous (5:39-48; Luke 6:27-36). The accumulation of heavenly treasures is the supremely worthy object of endeavor, while anxiety about the affairs of the earthly life will be swallowed up in one's confidence in God's care for his children (6:19-21, 25-33; Luke 12:22-34). One may be assured that the Heavenly Father will answer the requests of his children as generously as does an earthly parent (7:7–11; Luke 11:9–13). The true righteousness demanded by him requires genuine sincerity and fidelity to the will of God. To call Jesus "Lord, Lord," avails nothing in the absence of true purity of heart (7:16–21; Luke 6:43–46). Future safety for the disciple lies in obedience to Jesus' teaching about purity of life, singleness of motive, and loyalty to the will of the Heavenly Father (7:23–27; Luke 6:47–49).

In many sections of Matthew and Luke one might almost imagine that the evangelists had intended to let the teaching of Jesus stand accredited simply by the convincing power of its content. While both writers confidently affirm their belief in the unique supernatural equipment of Jesus and his consequent official authority to exorcise demons, to announce the presence of the Kingdom, or to establish the new Christian society, they have not always taken pains to superimpose these characteristically Marcan credentials upon the didactic materials derived from other sources. Had they been working more independently of earlier documents, it is not at all probable that they would have presented so much tradition lacking emphasis on the official significance of Jesus as

Christianity's founder. The writer of Mark had exercised a freer hand in the treatment of older tradition and consequently presented a much more uniform portrait of his subject. They, on the contrary, produced a more variegated picture because of extensive use made of previous works by the many who had "taken in hand to draw up a narrative concerning those matters which had been fulfilled among us" (Luke 1:1).

It is not to be imagined that the author of either Matthew or Luke would leave any section of his source materials absolutely free from the molding influence of interests that were uppermost in his own mind. Yet each of these evangelists has copied a considerable body of earlier tradition with so little alteration as to make possible a knowledge of the type of interest in Jesus therein reflected. Much of this tradition seems originally to have exhibited little or no concern with the unique authority and personality of Jesus. The demand for righteousness before God, purity of heart and sincerity of motive, and like features of ideal religious living, were left to make their own appeal to the conscience of the one who delivered the message and of those to whom it was addressed. It might be more true to say that the teaching authenticates Jesus than

[32]

that it derives its validity from the prestige of his official dignity as the inaugurator of a new order of things.

In this presentation the teacher is indeed highly revered, although he is not at all an object of worship. His message reveals his own standards for worthy living. This may make him an exemplary individual to be followed by his disciples, or he may indeed tower so far above them that they cannot hope to reach the pinnacle of attainment at which he has arrived. Be that as it may, the attitudes to be cherished by the disciples, the type of character to be cultivated, the deeds to be performed, and the ideals to be upheld derive their obligatory quality from a consciousness of direct relation between the individual and God. The ultimate norm set up for men's guidance is not Jesus' own word of command, not even his own model life, but the requirements of the Heavenly Father. Only remotely, if at all, is there any interest in hearing about the official dignity of Jesus as an object of the disciples' faith, an item that had been so prominent in Mark. Among the Christians who passed on this tradition portraying Jesus more specifically as the teacher, it was the religion of Jesus, religion as taught and lived by him, not the religion of which he was the object, that held the center of attention.

III

It is not difficult to forecast the impression that the Gospel of John would make upon a reader who took it up for the first time. If he were already familiar with Mark, Matthew, and Luke, whose general resemblance to one another has won for them the designation "Synoptic" Gospels, the novelty of the experience would only be heightened. The picture of Jesus in John differs so widely in detail from that contained in any one of the other three gospels, or in all of them taken together, that on first sight one might almost imagine that the Jesus of the Fourth Gospel was an entirely different person.

In comparison with the Synoptics, John is as surprising in its omissions as in its additions. Were we dependent upon it alone, numerous events in the life of Jesus and a large quantity of his teaching, now the common property of Christendom, would have been entirely missing in the New Testament. There would have been no record of marvelous incidents in connection with his birth and childhood, nor any reference to his life previous to the beginning of his public activity. His sojourn of forty days in the wilderness and his temptation by Satan would never have been imagined. One would not know that Jesus had opened his work in Galilee by issuing a call to repentance and gathering about him a group of chosen disciples from among fishermen in the vicinity of Capernaum, or that later Peter confessed belief in the messiahship of Jesus and then reproved him for predicting his crucifixion. His activity in conquering demons, his efforts to conceal from his contemporaries knowledge of his messiahship, the experiences on the mount of transfiguration, the agony in Gethsemane, and the cry to God from the cross are further examples of unrecorded incidents in John.

More striking still is the utter absence from John of that type of religious teaching reported of Jesus in the Sermon on the Mount. The imprisonment and death of John the Baptist and Jesus' remarks about the significance of John's work find no place in the Fourth Gospel. The parable of the sower and similar illustrations used by the Synoptic Jesus to describe the Kingdom of God are likewise missing. The command to the Twelve to go forth in pairs to carry on missionary labors, as well as the last great commission to evangelize all nations, is never men-

[35]

tioned. John knows nothing of any statement of Jesus regarding his return "in the glory of his Father with the holy angels." The conversation with the rich young man, the parable of the talents, the story of the good Samaritan and the prodigal son, and the discourse about the destruction of the temple are but representative of a wide range of Synoptic teaching which finds no echo in the Gospel of John.

From the Fourth Gospel one derives an equally elaborate array of new items nowadays familiarly associated with the career of Jesus. This is the only gospel to report that he was the incarnation of the divine "Word," the Logos of Greek philosophy. Without this book one would not learn that Jesus had ever said that it was necessary to be born again in order to secure admission to the Kingdom of God, or that God had revealed his love for the world by sending his only begotten son to hang on the cross. Here only do we find Jesus presenting himself as the bread of life and the light of the world, or calling himself the "Good Shepherd" and promising after his death to send his disciples the Comforter to lead them into all truth. The assurance that Jesus will return to take his disciples unto himself, the admonition that they are to preserve a union with him like that of the branch with the vine, and the commandment that they are to love one another even as Jesus had loved them are all distinctively Johannine information.

The activities of Jesus reported in John are as novel as his teachings. Here for the first time we hear that at the very outset of his ministry he appeared in Judea and that this territory rather than Galilee was "his own country" (4:43-45). Distinctive also are the accounts of his journey through Samaria, when he engaged in conversation with the woman at the well and proceeded to Cana of Galilee where he performed his first miracle by turning water into wine at the marriage feast. Additional miracles peculiar to John are the cure of the nobleman's son in Capernaum, the healing of the cripple at the pool of Bethesda, the giving of sight to the blind beggar, and the resuscitation of the deceased Lazarus. Likewise, it is from John alone one learns that the Roman soldiers cast lots for the garment of Jesus, that after the crucifixion they did not break his legs because he was already dead, that one of them thrust a spear in his side, and that Jesus while suspended on the cross had committed his mother to the care of the disciple whom he loved.

JESUS—A NEW BIOGRAPHY

In comparison with the Synoptic portrayal of Jesus, the uniqueness of the representation in the Fourth Gospel consists not simply in its omissions and supplements. It is a genuinely new and largely original product. Apparently the writer has not copied earlier sources with the same literalness and to the same extent as had the authors of Matthew and Luke. In this respect his book is more like the Gospel of Mark, although the new delineation of the person and work of Jesus differs widely from the Marcan. The Johannine Jesus is a striking figure whose uniformity and self-consistency contrast rather sharply with the composite features conspicuous in both Matthew and Luke. In planning his book the author set before himself a definite goal and moved toward it without those digressions into earlier documents that tempted writers of less independence. He devoted himself to the task of demonstrating from the story of Jesus' own life that he was the Christ, the Son of God, and that in the acceptance of this proposition on the part of mankind lay its only hope of salvation (20:30 f.).

The distinctive features of the Johannine portrait immediately arrest the attention of one whose eye has not been blinded by the varied colors in the Synoptic picture. While in John, Jesus is conspicuously the founder of the new religion, his equipment for his work is not endowment by the Spirit at baptism, as in Mark, nor supernatural authentication at birth, as in Matthew and Luke, but a unique constitution of personality. By a stroke of genius this evangelist turns to account, for the benefit of Christianity, an important phase of contemporary thinking. He sees in the earthly Jesus the incarnation of a pre-existent divinity who before the creation of the world had resided in heaven with God in the capacity of only begotten son, and to this being he applies the familiar Greek philosophical term, the "Logos." In Jesus, human flesh has received this divine inhabitant, bringing to the world power, enlightenment, and wisdom directly from the presence of God in heaven.

The course of action by which Jesus founded the new religion, like his equipment, is also strikingly original in John. Mark's imagery depicting an apocalyptic Jewish Messiah, who displays a preliminary triumph over Satan to be followed presently by a victorious return from heaven with the holy angels, is altogether absent from John. In its place a wholly new ideal of procedure has been substituted. Jesus' point of attack is not the demon-oppressed world, nor is there a single instance of casting out a demon in the Fourth Gospel. On the contrary, as pictured here, Jesus invades the darkened minds of men and seeks to dispel their darkness by convincing them that he has come down out of heaven with new redeeming light. It is his all-absorbing task so to act and so to teach that individuals in his own day and ever afterwards may be persuaded of the truth of his claim.

From the moment of his appearing upon the scene Jesus becomes, in this new rôle, the object of a new type of messianic faith. John the Baptist points him out to two of his own followers as the Lamb of God that takes away the sin of the world, and presently the immediate disciples of Jesus are testifying to their friends that they have found the Messiah of whom Moses and the prophets had written. In less than three days of public activity Jesus so impressed his contemporaries with his superior wisdom that the truly discerning recognized in him the "Son of God" and the "King of Israel" (1:49). This feature of the Johannine portrait contrasts sharply with the Marcan representation, in which Jesus so successfully veils his messiahship that even his closest disciples fail to attain belief in his official significance until shortly before the close of his ministry.

As a worker of miracles, the primary purpose of the Johannine Jesus is to manifest his own glory. The first occasion of this display is the changing of the water into wine at Cana, a sign which causes his disciples to "believe" in him. When, soon afterwards, he demonstrates his divine authority at the Passover by driving the money-changers out the temple, the confidence of his disciples is further fortified by seeing in this act a fulfilment of scripture. A few days later it is the superhuman knowledge of Jesus that leads the Samaritan woman to invite into his presence a number of her own countrymen who immediately recognize that "this is indeed the Savior of the world." Similarly, when the nobleman of Capernaum returns and finds his son healed in accordance with the word of Jesus, the father himself and his whole house "believed." The miracle of healing at the pool of Bethesda provides a further opportunity for Jesus to announce that those who see in his deeds evidence that he is the Son of God have already entered into eternal life. In brief, his miracles are performed for the purpose of bearing testimony to his heavenly origin in order that men may obtain salvation by believing him to be the incarnate Son of God.

As a teacher, the Johannine Jesus concerns himself with two principal themes. His first interest is to make clear to his contemporaries the unique type of person that he himself is. He bears witness to himself by uttering his own message of life-giving light, by performing miracles, and by fulfilling prophecies contained in the ancient scriptures. The words that he speaks are the very essence of saving-power and the new order of things which he thus inaugurates means the establishment on earth of the Kingdom of God, not a political kingdom, but a new régime of "truth." Jesus has come into the world to be the princely revealer of heavenly wisdom and "every one that is of the truth" hears his voice. While he announces himself to be the Messiah promised to the Jews, as portrayed in John he often resembles those savior-teachers who, by communicating words of light and wisdom to their fellow-mortals, had won the admiration and reverence of the gentile world. But for our author, this Christian savior is no pale replica of the gentile hero-philosopher; he is the climactic manifestation of divine revelation made by the true God originally worshiped only by the Jews.

A second aspect of Jesus' teaching, according to the Fourth Gospel, is great concern for the welfare of the continuing Christian society. Jesus takes pains to gather and train a group of disciples who will carry forward after his death the work begun by him. They learn from him both the method and the meaning of the new propaganda. In the foot-washing scene he sets them an example of that humble service which they in future will be called upon to render in their missionary labors. He remarks upon the regenerative significance of the baptismal rite and stresses both the ritual act and the accompanying endowment by the Spirit. No one can obtain entrance into the Kingdom of God who has not been "born of water and the Spirit." Mention is also made of the necessity of an appreciative observance of that sacred meal in which the disciples are to "eat the flesh" and "drink the blood" of Jesus. Only those who perform this act, and at the same time possess the guidance of the Spirit, "have eternal life." That the new movement should fail among the Jews and should pass to the Gentiles for its ultimate success is anticipated by Jesus in his pronouncement of doom on his Jewish contemporaries and his personal response to inquiring Greeks. He explicitly in-

[43]

forms the disciples that sheep from the gentile fold are his proper care. Before his departure from earth he takes special pains to speak words of comfort and assurance to those whom he leaves behind. With this task finished his teaching is complete.

No one who reads the Fourth Gospel, keeping it distinct from the Synoptics, can fail to be impressed with the daring originality of its portraiture. To be sure, the book was written while there was as yet no official collection of canonical gospels; and the author, had he been familiar with the Synoptic story, would not have felt a characteristic modern hesitancy in setting aside so much of Mark, Matthew, and Luke. In his day they had not yet become sacred scripture. A new interest on his own part and a conviction that a new type of biography was necessary for the further progress of the Christian movement constituted sufficient justification for the writing of his gospel. In this respect he moved in a much freer atmosphere than that which has enveloped the great majority of later biographers of Jesus. Yet in his underlying interests the author of John is not radically at variance with the other three evangelists. He, like the others, is primarily concerned to picture Jesus in the official rôle of founder of a new religion. He is a wonderful teacher and a unique personality, supernaturally qualified to inaugurate a new order. When his efforts among his own countrymen prove futile, he transforms seeming failure into a marvelous victory through his triumph over death and his continued care for the new movement which he had founded.

The Johannine representation certainly is no mechanical photograph. Nor is it a literary mosaic, such as one finds in Matthew and Luke. Rather, it is manifestly the work of an artist who, however true to life he may strive to paint, at the same time has an irrepressible genius for interpretative decoration.

IV

There were several ancient "Lives" of Jesus that were not included in the New Testament. These have survived only in fragments. Sometimes, indeed, little is known of them except their title. One hears of a Gospel according to the Hebrews, a Gospel of the Ebionites, a Gospel according to the Egyptians, a Gospel according to Peter, a Gospel according to Thomas, a Gospel according to Bartholomew, and the like.[1]

[1] M. R. James, *The Apocryphal New Testament* (Oxford, 1924), is the best English version of this literature.

Many such books were in circulation in various sections of Christendom during the second century, and some of them undoubtedly had arisen contemporaneously with our present New Testament gospels. They bear additional testimony to the creative energy of the early biographers of Jesus.

Of all the apocryphal gospels, that entitled "According to the Hebrews" is the most noteworthy. Possibly it had been composed at some time during the last quarter of the first century, but its failure to obtain a place in the New Testament is evidence of its restricted circulation from the outset. It seems to have suffered the disadvantage of having been composed in a Semitic language,[1] which would have been a serious handicap to its popularity regardless of any intrinsic merits that it might have possessed. Only minor groups within Christendom could use any language except Greek after the time of Paul, and particularly after the fall of Jerusalem in 70

[1] A. Schmidtke (*Neue Fragmente und Untersuchungen in den judenchristlichen Evangelien* [Leipzig, 1911]) thinks the original language was Greek, but this hypothesis fails to account adequately for the limited popularity of the book in early Christianity. Had it been a Greek gospel as early in date and as extensive in content as apparently it was, surely it would have been carried more widely about among the Christian congregations of the Mediterranean in the pre-canonical period.

[46]

A.D. Hence at first Hebrews could have been used only by inconspicuous congregations in Syria. Even subsequent translations into Greek and Latin were insufficient to offset its originally restricted circulation.

Had this gospel been preserved in full it might have commanded an interest equal to that of any one of the New Testament records. An ancient statistician estimates its bulk to have been about seven-eighths of that of our canonical Matthew, while the fragments that have survived indicate the comprehensiveness of the work and the interest of its author to portray both an earthly Jesus and a Christ worthy of faith. As in the canonical gospels, attention is given both to the deeds and to the teaching of Jesus, and the narrative covers the history at least from the baptism to the post-resurrection appearances.

The character of the book is apparent from the brief excerpts that have survived. It seeks to obviate the incongruity involved in the tradition about Jesus' baptism by offering a skilful explanation of why one presumably unconscious of fault should have responded to John's call to repentance. The author of Matthew was aware of this difficulty but offered a quite different solution. He said, in effect, that Jesus accepted this rite at John's hands in order to set an example for the practice of the ordinance by later generations of Christians (Matt. 3:15). Hebrews offers a less ecclesiastical motive: "Behold the mother of the Lord and his brothers kept saying to him, John the Baptist baptizes for the remission of sins; let us go and be baptized by him. But he said to them, What sin have I committed that I should go and be baptized by him—unless, perchance, this very thing that I have said is a sin of ignorance?"

The endowment of Jesus by the Holy Spirit at baptism is also described in original fashion: "And it came to pass when the Lord had come up out of the water the whole fount of the Holy Spirit descended and rested upon him and said to him, My son, in all the prophets was I waiting for you that you should come and I might rest in you. For you are my rest, you are my first begotten son that reigns throughout eternity." An echo of ancient prophecy also heightens the color of Jesus' reference to his temptation: "Then my parent, the Holy Spirit, took hold of me by one of the hairs of my head and bore me off to the great Mount Tabor" (Ezek. 8:3).

Marvelous happenings in connection with

[48]

the death and resurrection of Jesus seem to have been a subject of keen interest to this evangelist, and some of his information is quite new to one who knows only the four New Testament gospels. At the time of the crucifixion a gigantic lintel of the temple had fallen, an event which doubtless is linked in the author's mind with Isaiah's words: "The posts of the door moved at the voice of him that cried" (Isa. 6:4). The reality of his appearance to the disciples is confirmed by Jesus in the remark that he was not a "bodiless demon." But the most novel feature in the narrative is the explanation given of the way in which James became convinced of the resurrection of Jesus. Paul remarked that Jesus had appeared to James, but no particulars were given (I Cor. 15:7). One now learns that James had previously taken an oath to eat nothing until assured that his brother had risen. Accordingly Jesus, on leaving the tomb, visited James, commanded that a table and bread should be brought, and "took bread and blessed it and broke it and gave it to James the Just and said to him: My brother, eat your bread, for the Son of Man is risen from among them that sleep."

Yet in this gospel the risen Lord has not completely eclipsed the earthly Jesus. The narrative contains a number of realistic touches quite the equal of any similar features in the canonical books. Sometimes Hebrews has been discounted because "low in its Christology"—a theological vice but perhaps a historical virtue. The sympathies of Jesus are counted upon for a favorable response to the appeal of a man with a withered hand who, like Jesus, had been a laborer in the building-trade and pleads: "I was a mason earning my living by the use of my hands. Jesus, I pray thee to restore me my health that I may not basely beg my food." The realism of the conversation between Jesus and the rich man is also striking: "He [Jesus] said to him, Go sell everything you possess and distribute it to the poor, and come follow me. But the rich man began to scratch his head and was not pleased. And the Lord said to him, How can you say, I have kept the Law and the Prophets? For it is written in the Law 'Thou shalt love thy neighbor as thyself,' and behold many of your brethren, sons of Abraham, are enveloped in filth, dying of hunger, and your house is full of many good things and yet nothing at all goes out of it to them."

That frailties of human nature are to be condoned, even in the Christian communities, is made clear when Jesus teaches unlimited forgiveness on the ground that "in the prophets also after they were anointed by the Holy Spirit some sin still is found." In similar temper leniency is to be the refuge of the socially unfortunate, for it is from this gospel that the story of the woman taken in adultery, added to late texts of the Gospel of John (8:1–11), was originally derived.

Like Hebrews, various other ancient apocryphal books rehearse in their own way the deeds and words of Jesus. Sometimes they present a new version of incidents or sayings now familiar to us through our acquaintance with the canonical books, while at other points they contain entirely new materials. For example, the Gospel of the Ebionites gives a variant version of the call of disciples by Jesus: "There was a certain man named Jesus, and he was about thirty years of age, who chose us. And coming into Capernaum he entered into the house of Simon, surnamed Peter, and opening his mouth he said, As I was passing by the Lake of Tiberias I chose John and James, Zebedee's sons, and Simon and Andrew and Thaddeus and Simon the Zealot and Judas the Iscariot, and you Matthew while sitting at the toll-house I called and you followed me." On the other hand, an extra-canonical book known as the Preaching of Peter puts Jesus' commission to the disciples into quite new language: "If then anyone of Israel desires to repent and believe on God through my name his sins shall be forgiven him. After twelve years go forth into the [gentile] world lest anyone say, We did not hear."

Sayings of Jesus unrecorded in any canonical gospel have long been more or less familiar. Paul reports an otherwise unknown ordinance of the Lord to the effect that "we who are alive that are left until the coming of the Lord shall in no wise precede them that are fallen asleep" (I Thess. 4:15), and the writer of Acts is sole authority for the statement that Jesus said "It is more blessed to give than to receive" (20:35). References to uncanonical sayings of Jesus scattered along the byways of ancient literature mount into the hundreds, and in modern times the quantity has been considerably increased by the discoveries of new documents. Likely enough, some of these fragmentary traditions once belonged to one or another written gospel long since lost because it had failed to gain wide currency within Christendom.

In spirit and content these sayings are sometimes quite in the temper of a book like the Gospel according to the Hebrews, as when Jesus says: "Except you fast to the world you shall not find the Kingdom of God, and except you make the whole week a Sabbath you shall not see the Father." Or, again, "I stood in the midst of the world and in the flesh was I seen by them, and I found all men drunken, and none did I find among them thirsting, and my soul is afflicted for the sons of men because they are blind in their heart and see not." And, further, "Wherever there are two they are not without God, and wherever there is one alone I am with him. Raise the stone and you find me there, cleave the wood and I am there."

That unremitting antagonism between Jews and Christians, in which also the canonical gospels make Jesus a vigorous participant, reappears in a fragment from an early, but as yet unidentified, apocryphal book. A single paragraph will serve to illustrate its tenor. To the charge that the disciples have not properly purified themselves before entering the temple area, Jesus is said to have replied: "Woe unto you, blind that see not! You have bathed yourself in these waters that are poured forth into which, night and day, dogs and swine are cast, and after you have washed yourself you scoured your outer skin, which the harlots also and flute girls anoint and bathe and scour and beautify to arouse desire in men, but within it is filled with scorpions and all evil. But I and my disciples, of whom you say that we are not washed, have been washed in living waters which came down from God out of heaven."

Still other biographers were less interested in revising current tradition about the public ministry and teaching of Jesus, but devoted themselves to filling up conspicuous gaps in the earlier records. His birth and childhood, touched on only briefly in two of the canonical books, offered an open field for speculation. New infancy gospels dwelt upon the glorious and powerful personality of the divine child. When a lad only five years old, all nature obeyed his word, whether he commanded running waters to gather in pools, or bade clay sparrows soar aloft in flight, or struck dead those who offended him. In a more kindly temper he saved the life of a woodchopper whose foot had been cleft asunder, or miraculously lengthened a beam in his father's carpenter shop, or raised to life persons who had met an untimely death. Those who attempted to act as his teachers were overtaken by disaster, but in the presence of a more humble instructor

Jesus kindly disclosed his own superhuman wisdom and taught the Law to his elders who marveled at the "beauty of his teaching and the readiness of his words, in that being an infant he uttered such things."

Also the activities of Jesus after the crucifixion were passed over rather lightly in the earliest gospels. Later evangelists, indulging new flights of fancy, were able to add many incidents in this period of his career. It had been stated in I Peter that Christ after his death on the cross "went and preached to the spirits in prison" (3:19). This remark was elaborated into a detailed description of the Savior's descent to Hades to deliver Adam and his children: "And the Lord stretched forth his hand and made the sign of the cross over Adam and over all his saints, and he took the right hand of Adam and went up out of hell and all the saints followed him." Other narrators recounted words of instruction delivered by the risen Lord to his disciples. Sometimes he disclosed to them wonderful wisdom about the glories of heaven or the torments to be suffered by the wicked in hell. At other times, in more sober vein, as in the Epistle of the Apostles, recently brought to light, he revealed "things mighty and wonderful and true," rela-

[55]

tive to the status of his disciples in the present world. These extensive gospel supplements, crass though they often were, brought to the Christendom of the time in vivid fashion welcome accretions to the glory of its adored Savior. This was an age when piety fed on sacred legend and found genuine satisfaction in naïve supernaturalism.

Such are the features of Jesus exhibited in the total range of ancient portraiture. Its multiple character corresponds with the great variety of interests inevitably present in a new religious movement growing gradually more diversified and inclusive as its missionary propaganda extended more widely over the Roman Empire. The fruitfulness and efficiency of these ancient writers, working within the Christianity of their own age, may not be greeted altogether joyously by one today who seeks to recover from their books an accurate portrait of the earthly Jesus. But the task of the modern biographer is plain and imperative. He must devise a way to penetrate behind the varied imagery of the several gospels if he would rediscover the real Jesus of Palestine as he lived and labored among his immediate associates.

[56]

CHAPTER II
THE RETURN TO THE HISTORICAL JESUS

THE early biographers of Jesus performed brilliantly their chosen task. In their several ways they depicted an official Lord Jesus Christ who answered the needs of their own devotions and appealed effectively to their contemporaries. With each new recital of events the story of his life was enriched by fresh displays of his attractiveness. That these evangelists undertook seriously and enthusiastically to picture Jesus as each of them believed he might properly be presented is not for a moment to be doubted. But how far they employed what would now seem a scientific method of securing information, and the extent to which their own interpretations were allowed to heighten the effect of their portraiture, are inescapable problems.

A successful return to the real Jesus is possible only if one is able to distinguish clearly between unhistorical features in the documents and such objective data as may have constituted the raw materials, so to speak, used by his ancient biographers. How are the original elements in the gospel narratives to be separated from the interpretative accretions that accumulated year after year as this literature increased in quantity and variety? In short, how can the career of the earthly Jesus be rediscovered from the surviving written records of a later age?

I

There is one very simple and popular way of deciding the reliability of tradition about Jesus. For centuries it has been followed without misgivings on the part of a host of his biographers, and is even yet widely in vogue. To state this rule in its simplest terms, every item of information found in a canonical gospel is to be received as Simon-pure history, while every deviating or supplementary statement in an apocryphal book is to be unceremoniously rejected. Canonicity, it is assumed, insures historicity.

The view that a gospel is good history by virtue of its canonicity, while an apocryphal book is necessarily fictitious, will not bear careful scrutiny. The circumstances that brought about a formal collection of the New Testament books are not sufficiently reassuring. The second century was a period of vigorous expansion in the history of the Christian movement. During these years it attracted many new converts and absorbed an ever increasing variety of cultural heritages from its environment. Diverse and rival interests rapidly multiplied. Books on Jesus that would accommodate him to the heterogeneous tastes of the new generation of his more numerous disciples were much in demand. In fact, so conflicting were the forces within second-century Christianity that the new society was in serious danger of disruption unless it could devise a more efficient means of regulating the life and thinking of its members.

The beginnings of a New Testament canon of scripture answered to this necessity. The minor groups, called "heretics" by the more powerful majority, had cited Jesus in support of their own divergent opinions. They had not been slow even to compose new gospels that would display more clearly his alleged approval of their favorite views. Manifestly, there was a pressing need for standardization. To meet this crisis the orthodox majority by popular consent set up beside the Old Testament a new scriptural authority as part of a new machinery of control.

[59]

The leaders of Christendom insisted that only the most ancient and widely used gospels might properly be read in public worship. Four such books finally secured general recognition. Their prestige within the Christian society insured their perpetuity, and since they contained approved theology they were assumed to be good history.

The ultimate determination of the entire New Testament canon was not effected until the latter part of the fourth century. But the canonical status of the four gospels had been fully established by the year 200. Orthodox Christendom declared them to be the teaching which the apostles, under the direction of God, had committed to the church. Even their very number seemed a part of the divine economy. To quote a single spokesman of the time, Irenaeus of Lyons: "Since in the world where we dwell there are four points of the compass and four prevailing winds and the church is spread abroad over the whole earth and the gospel is the pillar and support of the church and its vital breath, accordingly it has four pillars breathing immortality on every side and kindling anew the life of men. Hence it is evident that the Logos, fashioner of all things, who sits upon the cherubim and holds together everything, when he was made manifest unto men gave us the gospel in four-fold form but held together by one spirit" (*Adv. Haer.* iii. 11, 8).

That the canonical gospels are true history because apostles sponsor their content is also a proposition of doubtful validity. The books themselves contain no explicit information about the identity of their several authors, but Christendom has provided each with an appropriate superscription. Since the latter half of the second century they have been universally entitled "According to Matthew," "According to Mark," "According to Luke," "According to John." About the middle of the second century Justin commonly referred to them indiscriminately as "Memoirs" composed by the apostles and their companions. Other early Christians sometimes showed an acquaintance with gospel language, yet had no concern for the names of the evangelists. But the formal process of canonization made it highly desirable to assign each book to a specific author.

Originally, gospels were prized primarily for their contents. Probably often the author's name was quite unknown to the earliest readers. In the pre-canonical period it was the subject matter of the narrative, not the revered name of the writer, that carried weight. This fact is interestingly illustrated in the case of the so-called "Gospel of Luke." The author's predecessors were the nameless "many" who had composed brief narratives which he so highly prized that he transcribed their contents with much fidelity. Yet he made no allusion to the name of any author, although the book now called the "Gospel of Mark" was among his array of sources. And his ambition, so he affirmed, was to write a fuller and more convincing account that would carry new conviction by its greater completeness. It did not occur to him either to speak in the authority of his own name or to claim to be the medium of divine revelation. His book was left simply to speak for itself, which is, after all, the ultimate test of value in ancient as in modern literature.

The custom today of prefixing to a volume a title page on which to display the name of the author, with his degrees and academic titles, the date of publication, and the address of the publisher who owns the copyright, was unsuited to the style and purpose of an ancient gospel written upon a ribbon of papyrus for use in the Christian communities. Indeed, no one of the early biographers of Jesus had been so self-assertive as Paul, who naturally followed the current epistolary style of prefixing his name to each of his letters. The gospels had not been put forth in this personal fashion. They were not letters written on the authority of any individual, but were a compendium of Christendom's common heritage from its savior-founder. Interest centered in the things said and done by Jesus, not in the name of their compiler. And authority resided in the convincing content of the compilation, as it was esteemed worthy of its hero and capable of serving his followers.

Interest in the apostolic authorship of gospel tradition was a development of the canonical period. Now it was assumed that a popular and widely used book could be further elevated in one's esteem if its origin could be traced back to some revered name among the older Christian worthies. When a gospel contained no indications to the contrary, its assignment to the Apostle Matthew or the Apostle John seemed no mere idle speculation, but a happy fact discovered by faith. Speaking generally, one may say that during the latter part of the first century biographical interest in Jesus aimed principally at expansion and elaboration of the content of written tradition. On the other hand, the second century saw a rapid growth of interest in attaching to both old and new "Lives" of Jesus the authority of some apostolic or near-apostolic name of repute.

Apparently, in some instances, desire to choose a suitable author for a well-known book was embarrassed by facts too familiar to permit of an absolutely ideal selection. In the case of the gospel called "Mark," a name of only second-rate authority was retained, although given added prestige by association with the greater name of "Peter". Mark, it was said, had been this apostle's companion and "interpreter." Hence this gospel was essentially a summary of Peter's discourses. One may surmise that if Mark's name had not already been intimately associated with the composition of the book, Petrine authorship would have been affirmed outright. Probably John Mark did write this gospel, but an examination of its style and content does not bear out the supposition that it is an unadorned compilation of excerpts from Peter's sermons.

Similarly, in the case of the Gospel of Luke the alleged author is not himself an apostle but only a companion of that other great figure in

[64]

the history of Christianity, the Apostle Paul. Here again tradition refrained from assigning a gospel directly to the greater name. Why this restraint? In the opening sentence of Acts one learned that it and the Third Gospel came from the same hand. Also in a later section of Acts the narrator spoke in the first person, while Paul was referred to in the third person. This circumstance implied that the book had been composed, not by the Apostle himself, but by one of his fellow-travelers. The writer had not mentioned his own name. But since "we" appeared first in Acts 16:10, when Paul left Asia for Europe, and recurred frequently until finally he arrived in Rome (28:16), it was appropriate to select a gentile author. The choice readily fell upon Luke "the beloved physician" referred to by Paul in certain of his letters (Philem. 24; Col. 4:4; II Tim. 4:11).

Today Lucan authorship of Luke-Acts is in serious doubt. The career and character of the Paul depicted in Acts sometimes deviates widely from what is now known of the Apostle through our acquaintance with his own letters. Of course, it must be granted that when Acts was written no collection of the Pauline epistles had yet been assembled. But a traveling companion, it is thought, could hardly have been so ignorant of the real Paul and so completely unaware of his correspondence. However that may be, were Luke in reality the author of the gospel it will have been the work of one who had no first-hand knowledge of the subject treated and whose "apostolic" authority consisted only in attachment to the person of Paul who himself had not been a companion of Jesus.

For the two remaining gospels, authors were found who from almost the very beginning of Jesus' public career had belonged to the inner group of disciples. One of these was the toll-collector Matthew (Levi), son of Alphaeus (Mark 3:14), and the other was the Galilean fisherman John, the son of Zebedee (Mark 1:19). Were it possible to accept this tradition, one could argue that the statements made in these books are historically dependable because they are recorded by eye-witnesses narrating a period of history in which they themselves had actively participated.

The grounds on which the First and the Fourth Gospel were supposed to have been written respectively by Matthew and John are today not apparent. The former book contains within itself no hint of its author's name. The same is true of the Fourth Gospel, except for the last chapter which is manifestly a later addition. Originally this gospel had ended with a reference to the self-attesting character of its contents: "These things are written that you may believe that Jesus is the Christ, the Son of God, and that believing you may have life in his name" (20:31). When the gospel was edited for canonical purposes, an appended chapter closed appropriately with the new emphasis on authorship: "This is the disciple that bears witness to these things and wrote these things and we know that his witness is true" (21:24). Johannine authorship was not explicitly affirmed, but it was very clearly implied. The same effect was secured by introducing the phrase, the "disciple whom Jesus loved," as though the author were modestly refraining from the mention of his own name (13:23; 19:26; 20:2; 21:7, 20).

The character of their contents is alone sufficient to refute the tradition of apostolic authorship for either Matthew or John. The makers of the canon were quite unjustified in selecting personal companions of Jesus to sponsor these books. There has been ample occasion already to observe the varied elements that entered into the making of the First Gospel. A large part of the material was copied substantially verbatim from earlier documents. Sometimes Mark was used extensively, while at other points the compiler drew heavily upon the many unnamed individuals who had composed the other narratives mentioned in the preface to Luke. The unknown author of Matthew gleaned very diligently from many sources a wide variety of materials, themselves often diverse in character, and strung them together in a none too solid unity. First-hand knowledge could hardly have been reported in this second-hand fashion. Such copying, sorting, and rearranging of existing tradition was not the work of one who had belonged to the company of the "Twelve" and had lived through that period of history in which the events he recorded had actually taken place.

In comparison with Matthew, the Gospel of John exhibits a far greater measure of unity, and may much more easily be thought the work of a single pen wielded by an author of marked originality. Yet there are insuperable objections to the tradition of its apostolic authorship. It is the very content of the gospel that testifies most eloquently against this hypothesis. John the son of Zebedee was a Galilean fisherman, unschooled even in the learning of the Jews. Christian tradition itself reputed him to be an "unlearned and ignorant man" (Acts 4:13). In the early church at Jerusalem he was one of the "pillars" who represented Jewish Christianity, in contrast with Paul and Barnabas who felt an irresistible urge to convert the Gentiles (Gal. 2:9). As befitted his heritage and previous experience, John belonged to that group of Palestinian Christians who some twenty years after Jesus' death were still restricting their missionary labors to their Jewish kinsmen (Gal. 2:9). In order to make him the author of the Fourth Gospel, one line of Christian tradition transferred his residence to Ephesus and kept him alive to a great age. But a variant tradition, early lost from view because now impracticable, left John in Palestine where he met death in consequence of his new faith, a fate that also overtook his brother James (Acts 12:2). The matter-of-fact manner in which Mark refers to the baptism of martyrdom in store for the two sons of Zebedee (10:29) suggests that they had both perished before this gospel was written.

When the canon-makers imposed the composition of the Fourth Gospel upon John the son of Zebedee, they so thoroughly transformed his inheritances and personality that no vestige of the

Galilean fisherman remained. He no longer regarded missionary preaching among Jews to be
the great task of his life, but clearly represented
that already in the lifetime of Jesus the new religion had passed beyond the pale of Judaism.
Nor was it to be preached in the thought-forms
of the Jewish people. This writer represents that
even Jesus fittingly phrased his message in such
abstract categories as "Light" and "Life" and
"Truth" and other forms of religio-philosophical
imagery characteristic of the Graeco-oriental
world. If the author of the Fourth Gospel had
been originally one of the Twelve, his former
outlook and interests had become so thoroughly
altered before the writing of this book that he
could no longer be regarded as a dependable
witness for events within the strictly Palestinian
Jewish setting where Jesus had lived.

Neither the prestige of canonicity nor the hypothesis of apostolic authorship can insure the
accuracy of any ancient biography of Jesus. The
inescapable fact remains, evident to every at-
tentive reader, that even the four New Testament gospels diverge widely from one another in
content and represent successive stages of literary evolution. They betray a constant interest
to interpret anew to different groups of readers

and to varying types of mind the latest interests of the expanding Christian movement. To distinguish between the genuinely historical elements in this body of literature and the interpretative additions of successive evangelists, it will be necessary to seek a more competent test of value. Canonical dignity and apostolic authorship are insufficient guides. Yet these notions are still serious mental hazards for not a few present-day biographers of Jesus, even when they aim to conform strictly to the standards of modern historical science.

Conversely, lack of canonical dignity does not prove the worthlessness of an apocryphal gospel. No modern historian can slight a document simply because ecclesiastical custom stigmatizes it "apocryphal." There is no valid reason for assuming that reliable reminiscences about the life and teaching of Jesus could not have survived in more than four of the ancient books composed to perpetuate his memory. The author of Luke explicitly mentioned the fact that he had before him several older compositions in which deeds and words of Jesus were recorded, and it is not at all likely that his new book immediately supplanted all its predecessors, even though some of them had been extensively embodied in his pages. Quite possibly some congregations were using still other ancient books of the gospel type with which the writer of Luke was unacquainted. In his second treatise, the Acts, he worked without any knowledge of the letters of Paul, copies of which evidently he did not have at hand. And it is very probable that he was similarly unfamiliar with some of the tradition about Jesus which, on his own showing, was already in wide circulation.

Indeed, Christianity was still enjoying something of the spontaneity that had characterized earlier days before the spoken word had given place to the written page. Even in the second century there were Christians who prized the fluid oral teaching—the "living and abiding voice," as they termed it—over any shrunken form of the tradition that could be set down in the ordinary papyrus-roll used in the book trade of that time. Instead of the written gospels representing a comprehensive embodiment of information about Jesus, to many Christians at first they seemed rather an example of shrinkage. And this feeling was of course true to fact. That what these authors had omitted might have found its way into some book which never attained a place in the canon is altogether probable.

The judgment to be pronounced upon the historical character of the early church's extra-canonical literature cannot be settled by assuming that a canon when formed rendered all remaining writings historically worthless, any more than that it insured the historicity of everything in the approved collection. Undoubtedly, the writers of the older apocryphal gospels, had they employed competent methods of research, could have gained access to much new and reliable information. But these books, like the canonical gospels, must ultimately be judged by the character of their contents. In the last analysis their dependability is conditioned by the extent to which their authors recreated the story of Jesus' career to meet the immediate interests of their own age as the expansion of the new religion carried the name and fame of its founder farther and farther afield.

II

Neither the canonicity of a gospel nor tradition about its authorship is of any real value for determining the historical quality of the narrative. Not what the church has said about a book, but what the document lying before us to-day contains, remains the sole ground for judging its historical worth. It is doubtful whether the ancients had any other basis than this for their conclusions, and certainly they lacked the technique of present-day historical method for testing the accuracy of their views. Thus one suffers no real loss in abandoning traditional opinions. Rather, the way to better knowledge is thereby cleared of certain obstructions by which it has been too long encumbered. All is gain for genuine history. The documents may now bear testimony for themselves directly to their present readers.

Incidentally the various gospels tell a great deal about themselves, although professing only to give information about Jesus. By reading between the lines we are able, for example, to determine approximately the dates of the gospels.

Since Mark was used in the composition of both Matthew and Luke, its priority in time is self-evident. Among the more conspicuous indications of its date are references to the overthrow of the Jewish nation and the destruction of the temple in the year 70 A.D. Teaching of Jesus relative to events that occurred after his death, was necessarily recorded in the form of prophecy. But when the narrator had lived through the predicted occurrences, his description took on the realistic quality of actual history. Now his own experiences enabled him with unerring certainty to point a moral for his readers. Thus the parable of the wicked husbandmen (Mark 12:1–9) seemed to be a clear forecast of the fate that overtook the Jews for rejecting the "beloved son," a dignity bestowed on Jesus at the time of his baptism (Mark 1:11). In consequence of this rejection the vineyard was to be given "unto others," a prophecy that the author had seen fulfilled when God permitted the Roman conquerors to dispossess the Jews of the Holy Land.

Now that the evangelist looks back upon the end of the Jewish state and the destruction of the temple, in accordance as he believes with an explicit prediction of Jesus (13:2), he must explain why the end of the world and the coming of the Messiah from heaven had not immediately followed these frightful calamities. Certainly this would have been an appropriate setting, in conformity with current Jewish apocalyptic imagery, for the advent of "the Son of man coming in the clouds with great power and glory" (Mark 13:26; cf. 8:38). The delay needs explanation.

But a Christian writer, already engaged in spreading the new religion over the Roman world at large, finds a ready answer. More time is necessary to complete this task: "The gospel must first be preached unto all the Gentiles" (13: 10). Just when Jesus will return to reveal himself in messianic triumph, God alone knows, but the evangelist is convinced that this grand consummation of world-history is not far distant. There will be men of Jesus' own generation still living—and the evangelist seems to count himself in this class—when the impending divine event transpires (13:30–32).

When Mark was written, the fatal Jewish revolution was a thing of the past, but not of the remote past. The book must have been composed soon after 70 A.D.[1] In the decades that followed, two later evangelists, working independently of one another, expanded Mark into the more detailed gospels now known as "Matthew" and "Luke." John is not so evidently dependent on Mark and therefore is not so easily allocated in the chronological succession. But the complete abandonment in John of teaching about

[1] The date and authorship of this gospel have recently been examined in a very thorough manner by B. W. Bacon (*The Gospel of Mark* [New Haven, 1925]).

the early end of the world, and the absence of interest in an apocalyptic advent of the Son of
man, would imply a date well beyond the year
70 A.D. This book can hardly have come into existence before the close of the first century. And
most of even the older apocryphal gospels fall
within the second century.

As evidence for the accuracy of any gospel's
information about Jesus, the date of its composition is a very uncertain witness. He had lived
and died at least forty years before the oldest
surviving account of his career, the Gospel of
Mark, was composed. How can one today hope
to bridge that ominous gap of silent years separating the earthly Jesus from the later age in
which the gospels were produced?

The darkness of the forty-year chasm lying
between the death of Jesus and the writing of
Mark is not utterly impenetrable. Early in this
period Paul had been converted, and in the
course of his missionary labors sent letters to
various churches. Several of these epistles are
still extant, most of them coming from the decade 50–60 A.D. Although composed principally
for the purpose of solving problems recently
arising within the communities addressed, one
may reasonably expect that incidentally the let-

[77]

ters will reveal something of the contemporary
status of Christian tradition about the life and
teaching of Jesus. The Book of Acts, on the
other hand, was a deliberate effort to narrate the
history of the Christian movement from the
time of Jesus' death until Paul arrived in Rome.
Surely one may hope to find here many a valuable clue to the manner in which tradition about
the earthly Jesus had first taken shape and the
process of evolution through which it had passed
prior to the year 60 A.D.

In the narratives of Acts early Christian
preachers are frequently brought upon the scene.
Peter is the chief spokesman, until this rôle is assumed by Paul. Other less conspicuous persons
—Stephen, Philip, Ananias of Damascus, Barnabas, Priscilla and Aquila, and Apollos—discourse more or less at length by way of defining
and defending Christianity. It is the primary
function of Christian leaders to devote themselves to "the ministry of the word" (Acts 6:4),
the very type of person from whom the writer of
Acts had derived information for his earlier
book, the Gospel of Luke (Luke 1:2). This situation should have furnished an excellent opportunity to show how memories of the life and
teaching of the earthly Jesus had been turned to

[78]

practical account both in the nurture of the new communities and in the missionary preaching.

One turns with keen expectation to Acts, only to be rudely disillusioned. We read the book from beginning to end and discover that no Christian preacher whose words are there recorded concerned himself, except in the most casual way, with the career of Jesus prior to the crucifixion. Only incidentally, and very infrequently, is any reference made either to his deeds or to his teachings. Once the story of his miracles is told in a single verse: "Jesus of Nazareth, a man approved of God unto you by mighty works and wonders and signs which God did by him in the midst of you" (2:22). On another occasion the whole record of his career from the baptism to the cross is summarized in a couple of sentences (10:37–39). We learn that the primitive group of believers continued steadfast in the "apostles' teaching" (2:42), but nothing is said about any attempt to assemble a body of instruction uttered by Jesus. Except for a single saying of his, to the effect that it is more blessed to give than to receive (20:35), no word spoken by him prior to his death is cited anywhere in the book.

[79]

On the basis of Acts one might easily infer that for thirty years after the death of Jesus his followers had shown little or no interest in rehearsing the story of his earthly career. It might seem that they had busied themselves with bearing witness to their own belief in him and had made no effort to substantiate their message by references to occurrences in his lifetime. They deduced evidence for his resurrection sometimes from their own observation and sometimes from ancient scripture, but never referred to any anticipations of this event by him. They declared him to be the savior promised to the Jews, and clinched their argument by citations from prophecy, but did not mention any teaching of his on this theme. They cited their own possession of the Holy Spirit in evidence of his exaltation to a position of messianic dignity in heaven, whence he presently would descend to establish the new Kingdom of God on earth, but they never reported that he himself had predicted his messiahship. A particularly favorite theme with them was the evidential value of wonders which they were now able to perform in the name of Jesus, but they never credited him with having commissioned them to work miracles. In all of this they spoke on behalf of the exalted Lord Jesus Christ of their present faith; they never brought forward the earthly Jesus to speak for himself.

For the purposes of a biography of Jesus, the Book of Acts has almost no positive value. If the early Christians had not said more about him than is contained in this narrative purporting to be a history of the new religion during the first three decades after the death of its founder, one marvels that any information at all about his earthly career should have survived. From Acts alone one would never suspect that the same individual who composed this book would have had any interest whatsoever in writing the detailed account of Jesus' life previously set forth in the Gospel of Luke. Evidently the author had deliberately adopted the plan of assembling in his first treatise all the information about Jesus that he had learned—and it was considerable in extent—from those "ministers of the word," some of whose activity belonged in reality to the period of history covered by Acts. Having told their story in his previous work, he devoted the space in his second treatise to demonstrating the supernatural character of the new religion. He would convince Theophilus that its success was further assured in consequence of the present position of heavenly authority held by the official Lord Jesus Christ of Christian faith.

Paul was in a more favorable position than the author of Acts for knowing the early history of Christianity. He was an actual contemporary of the first disciples. At the outset he had been a persecutor of these new religionists and must have known enough of their activities and interests to inspire his hatred of them. Immediately after his conversion he was intimately associated with the Christians of Damascus, some of whose number probably were refugees from Palestine. Three years later he spent two weeks in Jerusalem with Peter. Then for a period of fourteen years he preached in the neighboring territory of Syria and Cilicia. During a part of this time he was closely associated with Barnabas, who earlier had been a member of the Christian group in Jerusalem. About the year 50 Paul was again in Jerusalem, where he came into close contact with several individuals who had been personal companions of Jesus. In later years his chief helper was Silas, who also had come from Palestine. For upwards of a decade and a half before the writing of any of his epistles, Paul had enjoyed ample opportunities to learn the manner in which memories of Jesus were being made to serve the new cause.

While no one of Paul's letters is in the nature of a history, incidentally they reflect a measure of his debt to Christian predecessors. Sometimes he explicitly indicated these obligations. He commended the Corinthians for holding fast the "traditions even as I delivered them to you," particularly the observance of the Lord's Supper which, he had been informed, went back for its authority to the events of the last night of Jesus' life (I Cor. 11:2, 23 ff.). The scriptural justification for the death of Jesus, and the most complete extant list of his appearances were among the things Paul had "received" (I Cor. 15:3–7).

At other times, without specifying the source of his information, Paul alludes to the life and teaching of Jesus, but in a manner to make clear that he is employing current tradition already familiar to his readers. He admonishes the Philippians to model their lives after the example of Jesus, whose earthly humility had now been rewarded by exaltation to lordship in heaven (Phil. 2:5 ff.). Paul never questions the tradition that Jesus had gathered about himself during his lifetime a group of special disciples, who now were the "pillars" in the Jerusalem church,

[83]

even though enemies of Paul used this fact to undermine his own prestige. He knew a brother of Jesus, James, who was the leading person in the church at Jerusalem about the year 50 A.D. (Gal. 2:12). That Jesus had suffered death by crucifixion is another historical item so familiar to Paul that he made it the basis of his gospel of redemption (I Cor. 2:1–8). In actual bulk the Pauline references to events of Jesus' lifetime are relatively meager, but the unstudied character of Paul's remarks implies that this type of tradition was common property even in the gentile churches.

Paul also knows that reported teachings of Jesus carry an unquestioned authority in both Jewish and gentile Christian circles. He cites such instruction himself for the benefit of the Corinthians, even though he adds advice of his own on questions not covered by any reported words of Jesus (I Cor. 7:10 ff.). Also he grants that his critics are right in quoting Jesus in support of their claim that the Christian missionary may demand his living from the congregations which he serves (I Cor. 9:14). On another occasion he uses a reputed saying of Jesus to justify the view that deceased Christians will not be at a disadvantage in comparison with those still alive when the Lord comes in apocalyptic triumph (I Thess. 4:15). Scanty as these citations are, they nevertheless attest very clearly that for Paul and his contemporaries teachings of Jesus, when they can be cited, are decisive and final.

Paul had never been associated with the historical Jesus and had not allied himself with the Christian movement until a year or more after its founder's death. Yet his later contacts with the disciples had been sufficient to make him well aware of whatever interest they may have had in rehearsing the story of Jesus' career. His infrequent reference to this subject is a great disappointment, which is only enhanced by the fact that it is not chargeable to mere ignorance. Even as it stands, the Pauline correspondence is a richer source of information for the life of Jesus than is the Book of Acts. Had Paul undertaken the task, undoubtedly he could have written a gospel that would have been quite as accurate and extensive as the Gospel of Luke. Unfortunately, he had no interest in such an enterprise.

It is easy to understand why Paul concerned himself so little with tradition about the earthly Jesus. For him, even more than for the writer of Acts, the heavenly Christ was the object of supreme concern. Paul was engrossed with events

[85]

that had transpired since the crucifixion, and with still more significant happenings to occur in the near future. Believing that the end of the "present evil age" was near, he looked for the early coming of the Son of God from heaven (I Thess. 1:10; 3:13; 4:15–18). On various occasions his readers were warned of this impending "day of our Lord Jesus Christ" (I Cor. 1:8; 5:5; II Cor. 1:14; I Thess. 5:2; Phil. 1:6, 10; 2:16). Watchfulness was the proper Christian attitude, for "the Lord is at hand" (Phil. 4:5). Present earthly activities were of minor importance, since only a short time would elapse until, "the fashion of this world passes away" (I Cor. 7:29 –31). This futuristic psychology was not conducive to historical research. It was quite out of place in a world that hung on the brink of the great transformation. Indeed, this attitude was so characteristic of Christianity in the early days that no extensive gospel records were produced until a generation after the time of Paul.

Furthermore, in Paul's case there was yet another hindering circumstance. Since his opponents denied his right to be counted an authority because he had not been a follower of the earthly Jesus, it behooved him to minimize the significance of any such historical contact. A vision of the risen Christ must be held all-sufficient, as indeed it was in Paul's own conviction. Moreover, he knew what it was to experience immediate "visions and revelations of the Lord" (II Cor. 12:1). Communications received directly from the present heavenly Christ rendered unnecessary for one of his temperament any wearisome search into the past for authentic Christian instruction. Since Paul believed himself to possess the very mind of Christ (I Cor. 2:16), and to be under the perpetual guidance of the Spirit, it is hardly to be imagined that he would concern himself with any diligent quest for traditional information about the life and teaching of the earthly Jesus.

III

Neither from Acts nor from the letters of Paul do we derive any appreciable help for retracing the course of evolution through which tradition about Jesus had passed between the years 30 and 70. Again, it is to the gospels themselves that we must turn for further light. For upward of half a century students have been diligently investigating their relations to one another. Substantial results have now been reached.

A key to gospel origins is found in the nota-

ble preface of Luke. Originally an early generation of preachers active in the missionary enterprise had put into circulation stories about the
doings and teachings of Jesus. By degrees these
orally transmitted narratives passed into writing. The author of Luke had collected a number
of such documents, but with no one of them did
he feel fully satisfied. They were too fragmentary, perhaps even too contradictory, and at
least not competent to produce that conviction
which he desired to establish in the mind of
Theophilus. Accordingly, he undertook the composition of a new treatise. This was based upon
a careful examination of earlier works but was
designed to correct their seeming defects and to
constitute a story of Jesus' career that would
serve better the needs of the hour.

The Gospel of Mark proves to have been one
of the documents referred to in the Lucan preface. The new evangelist copied it in large part,
sometimes verbatim and at other times more
freely. It supplied the general outline for his
story of Jesus' career, and evidently it was
thought one of the most valuable of the "many"
narratives to which reference was made. Yet the
writer of Luke felt no hesitation in deviating
from Mark. He omitted at will longer or shorter

[88]

sections of the book. Occasionally he rearranged its order of events or deliberately altered its statements. And an important feature of his work was his elaborate supplementation of the Marcan story.

An examination of Matthew shows that it also was built largely on Mark. Various sections of Mark were transcribed with only slight changes of wording. In Matthew, as in Luke, Mark furnished the geographical and chronological outline for the narrative, but into this framework large bodies of new material were incorporated. Nor was the process of enlargement hindered by any policy of slavish adherence to Mark. The author of Matthew felt no obligation to follow this source when his own interests called for a different procedure. Frequently its narrative was freely condensed; sometimes its order was altered; occasionally it was more or less elaborately expanded; and a few sections were entirely omitted. Yet, on the whole, Mark appears to have been one of the most highly prized of the sources used in the composition of Matthew.

A reader who will take the trouble to expunge from Matthew and from Luke those portions of their respective narratives that were derived from Mark will find himself left with a very interesting residuum. In both substance and diction a large part of this remainder still proves to be closely parallel in both gospels. Matthew may state that John the Baptist addressed "Pharisees and Sadducees," while Luke has him speak simply "to the multitudes"; but both agree that on this occasion his message to his audience opened with the challenge "Ye offspring of vipers, who warned you to flee from the wrath to come?" Throughout this whole paragraph the verbal agreement is very close (Matt. 3:7–10; Luke 3:7–9). Sometimes there is a substantial agreement in content but a variation in phraseology. Matthew reports that on a certain occasion when the disciples were assembled Jesus "opened his mouth and taught them saying, Blessed are the poor in spirit for theirs is the kingdom of heaven"; while in Luke the language runs "he lifted up his eyes on his disciples and said, Blessed are ye poor for yours is the kingdom of God" (Matt. 5:3–12; Luke 6:20–23). An extended survey of the non-Marcan parallels in Matthew and Luke proves that the writers used, more or less freely, a considerable body of common source material for these portions of their books.

THE RETURN TO JESUS

Efforts to reconstruct the content of the ancient non-Marcan tradition about Jesus have been measurably successful. Whether it stood in only one of the "many" documents mentioned in Luke's preface, or was a combination of two or more, is still subject to doubt. Sometimes the agreement between Matthew and Luke is so close as to attest beyond question their use of the same written source. Conspicuous illustrations of this resemblance may be seen in Jesus' discourse on freedom from anxiety (Matt. 6:25–33; Luke 12:22–31), in his remarks about the mote in the eye (Matt. 7:3–5; Luke 6:41 f.), in the exchange of communications between Jesus and the imprisoned John (Matt. 11:2–19; Luke 7:18–35), in Jesus' prayer of gratitude for God's favor (Matt. 11:25–27; Luke 10:21 f.), or in the lament over Jerusalem (Matt. 23:37–39; Luke 13:34 f.).

At other times the agreement between Matthew and Luke is so free that one may easily assume their dependence on sources that were already current in variant forms before falling into the hands of these evangelists. Examples are fairly numerous. Among the more striking are the divergent accounts of the Lord's Prayer as reported in Matt. 6:9–15 and Luke 11:2–4, or the variant lists of beatitudes assembled in Matt. 5:3–12 and in Luke 6:20–26. Often, also, there is wide disagreement between Matthew and Luke in the setting given to the same incident, even when there is close verbal agreement in their several narratives. To illustrate this point, take three familiar topics, "the lamp of the body is the eye," "no man can serve two masters," and "be not anxious for your life." In Matthew, Jesus' words on these subjects are grouped together in an immediate sequence as part of the Sermon on the Mount (6:22–33). In Luke, on the contrary, they are not in the "Sermon" at all (6:20–49), but stand in a different context entirely separated from one another (Luke 11:34 f.; 16:13; 12:22–31).

Such phenomena have left us in much doubt about the original form of this lost non-Marcan source. Have we here to do with a single document, sometimes copied closely and at other times liberally altered or rearranged according to individual taste by the authors of Matthew and Luke? Or did they employ several documents, some of which were identical, while others had already gained circulation in divergent forms before these authors wrote? On the whole, the latter seems the more probable supposition, yet doubt as to the literary unity of this material does not seriously affect one's appreciation of its unique character and content. Whether circulating originally in one or more documents, it embraced mainly—but not exclusively—teachings of Jesus; hence for a long time it has been called "Logia," that is, "Sayings." Nowadays it is often called "Q", the first letter of the German word *Quelle*, meaning "source."

When Mark and the Logia have been exscinded from Matthew and from Luke, there is still a substantial remainder left over in each of these two books. Whether this residuum was also derived from earlier tradition or was an original composition of the final author cannot always be determined. But ordinarily it is now taken to be a late addition to gospel literature, and for that reason to have little if any historical value as a source of information about Jesus. Similarly, the independence of the Fourth Gospel, when compared with the Synoptics, has resulted in an unfavorable judgment regarding its worth as a witness to the historical Jesus. One finds it quite impossible to graft John on to the genealogical tree constructed to explain the rise of the other three gospels. While its author seems to have been familiar with narratives of the Synoptic type, so divergent is his story of Jesus' career that today his book is widely believed to have been a late composition made with little or no reference to older documents.

The two-source hypothesis, which thus resolves the Synoptic gospels into Mark and the Logia, is thought by many scholars to furnish a sure way of return to the real Jesus of history. One passes hastily over John and the sections of the Synoptics peculiar to Matthew and to Luke. Appeal is made to the older units of tradition. Mark is trusted, especially for geographical and chronological data about Jesus, and the recoverable sections of the Logia are assumed to be almost a verbatim account of his teachings.

IV

Historical certainty must not be too hastily inferred from the current two-source theory of gospel origins. Great indeed is the debt of gratitude due those investigators who have labored diligently upon the Synoptic problem. Minute comparison of parallels in the first three gospels has made clear the earlier currency of Mark and has also demonstrated the independent existence of a more or less extensive body of non-Marcan materials used in the composition of Matthew and Luke. These two general conclusions stand unquestioned. But new problems immediately emerge. What was the state of affairs before Mark, and before documents of the Logia group arose? The tradition that went into the composition of these writings certainly had a previous evolution. To halt one's quest with them and immediately to reconstruct therefrom a "Life" of Jesus, as though they carried one straight back to him, is simply historical myopia. A more penetrating investigation into the earlier stages of gospel history is needed to insure a safe return to Jesus.

Taken singly, as literary compositions the gospels exhibit some very striking characteristics. Mark, for example, is largely a congeries of short paragraphs depicting Jesus in rapidly varying and frequently recurring rôles. First he is a prophet declaring the imminence of the Kingdom of God (1:14 f.). Then suddenly he changes into the founder of a new religious movement who authoritatively selects disciples to perpetuate its existence (1:16–20). Immediately and without warning he is transformed into a worker of wonders piled one upon another in rapid succession (1:21—2:12). Abruptly again he becomes a model controversialist, con-

[95]

tending for the independence of himself and his disciples (2:13—3:6). Then the miracle motif comes into play once more (3:7-12), only to be followed immediately by another account of his choice of disciples to represent officially the new Christian society (3:13-19). Next he passes again into the ideal controversialist, defending himself against the charge of collusion with Beelzebub (3:20-35). Suddenly he changes form once more, becoming a teacher of parables (4:1-34). Similarly diversified phenomena recur throughout the book. What a variety of structural units make up the literary mosaic that we call the Gospel of Mark!

It is easily conceivable that an evangelist might have set himself a very different sort of task. He might have chosen to write a unified and comprehensive story of Jesus' career as a worker of miracles. Or he might have attempted a detailed biographical narrative setting forth the activities of Jesus from year to year and tracing in succession each movement made by him during the course of his public and private life. Again, he might have proposed a treatise unified around the content of Jesus' teaching. Indeed, he might have dwelt exclusively, as sometimes moderns have done, on the parables of Jesus. But it is an arresting fact that no gospel writer, particularly no one of the Synoptists, composed a work designed to have any such unified literary character. Matthew and Luke are even more diversified in content than Mark. They are characterized by abrupt transitions that indicate the presence of numerous blocks of tradition, like groups of beatitudes, model prayers, proverbial sayings, or collections of imprecations, readily betraying earlier stages in the growth of gospel books. Even though the units of the mosaic are often carefully cemented together, the outlines of the several pieces in the composition are still clearly discernible.

The choppy quality in the present gospels tells its own story. The rehearsal of memories about Jesus did not at first assume the form of continuous narrative. It was left for Christians of a later generation to assemble earlier, fragmentary traditions into a formal biography and supply a measure of solidarity to the whole. At the start, activities and teachings of Jesus were recalled only in isolated fashion. References to time and place were quite incidental, if not indeed entirely wanting. It was a sufficient introduction to say "and it came to pass," or "in those days," or "on a certain occasion." These

first accounts owed their origin, not to the literary impulses of outstanding authors, but to the
activity of various inconspicuous disciples who
rehearsed individual sayings or incidents from
the lifetime of Jesus for practical use in the
Christian cause. First orally, and then in written
form, these fluid memories gradually crystallized into more formal units of tradition that ultimately were embalmed in our present gospels.

The Gospel of Mark was one of the first efforts at continuous narrative. The writers of
Matthew and Luke undertook a more comprehensive gathering of material and revised the
Marcan scheme of unification. They both
showed not a little originality in grouping their
subject matter. Particularly was this true of the
author of Matthew. But their general dependence upon the Marcan sequence of events, un-
satisfactory though it was, proves it to have been
the best model at their disposal. Each of these
evangelists ran his traditional materials together
like beads of different size and color strung on a
single thread. A few of the beads may have been
shaped by his own hand, but most of them had
been bequeathed to him from the accumulated
stores of earlier tradition. Some had been made
at one bench and some at another, in each case

according to the skill and taste of the artisan. Missionary fields and Christian communities were the workshops, while preachers and teachers were the laborers.

The earliest stages in the gospel-making process are now to be recovered only by resolving the present documents into their constituent parts. We unstring, let us say, Mark's beads. We lay aside the string itself, which in this case is the rather flimsy thread of topographical and chronological sequence superimposed on the originally unlocated and untimed incidents derived from the older tradition. A similar procedure in the case of the other gospels is attended by a like result. When the process has been completed, the elemental units thus recovered become themselves the object of chief attention.

The isolated blocks of tradition have now to be reclassified according to their own inherent likenesses. One group is distinguished by a dominant interest to depict Jesus as a hero in action. Such are the narratives of his baptism, his temptation, his miracles, his transfiguration , and his resurrection. In these stories the unifying motive is an interest in legend. In another group the aim is more specifically didactic. Here Jesus sets an example to be imitated. He resists Jew-

[99]

ish religious leaders, he ignores legalistic refinements, he forsakes even his nearest of kin to espouse the new cause, he blesses little children, he pays the temple tax required of all Jews, he submits to the Roman demand for tribute, and he goes about doing good whenever the opportunity offers. These incidents made him the model to be copied by disciples in pursuing a similar course of action.

Reported sayings of Jesus also belong in different categories. One type of discourse is framed about an interest in the future of the Christian movement. Such are the parables forecasting the final triumph of the Kingdom of God and the prophecies regarding the end of the world. Other groups of sayings have the character of proverbial expressions that readily stick in the memory and are appropriate for citation on various occasions. Examples are numerous: "Sufficient unto the day is the evil thereof," "Out of the abundance of the heart the mouth speaketh," "If any man hath ears to hear let him hear," "There is nothing hid that shall not be revealed," "Wheresoever the carcass is there will the eagles be gathered together." Many sayings are cast in hortatory form. Admonitions of Jesus, like decisions of the rabbis, constitute a rule of life for the guidance of disciples. He teaches proper methods of almsgiving, prayer, and fasting. He defines correct procedure with reference to the question of divorce. He lays down rules for settling disputes within the Christian communities. He advises missionaries about a suitable equipment for their journeys and prescribes the ideal form of conduct for the traveling preacher.

When the several units in the gospel mosaic have been regrouped according to similarity of form, is the result of any service to the biographer of Jesus? There is today a new "school" at work on this problem. Its task falls chiefly in the period before any continuous gospels were written, even before Mark and the hypothetical compilation called the Logia arose. By classifying the earlier fragmentary narratives according to their various forms—legends, paradigms, proverbs, exhortations, or whatever else they may be—an effort is made to distinguish between earlier and later pieces. It is thought possible to discover a law of evolution in the forms which a religious literature assumes in the course of its growth, and so to determine successive stages in the rise of tradition about Jesus. By tracing the course of expansion from Mark through the later gospels, both canonical and apocryphal, one may easily distinguish typical forms in the history of Christian literature after the year 70 A.D. For this period there are extant documents.

Materials for the interim between Jesus and Mark are less objective. To make a comparative study of Jewish literary forms is of some assistance. They furnish a standard for judging as to whether a particular piece of Christian tradition is Palestinian in character, while other blocks may be tested by comparison with corresponding gentile types of cult-story. For example, Jesus as prophet or rabbi conforms more closely to a Jewish motif than does Jesus in the rôle of miracle-worker, a motif more characteristically gentile. By these and other like means, one endeavors to penetrate behind the present gospels, even beyond the paragraphs of which they are composed, to the primal elements in the literature. When the most primitive blocks have been isolated, they become stepping-stones on which to follow up the gospel stream a little nearer to its source, and thus to effect a closer approximation to the times of Jesus.[1]

[1] More than a decade ago E. W. Parsons (*A Historical Examination of Some Non-Markan Elements in Luke* [Chicago, 1914]) explained the rise of certain sections in the gospel by reference to

THE RETURN TO JESUS

V

The test of literary *genre*, although more penetrating and discriminating than that of chronological priority for Mark and the Logia, still falls short of complete satisfaction as a norm for distinguishing historical from unhistorical items in the present gospels. There is yet a more fundamental consideration to be borne in mind. This is the social experience reflected in the tradition, whatever its age or form.

"problem-situations" in the life of the Christians. By such study he endeavored to fix the probable date and place at which selected portions of tradition arose. He was not concerned, however, with its specific literary forms. C. W. Votaw ("The Gospels and Contemporary Biographies," *American Journal of Theology*, XIX (1915), 45–73, 217–49) examined the gospels beside other biographical literature of the age but did not carry the discussion into the field of origins. This phase of research has been pursued with especial vigor in Germany, where it is known as *Formgeschichte*. Its first exponents were K. L. Schmidt (*Der Rahmen der Geschichte Jesu* [Berlin, 1919]), who sought to demonstrate that the tradition incorporated in the gospels was originally devoid of any chronological and topographical scheme of unification; and M. Dibelius (*Formgeschichte des Evangeliums* [Tübingen, 1919]), who attempted a classification of different forms of early tradition as shaped by the practical needs of the Christian communities. This tradition was found to be the work of unliterary men who framed unconnected narratives—paradigms, short stories, apothegms, exhortations, legends—in accordance with the immediate necessities of their cult-life and missionary propaganda. R. Bultmann (*Die Geschichte*

JESUS—A NEW BIOGRAPHY

The Christian movement was the matrix that nourished into life all tradition from the earliest fragment to the most complete biographical narrative. Throughout the entire period of its growth, the gospel tree remained firmly rooted in the soil of the Christian society. The portions of the literature that have survived, whether in canonical or apocryphal books, are quite as truly sources of information for the contemporary status of the new religion as for the history of Jesus'

---

der synoptischen Tradition [Göttingen, 1921]) made his point of departure not the life-situations within the Christian society but the specific types of different units discoverable in the present gospel books. The result was the differentiation of distinctive forms not essentially dissimilar to those specified by Dibelius. This general line of investigation has been pursued by M. Albertz, *Die synoptischen Streitgespräche: Ein Beitrag zur Formgeschichte des Urchristentums* (Berlin, 1921) and "Zur Formgeschichte der Auferstehungsberichte," *Zeitschrift für die neutestamentliche Wissenschaft*, XXI (1922), 259–69; G. Bertram, *Die Leidensgeschichte Jesu und der Christuskult: Eine formgeschichtliche Untersuchung* (Göttingen, 1922); E. Fascher, *Die formgeschichtliche Methode: Eine Darstellung und Kritik* (Giessen, 1924); R. Bultmann, *Die Erforschung der synoptischen Evangelien* (Giessen, 1925); K. Kundsin, *Topologische Überlieferungsstoffe im Johannes-Evangelium* (Göttingen, 1925); see also three papers in Gunkel's "Festschrift," *Eucharisterion*, 2. Teil (Göttingen, 1923), one by M. Dibelius, "Stilkritisches zur Apostelgeschichte" (pp. 27–49), another by K. L. Schmidt, "Die Stellung der Evangelien in der allgemeinen Literaturgeschichte" (pp. 50–134), and the third by H. Windisch, "Der Johanneische Erzählungsstil" (pp. 174–213).

career. Doubtless these books are most frequently read simply for information about him. But it would be entirely appropriate to consult them for data regarding the history of Christianity from the time of Jesus' death until early in the second century. The themes that interested an evangelist, the drift of his argument, his choice of selections from older tradition, his arrangement of materials, his interpretative emphases—all are windows through which a modern reader may look upon different scenes in the evolving history of Christianity during the gospel-making age.

Our earlier survey of the content of the several gospels should have made sufficiently evident the immediate interests of the different evangelists. In producing their respective portraits of Jesus they were seen to be simultaneously, though perhaps unconsciously, recording the history of their own times. They were all immensely concerned to establish the divine authority of the new religion which at the moment was competing with rivals for the allegiance of both Jews and Gentiles throughout the ancient world. This fact could not have been one whit plainer had each author explicitly affirmed that Christianity was now an independent movement, organized for missionary purposes, equipped with the rites of baptism and the Lord's Supper, served by recognized leaders, resisted in its expansion by powerful enemies, and destined in the opinion of its advocates ultimately to triumph over all its foes.

For each evangelist the Christian society was a going concern, from which he drew his immediate enthusiasms and whose interests lay close to his heart. By recasting the story of Jesus' career as it had been transmitted to him through inheritances from the past, he would forge a better instrument for serving the present and the future of the new religion. Differences of individuality, of inheritances, of time, of provenance, and of outlook among the several authors resulted in the production of books that varied widely from one another. Each gospel revealed the distinctive social experience of its particular writer and his immediate associates within one or another area of growing Christianity. While formally his work was a biography of Jesus, virtually it was also a treatise dealing with issues and interests of the author's own day.

The primal units into which the present written gospels must ultimately be resolved are no less closely bound up with the life-interests of the earlier Christian society. Everywhere in evidence are indications of exigencies that prompted rehearsals of Jesus' words or deeds. At one time it might be a celebration of the Eucharist that led someone in the assembled company to recall an occasion when Jesus had fed a multitude of people with a few loaves and fishes. The observance of the eucharistic rite was so frequently repeated, and in so many different places, that the accompanying story of the feeding soon took on a number of variations. The author of Mark knew it in at least two forms, one mentioning five thousand participants and another four thousand (6:34–44; 8:1–10). Happily, he included both in his book, even though he had no distinctive setting for the second account but was content to introduce it with the vague phrase "in those days."

Perhaps, on another occasion, free intercourse with Gentiles in the prosecution of missionary work met severe criticism from Jews, or from Christians with strong Jewish leanings. Then it was especially in point to recall controversies between Jesus and his adversaries, and to note that he had virtually eliminated the distinction between clean and unclean meats (Mark 7:1–23). Or, again, wearied by the struggle to save a world that responded none too eagerly to

the Christian message, a discouraged congregation revived its drooping spirits by reciting a
parable of Jesus likening the Kingdom of God to
a diminutive mustard seed growing from small
beginnings into a plant with great branches
(Mark 4:30–32).

When enemies cast doubt upon the divine
character of Christianity by alleging that its expulsion of demons in the name of Jesus was
simply Satan-magic, such as might be performed
by other exorcists of the time, again appeal was
made to an incident in the lifetime of Jesus. His
work had been similarly disparaged. Opponents
had said that his wonders were accomplished
through an alliance with Satan, and not through
the power of the Holy Spirit. But with great emphasis he had affirmed that such blasphemy was
the one unforgivable sin (Mark 3:22–30). Thus
Christians sought to turn the edge of hostile criticism, and the divergent forms in which this incident has been reported suggest the frequent re-
currence of the situation in the experience of the
disciples (Matt. 9:33 f.; 12:22–32; Luke 11:14–
23).

Were it necessary, additional illustrations to
demonstrate the vital social connections of a
wide range of gospel tradition could easily be ad-

duced. As it now stands, this literature is intimately bound up with the evolution of the new religious movement from the days of its very beginnings in Palestine down to the period of its spread over the Mediterranean world at large. The wealth of local color in the gospels, gratifying though it is to the historian of early Christianity, greatly enhances the difficulty of isolating exactly the figure of the earthly Jesus. On the other hand, a full recognition of the presence in a gospel of interests vital to the contemporary Christian society is the only sure basis from which to assay the genuineness of its tradition. Negatively at any rate, the significance of such interests is self-evident. That which is peculiarly apposite to a situation realized first in the social experience of the disciples after Jesus' death can hardly be taken to represent a well-established fact of his own career.

Positive results are also available. Jesus, too, lived in a very real social environment. Conditions within Palestine during the first third of the first century, and tendencies which later culminated in the disastrous revolution of the year 66 A.D., are hardly less significant for the life of Jesus than they are for the history of Judaism. Contemporary religious activities among Jews, the attitudes characteristic of various strata in Palestinian society, and the outstanding problems to engage the attention of Jesus and his associates must be made the ready possession of his modern biographer. It is as true of the religious genius, as of the poet, that he may not be understood by one unfamiliar with his native environment.[1]

No return to Jesus will be adequate that is not at the same time a return to the living conditions of his own time, with all that they signified for the determination of his course of life and the shaping of his experience. To visualize in concrete fashion the social setting in which he did his work will carry one a long way toward a genuine understanding of the tasks that confronted him and the line of conduct he chose to adopt. Since he made immediate connections with the life of his age, the issues he faced and the ideals he upheld must have been of vital concern to his contemporaries. Had he talked of things remote from their interests he would hardly have created enemies, much less would he have won disciples. The attitudes taken toward

---

[1] Wer den Dichter will verstehen,
Muss in Dichters Lande gehen.
—Goethe.

him, whether of friendship or of hostility, were an outcome of circumstances to be understood only when viewed in connection with the life-situation by which he was environed and of which he was a moving part.

When the framers of gospel tradition have been socially integrated within the early Christian movement, and Jesus has been vitally linked with the Palestinian society of his day, the problem of recovering dependable historical information about him becomes more readily soluble. Gospel traditions that dovetail normally into his experience within a Palestinian environment need not be called in question. On the other hand, when he is made to sponsor interests or opinions whose social appositeness emerges first in the later history of the Christian movement, one will be very hesitant about accepting the historical reliability of such data. A gospel-writer may, to be sure, correctly represent what Jesus would have said or done had he been present on the later occasion. But this possibility must not be confounded with historic fact. To feel justification in assuming that Jesus would have met a future contingency in a particular way is one thing; to affirm that it was a part of his actual experience is quite another.

The assumption may represent perfectly good interpretation, but it is not valid history. The particular situation in which Jesus lived is never to be confused with the different situations in which the disciples found themselves during the later years when gospel literature was a-making.

At the outset, however, the social experience of Jesus, and that of the disciples who first perpetuated his memory, largely coincided. Their Palestinian setting was identical with his: they had inherited a similar range of religious interests, and they were enveloped by the same general conditions of life. In recalling incidents from his career, the occasion for interpretative elaboration, while present from the start, operated under significant limitations. The vividness of the disciples' own recollections and literalness of memory on the part of their contemporaries, together with the general sameness of social environment, tended to compel the earliest Christians to paint Jesus in the main true to life. Gospel tradition at its inception was of necessity essentially historical in character. But the new religious movement did not long restrict itself to Palestinian territory. With the widening of the missionary enterprise to include, first, Jews of the Diaspora and then Gentiles as well, it was found necessary to translate the preachers' message into new language and recast even its content, in accordance with the requirements of the new situation. To what extent the quality of genuine history was lost in this transition is ultimately determinable only by the character of the social experience reflected in the later forms of the tradition.

The decisive consideration in dealing with all gospel tradition is the extent to which the narrative reveals the dominance of interests suitable to the distinctive situation of Jesus, in contrast with conditions characteristic of later stages in the growth of the Christian movement. Such norms as canonicity, supposable apostolic authorship, the fixing of the earliest written sources, or the determination of distinctive literary forms, are only preliminary to the more fundamental test of social experience as revealed in the content of the narrative. Every type of tradition, whether an entire gospel or a documentary source or a more primitive fragmentary block, is subject to the same test; and no supposable date of origin is early enough to secure immunity for any portion of the gospel. Not only Mark but the most primitive sections of the Logia have to be subjected to this same test.

Likewise, later portions of the literature, such as material peculiar to Matthew, to Luke or to John, are entitled to a hearing in the same court of appeal. To declare offhand their unreliability, just because of their late emergence in the written records, is an improper procedure. The conditions within the early Christian society do not warrant the assumption that there could have been only one or two original sources, such as the Logia and Mark, whence reliable data were derivable. In the ardor of their devotion to the two-source solution of the synoptic problem, scholars all too readily imagined that true gospel history flowed down in a single channel from one head. When one visualizes the actual conditions under which gospels arose, no such simplicity is imaginable. When the crystallization of tradition first set in, the memories of different persons in various communities were at work on the task; and it is not at all improbable that some rivulets from a perfectly genuine fountain-head may have been much later than others in joining the swelling stream that ultimately constituted the present gospels. Except for the mechanical inconvenience which it causes the modern student, there would seem to be no reason for supposing that the author of Matthew or of Luke, and even of John or of an apocryphal book, might not have embodied new materials that were quite as reliable as anything in Mark or the hypothetical Logia.

Every statement in the records is to be judged by the degree of its suitableness to the distinctive environment of Jesus, on the one hand, and to that of the framers of gospel tradition at one or another stage in the history of Christianity, on the other. When consistently applied, this test will prove our safest guide in recovering from the present gospel records dependable information regarding the life and teaching of the earthly Jesus.

CHAPTER III
JEWISH LIFE IN PALESTINE

IN THE time of Jesus, Palestine was a comparatively small country, even within the
narrow confines of the world known to the
ancients. On a map of the Roman Empire, of
which the Holy Land was now a part, it was a
mere speck on the eastern frontier. Its scant ten
thousand square miles of territory measured less
than a hundred and fifty miles from north to
south. Toward the north and west it was
hemmed in by the more extensive country of
Syria and Phoenicia; while on the south and east
lay Arabia and the desert. In the more pros-
perous periods of its history access to the
Mediterranean was made possible through the
control of certain coast cities such as Joppa and
Caesarea, but the maritime plain was not itself
a part of Palestine proper. The waters which
its inhabitants counted as their own were the
Lake of Galilee and the Dead Sea, with the

connecting river Jordan. For a Roman geographer this country was only one of the minor units of the Empire, but for Jews it was the land of promise which, to their ancestors emerging from the frugal life of the desert, had seemed to flow with milk and honey.

I

Although confident that God had promised them ultimate possession of Palestine, the Hebrews experienced repeated disappointments in their efforts to secure the fulfilment of the divine intention. Their initial success under the leadership of David early in the tenth century was quickly followed by a division of the territory into the kingdoms of Israel and Judah. Weakened by disunion, the northern kingdom went down before the Assyrians in the last quarter of the eighth century. Judea only was left to perpetuate the ideal of political independence. But Judea itself was overrun by the Babylonians less than a century and a half later, when the bulk of its inhabitants were carried away captive into Mesopotamia. After the lapse of half a century, a group of the captives' descendants returned in the hope of repossessing the country and establishing a true kingdom of God's people. For them Palestine still was the land of hope where the Jews were yet to fulfil their heaven-decreed destiny. But the succeeding years were marked by hardship and failure contrasting sharply with that realization of national prosperity and distinction toward which the returning pilgrims had aspired. In the fourth century Palestine fell before Alexander the Great, and with the subsequent division of his empire this exposed land became a bone of contention between the Ptolemies of Egypt and the Seleucids of Syria.

The slumbering discontent of the Jews burst into a new flame of national zeal in the second quarter of the second century B.C., when the Syrian rulers had carried oppression to the point of endeavoring to wipe out the Jewish religion. That heroic struggle, known as the Maccabean revolution, continuing for approximately twenty-five years, finally issued in temporary political independence. Henceforth this was a period of history to be enshrined in memory along with the now idealized national triumph under David. It must have seemed to many Jews that they were now on the verge of realizing a happy theocracy, a veritable kingdom of God on earth. At no previous time since the Babylonian exile had the prospects for Jewish autonomy been so bright.

Under the leadership of a John Hyrcanus (135–104 B.C.) the national fortunes of the Jews rapidly approached their zenith. Samaria on the north and Idumea on the south were added to the kingdom, although neither country ever became dominantly Jewish in its population and sentiment. Farther north, in Galilee, reconquest went on more slowly but with greater ultimate success. The resistance of the Samaritans to distinctively Jewish culture made it impossible for Samaria ever to become genuinely holy land, but such was not the case in Galilee. By the middle of the first century B.C. this portion of David's kingdom had been effectively reclaimed for Judaism. Doubtless its population retained a large residuum of those foreign elements whose presence had once caused it to be known as "Galilee [i.e., "Region"] of the Gentiles," yet here the Maccabeans found themselves able not only to enforce their claim to political supremacy but also to settle in the territory many persons of pure Jewish blood. Jews secured the general recognition of their religious rites, and the inhabitants cultivated a genuinely Jewish type of patriotism.

Jewish aggressions to the east of the Jordan were also attended with success. Particularly along the southern portion of the river was the program of reconquest effectively enforced. During the first century B.C. the population and the customs of this territory, known as "Perea," became prevailingly Jewish. It, along with Galilee and Judea, made up the real Palestine of the Jews, the Holy Land proper. Jewish princes might rule contiguous territory, such as Samaria, Idumea, or Trachonitis, but only in Judea, Galilee, and Perea were Jewish peoples and customs in the ascendant.

The hope for permanent political autonomy under the Maccabean rulers was soon dispelled. Internal dissensions again rendered the Jews an easy prey for the conqueror, who this time was the Roman general Pompey. In 63 B.C. Palestine became a possession of the Romans. On the whole the new overlords were more lenient with this subject people than the Assyrians, Babylonians, or Syrians had been. Yet Pompey carried off many captives to Rome, and in subsequent years Palestine was to feel ever more heavily the yoke of the foreigner. The nearest approach to independence came during the reign of Herod the Great (37–4 B.C.). He would have had his subjects regard him as a true Jew, but they saw in him only a half-Jew hireling of Rome.

Even the semblance of national unification vanished when Herod's will, bequeathing Palestine to three of his sons, received the approval of the Roman emperor Augustus. By this division Judea, separated from Perea and Galilee, was grouped in a unit with Samaria and Idumea. Its ruler, Archelaus, proved so incompetent that the Jewish people themselves clamored for his removal. When in the year 6 A.D. he was deposed and his dominions were assigned directly to a Roman procurator, the most important section of the promised land lost its last vestige of political autonomy. That spot of earth which should have been the very center of a theocratic kingdom, more powerful and glorious than even David's had been, was now desecrated by the presence of a foreign government that knew not the god of the Jews.

In Galilee and Perea, where Herod's son Antipas continued in authority throughout the period of Jesus' career, popular feeling was hardly more reconciled to the existing state of affairs. Indeed, in Galilee the spirit of restlessness was particularly in evidence, even though Antipas himself conducted his administration with no little skill. But he never appealed to the popular imagination in the rôle of a Davidic prince. Rather, he was looked upon as the agent of the hated Roman government and hence in reality an obstacle to the realization of that national autonomy which was still believed to be the true destiny in store for God's chosen people.

The Jews might have congratulated themselves on their privileges under the Imperial régime. They, along with all other peoples in the Empire, enjoyed those opportunities for cosmopolitan intercourse that orderly government, the maintenance of excellent roads, and the driving of pirates from the sea had made possible. Nor did Jews fail to make themselves at home all about this newly unified Mediterranean world. Even in Palestine the blessings of Roman government were clearly in evidence. The Roman soldier maintained order, the administration of justice was insured by the presence of the Roman court, and the taxes were placed on a scientific basis by means of the characteristic Roman method of taking a census. At the same time the local Jewish community was left great freedom in the conduct of its own affairs. While individual procurators might on occasion prove incompetent and irritating, it nevertheless must be said that the physical benefits accruing to the Jews under Roman rule were not a few, and the inconveniences probably were less numerous and aggravating than had been the case in any previous period of Jewish subjection to foreign powers.

But the Jews themselves, particularly in Palestine, could hardly be expected to appraise favorably the actual benefits of Roman domination. And the more effectively Rome administered the affairs of the country, the more conscious were the chosen people of having lost the right to that self-determination which alone was consistent with their inherited ideal of a theocratic kingdom. The presence of the Roman police, the payment of the Imperial taxes, and the intrusion of foreigners in their midst only augmented popular longing for national rehabilitation. The spirit of revolt matured rapidly, particularly in Galilee. For over half a century this restless state of mind had been assuming revolutionary proportions until it finally flamed out in open rebellion in the great war of 66–70 A.D. The longing for deliverance from the yoke of the foreigner and more perfect realization of God's dominion over his own people, in fulfilment of long-awaited promises, was an item of pre-eminent and universal interest among the contemporaries of Jesus. It is not in the least surprising that he should have concerned himself very immediately with the problem of the establishment of the Kingdom of God. This was the crucial issue of the hour.

II

No single interest, however, had sole right of way in the Palestinian society of Jesus' day. Life had become far too complex to make possible absolute uniformity of opinion or action even on a matter of so general concern as the political issue. Indeed, the disastrous outcome of the revolt in the year 66 A.D. was due in no small measure to the presence of bitterly rival factions within Judaism itself. In consequence of the growing complexity of the social fabric and the wide interplay of rival wishes it had been impossible to win general assent for any single program of action. This variety of interests and attitudes was already characteristic of the time of Jesus. Doubtless the Jewish people were still essentially one in their desire to realize more perfectly the fulfilment of their national aspirations, but individuals and groups differed widely from one another in their notions of the course of conduct likely to effect the speediest realization of their common wish.

Probably Palestine was never more densely populated than in the first half of the first century of the present era. The Jewish historian Josephus estimates that there were three million persons in Jerusalem at the time of the Passover in the year 65 A.D. These figures are not impossible if one may assume that great numbers of the people from all over Palestine and also many from the Dispersion were in attendance upon the feast. But it is quite unimaginable that the city of Jerusalem could ever have contained any such numbers in its normal population. Galilee seems to have been even more thickly settled than Judea. Its cities were large and its villages very numerous, while the smallest of them is said to have had from ten to fifteen thousand inhabitants. Lacking official figures, modern statisticians have differed widely in their estimates of the number of Jews residing in Palestine at the time of Jesus, but all indications point to a dense and varied population.

A wide range of different interests is manifest in the various occupations by which people sought a livelihood. Many persons were engaged in the cultivation of the soil. Judea, though rocky and irregular, was moist enough for agriculture, and is said to have been very fruitful. The rain caught by the Judean hills compensated for the lack of springs and streams, and the cattle which fed upon the excellent grass in these regions were famed for their milk-producing capacity. An ancient writer describes the land as thickly planted with olive trees and yielding abundantly corn, pulse, and grapes. Honey also was produced in large quantities. Galilee in particular was noted for its fertile soil, which was said to be so universally rich and fruitful as to invite the most slothful of its inhabitants to take pains in its cultivation, with the result that no part of the land was permitted to lie idle. Perea, on the other hand, was largely waste land and desert. Yet there were productive portions where trees of all sorts grew, principally the olive and the palm. Also there were vineyards in Perea.

Even in the relatively simple life of the country, Jewish society was far from homogeneous. He who owned olive orchards, vineyards, or flocks, might have shared heartily with his servants and hired laborers in a feeling of dissatisfaction with their present political status. He and they might have entertained a common longing for the establishment of a new régime more directly controlled by their own God. But it would have been much less easy for them to agree upon a specific program for accomplishing their common desire. One person might be interested in a course of action that would conserve his home, his flocks, and his harvests, while for another it would be only a bare livelihood or a meager daily wage that was at stake, to say nothing of different attitudes toward the more subtle cultural values that distinguish the social strata of even a rural community.

Still more complex were the varied interests of urban life. In Judea, Jericho and Jerusalem were the principal cities. Every grade of social position from that of the poverty-stricken beggar to that of the priestly aristocrat or high government official was represented in their populations. Jerusalem especially was a center of commercial activity where men of all races mingled in the pursuit of business. Jewish merchants exported native products to foreign lands and imported merchandise from all parts of the Mediterranean world. Next to Jerusalem the most important city of Palestine was Sepphoris, an easy hour's walk from Jesus' home in Nazareth. Sepphoris too was a thriving commercial center and was the capital of Galilee until supplanted by Tiberias in the first half of the first century A.D. Probably Capernaum was the most significant among those towns where the busy life about the Sea of Galilee congregated, but such names as "Chorazin," "Bethsaida," "Magdala," "Gamala," and "Taricheae" must not be forgotten. The numerous villages that Josephus mentions, ranging in population from ten to fifteen thousand, must also have supported a type of life that would be more truly urban than rural. The largest of these Galilean villages was Japha, a half-hour's walk south from Nazareth, on one of the principal roads from Galilee through Samaria to Jerusalem. By this route the journey could be made in only three days.

The pursuit of a livelihood within the city gave rise to a great variety of interests. Although the Jews are credited with having forestalled the danger incident to the growth of cities at the expense of healthful rural communities, it is nevertheless true that by the beginning of the Christian Era Palestine had become in a marked degree a land of city dwellers. Here some persons lived as slaves, others as menials, others as skilled laborers, others as merchants and bankers, others as teachers, others as physicians, others as religious or political officials, not to mention those extremes of poverty and opulence whose representatives had no professed occupation. People in these various walks of life could not be expected to agree upon any single scheme for inaugurating the Kingdom of God. What seemed advantageous for a group of individuals in one station, might appear to another group highly undesirable.

The complexity of Palestinian society was further augmented by the presence of the foreigner and his customs. When Alexander the Great overran Western Asia, numerous Greek settlements were formed in the wake of his conquest. Not even Palestine escaped Greek colonization. In almost the very heart of the Holy Land stood the Hellenistic city of Scythopolis, the Bethshan of biblical times. Beyond the Jordan were nine other such foundations, the ten together constituting the well-known Decapolis. They formed themselves into a league to maintain their own interests in the midst of their Semitic environment, and thus they retained their Greek character although they were now subject to Rome.

Undoubtedly the Jews would have been quite happy to have all foreigners in Palestine live in segregated communities, but this arrangement was not at all agreeable to the invaders. The Romans were in this territory by right of conquest, just as in earlier years the Babylonians, the Persians, and the Greeks had been. The foreigner was there primarily to discharge the business of government, but he also made his presence felt over a wide range of social contacts. He brought his own language, his own customs, his own money, his own wares, his own forms of entertainment, his own taste in food and clothing, and even his own religion, into every important center of population in the land. Notwithstanding the natural disposition of the Jews to resist foreign contacts, complete isolation was quite impossible.

The extent to which gentile influences had penetrated Palestine by the beginning of the present era must not be measured simply by the negative attitude of those purists who inveighed against the presence of the foreigner. In fact, the vigor of this protest is itself testimony to the success that had attended the introduction of foreign culture. After the Maccabean princes had gained political independence, the bitter hostility toward all things Greek that had accompanied the revolution gradually subsided, particularly among the aristocrats. Jewish princes now learned to appreciate the value of living on friendly terms with their gentile neighbors, and to enjoy the products of Hellenistic civilization. Under Herod the Great this stream of foreign invasion rapidly increased in volume until Palestine was virtually flooded with cultural importations from the Graeco-Roman world. These alien influences were to be seen in its industries, its trade, its festivities, it public buildings, its politics, and its religion.

Through still another channel the life of the outside world filtered into Palestine. For centuries many Jews had been in foreign lands, but at the same time had maintained close relations with their kinfolk at home. Wherever they might reside they still remained loyal Jews, but their more intimate contact with gentile life had necessitated on their part a more or less extensive Hellenization. When representatives of this Dispersion returned for the religious festivities, to visit friends, or to take up permanent residence in the Holy Land, it was inevitable that they should bring with them numerous marks of the foreign culture by which they had previously been environed. There was in Jerusalem itself at least one synagogue, and perhaps more, where

worship was conducted in Greek for the benefit
of these returned Jews who had been so long
away from the land of their fathers that they
were now unable to use the native Aramaic
speech. The Jews of the Diaspora were a bridge
by which contemporary Graeco-Roman civilization reached Palestine without incurring that
conscious antagonism so often aroused when the
foreigner forced his own physical presence upon
the people of the Holy Land.

Contact with aliens was not bitterly opposed
by every Jew, even though ideally the foreigner
and his culture had no rightful place among
God's own people. Upon this ideal they all could
have agreed, but in the immediate relations of
daily life various practical considerations affected the situation. The priestly aristocracy and
those who held government offices could easily
believe that the Jews would profit by cultivating
rather than by antagonizing the Romans. And
the common laborer, although chafing under the
payment of tribute to Rome, might appreciate
the opportunity for employment which the presence of foreign capital insured. Also, the new experiences that acquaintance with gentile culture
afforded were not always unwelcome. The baths,
the theaters, the amphitheaters, and the Roman

festivals, introduced into Palestine in the time of
Herod the Great, certainly were not entirely
lacking in Jewish patronage.

The presence of these gentile features in Palestinian life increased still more the complexity
of current social attitudes. All of the people
could not agree even upon a platform of hostility
to Rome as the way to a better realization of the
Kingdom of God. This issue engendered great
warmth of feeling, but it is not at all probable
that aristocrats were alone in their opposition to
the program of revolution. For example, the citizens of Sepphoris, refusing to participate in the
revolt of the year 66 A.D., stood out boldly for
peace with the Romans. Undoubtedly there
were aristocratic influences present to shape this
conciliatory policy, even though Sepphoris was
no longer the capital of Galilee. But the whole
city and even the many neighboring villages—
none is specifically mentioned in this connection,
but Nazareth was one of them—are said to have
united in this attitude. Earlier in its history
Sepphoris had suffered the consequences of revolt but had recovered its prosperity and been
magnificently rebuilt, and its inhabitants no
longer looked favorably upon revolutionary agitation against Rome. They recognized the futil-

ity of a procedure that previously had ended in disaster and in their opinion would only result in a new devastation of the city. The artisans, the shopkeepers, the merchants, the bankers, and the citizens in general, saw no advantage to be gained from plunging the country into another war. This does not mean that the Jews of Sepphoris and its neighborhood had abandoned all hope in the promises of divine favor, but only that they disagreed with many of their kinsmen elsewhere in Galilee on the correct method for securing the establishment of the Kingdom of God.

III

The complex elements in Jesus' social environment no longer existed in a mere fluid state. On the contrary, an extensive degree of crystallization had set in. Definite groups had formed themselves around focal points of special interest, a situation that increased the difficulties attending any new attempt at the solution of a current vital issue such as the way to secure God's deliverance for his chosen people.

Even before the Maccabean revolution there had been among the Jews of Palestine a definite disposition on the part of a certain group of leading men to court the favor of their Syrian

overlords. After the Maccabean revolt had suc-
ceeded, and John Hyrcanus had made himself
both king and high priest, there gathered about
him individuals of the aristocratic and priestly
class who favored John's policy of negotiation
with foreign governments, particularly with that
of the Romans. Many Jews sympathized with
John's disposition to build up a kingdom in Palestine marked by worldly prosperity and display
essentially gentile in character. These supporters of the king were the ancestors of the Sadducees.

By the beginning of the present era the Sadducees had come to be a well-recognized class in
society. Josephus says that they were particularly influential among the rich, but had practically no following among the populace. They devoted themselves especially to political affairs
and were always strongly in favor of friendly relations with foreigners. They were not overly
meticulous in religious observances, especially
when it came to supplementing the Old Testament scriptures with that body of oral interpretation produced by later generations of religious
teachers. According to the Sadducees, the hope
of the Jewish people lay in making the most of
the present opportunity for obtaining favors

from threatening foreign powers. Owing to their relatively scanty numbers as compared with the total population, and their lack of a constructive policy for securing release from Rome, the Sadducees were fast losing their prestige in the Jewish society of the time of Jesus.

The success of the Maccabean revolution had been due in large measure to the loyal support of that part of the Jewish people who were ready to die rather than abandon their ancestral religion. These pious enthusiasts participated in politics primarily for the purpose of insuring religious freedom. When the Maccabean princes had attained a position of independence and the Jewish religion was no longer threatened by foreign foes, these supporters of the revolution quickly lost interest in national affairs, except as they might take offense at the worldly character of the Jewish government. These religious purists are the ancestors of the party known in the time of Jesus as "Pharisees."

During the successful reign of John Hyrcanus, the Pharisees, as a group in society, appear clearly differentiated from the Sadducees. The latter are supporters of the policy of internationalism in politics and the maintenance of a typical royal court by the king of the Jews.

They are the priests and aristocrats upon whom the king depends for assistance in the administration of his government. On the other hand the Pharisees, although appreciative of the king's success in re-establishing the political prestige of the Jews, are offended by the fact that he has assumed also the high priesthood and has admitted within Judaism worldly features which to them become increasingly offensive. They stress rigidity in the observance of religious rites, and would have royalty understand that its primary function is to protect the integrity of the national faith.

Henceforth the Pharisees and the Sadducees, according to the Jewish historian Josephus, constituted the two principal parties in Judaism. In contrast with the Sadducees, who are said to have been strikingly lacking in the consciousness of a group spirit and who often were as contentious with one another as they were with outsiders, the Pharisees felt keenly a sense of united purpose and regarded themselves as guardians of the common good. Their influence with the populace was powerful and far-reaching. They were zealous students of the scriptures, and taught the people to observe not only the injunctions of the written Law, but also the interpretations that had been worked out in the oral tradition of the scribes. Among the contemporaries of Jesus, the Pharisees were the largest and most influential single group in the social structure.

The well-being of the Jewish people was the Pharisees' primary concern, and complete devotion to God was their fundamental religious ideal. While placing great reliance upon God to insure the future good of the Jewish race, they also stressed the importance of human action. When the sanctity of their religion was threatened by a foreign ruler, no one was more ready to take up the sword in defense of the faith. But the hope of Judaism, as interpreted by the Pharisees, was fixed on God. The disillusionment that had followed the war of liberation in the time of the Maccabees seems to have restrained the Pharisees of later times from placing great confidence in worldly princes. Their characteristic emphasis was the cultivation of righteousness by means of a rigid observance of God's will as revealed to them in their sacred scriptures. To fulfil this divine requirement was man's distinctive task. To elevate the chosen people to their rightful position of supremacy among the nations was distinctively God's affair. The

Pharisees were from the start essentially a religious rather than a political group. As an association of purists, they stood in sharp contrast to the "people of the land" (*'Amme ha-'aretz*), who made up the rank and file of the population.[1]

The desire to live pleasing to God sometimes inspired attempts to discover new ways to cultivate righteousness. Certain groups came to represent one or another specific type of procedure for winning the divine favor. One of these reforming movements within ancient Judaism is now called, for lack of a better name, the "Zadokite sect." Its representatives were offended by the impurity of the Sadducean priesthood and were dissatisfied with the religious leadership furnished by the Pharisees. The Zadokites therefore formulated a program of their own in the interests of a more specialized righteousness. From their point of view they were the true Israel, performing the divine will more perfectly than did their neighbors, and thus were in a position to claim that they were especially pleasing to God.

Before Jesus began preaching, the Zadokites had already crystallized into a well-defined social unit, independently organized to carry on a

[1] See below, pp. 303 ff.

[139]

distinctive propaganda. Between its representatives and the Pharisees the hostility was bitter, if not indeed violent. Both groups were devoted to the Law of Moses, but the Zadokites gave it their own interpretation and maintained that the present unhappy condition of the Jews was a consequence of failure to keep the Law. Since customary ways of doing God's will had proved abortive, hope lay only in the new program proposed by the Zadokites. They condemned the sins of the people whom they summoned to repentance. Membership in their order, the adoption of their stricter way of living, and the maintenance of their cause were thought to offer the only prospect of relief for the Jews. This new reform movement had entered into a special covenant with God, against that day when in his wrath he would destroy the wicked and establish a victorious kingdom for the righteous.

The Essenes constituted another element in Jewish society bent upon attaining a unique degree of righteousness. Their movement too had become definitely institutionalized before Jesus undertook his work. Their community life was under the management of one of their members appointed by the group. They held all their worldly possessions in common; they rejected marriage but took the children of others to rear; and as far as possible they formed their communities outside the cities, whose moral atmosphere seemed to them to be particularly bad. They adopted various ascetic practices such as fasting, frequent bathing, and rigid self-discipline. Those who joined the society solemnly pledged themselves to a life of piety toward God. Next to God, the lawgiver Moses was revered, and to blaspheme his name made one liable to capital punishment.

Communities of the Essenes were numerous and widely distributed among the Jews in the first century A.D. They cultivated the spirit of fellowship in a high degree. Each community provided food and clothing for any member of the sect, even though he were a complete stranger on appearing in their midst. They possessed also a keen sense of loyalty to the Jewish religion, of which they doubtless regarded themselves the truest representatives. They steadfastly endured torture or death rather than violate the injunctions of their sacred Law. They were distinctly pacifists in their attitude toward government, believing that God overruled all things for his own purposes. Yet when on a journey they carried weapons to protect themselves from the attack of thieves. But apparently their hope for a new order lay in keeping their own particular program for the attainment of individual and community righteousness.

The passion for political independence, which was ultimately to express itself in an organized revolt against Rome, had not yet in Jesus' day become the distinctive interest of an established group with the same clear marks of differentiation that characterized Sadducees, Pharisees, Zadokites, or Essenes. But all through the period of Jesus' life the atmosphere of Palestine was surcharged with the spirit of revolution. Occasionally this restlessness found leaders whose premature efforts to force the issue were attended with failure, but these adventurers were the forerunners of the movement later to crystallize in the strong revolutionary party called "Zealots."

The death of Herod the Great had been the signal for numerous uprisings in different parts of the country. In Jerusalem at Pentecost the revolt assumed threatening proportions, while agitators were active at many other points in Judea. In and about Jericho the revolutionists were led by one named "Simon," who had in his band of followers many persons from Perea. In

Galilee a certain Judas captured the military equipment stored at Sepphoris and made it the center of a threatening revolt. Adventurers were active all over the country, but as yet no well-organized party had emerged and the movement lacked official leadership. It was, however, a very definite expression of Jewish longing for the recovery of the country's ancient liberty. When the Romans finally restored order and punished only those who were believed to be the most guilty authors of the disturbance, they found two thousand persons to be crucified. Although there was as yet no formal revolutionary party, it is clearly apparent that there was a very strong revolutionary disposition.

A decade later the spirit of national discontent came more definitely to a head under the leadership of the same Judas who had raised the previous revolt at Sepphoris. Closely associated with him was a Pharisee named "Saddokos." The taking of a census by the Romans provided the opportunity so readily embraced by Judas and Saddokos. The high priest in Judea, with his Sadducean inclinations, had persuaded the people to submit peaceably to the census as a basis for taxation. This gave Judas and his followers a new slogan. They called the taxation a species of slavery and exhorted the people to show their loyalty to God by readiness to take up the sword and fight for liberty. On no other condition, they alleged, could God be expected to render them any assistance. They were one with the Pharisees in their zeal for the Jews' religion but in advocating revolution they went quite beyond the characteristic Pharisean reserve. They set the ideal of political freedom in the foreground of attention and made it their motto that God only should be their ruler and lord.

The agitation for national freedom appealed particularly to the younger element in the population and rapidly gained strength. It now became the definite concern of a specific group. As yet perhaps it bore no distinctive name, and many who were interested in its success may at first have classified themselves definitely in some other existing sect, particularly in that of the Pharisees. But the new party grew so rapidly that within sixty years it was able to dominate all other interests and precipitate a well-planned revolution against Rome. In the meantime the descendants of Judas remained prominent in its leadership. Two of his sons were crucified by the Romans shortly before the year 50 A.D., another son became a martyr to the cause a decade later, and still another of his descendants, Eleazar, was an outstanding leader in the final revolt.

The failure of any single party to unify public sentiment around its own distinctive program left room for the proposal of new schemes by which the will of God could be done more perfectly. A Bannus might with complete propriety retire to the desert to cultivate the ascetic life independently of the Essenes and receive such persons as resorted to him to discipline themselves in his special way of living. Also a John the Baptist was quite in line with the temper of his environment when he summoned his contemporaries to a baptism of repentance in preparation for an early advent of a new order. And Jesus was not at all out of harmony with the spirit of his age when he launched a new propaganda on behalf of righteousness and assembled adherents to his cause. But with the multiplication of recognized parties, the pathway of the individual reformer became constantly more difficult and hazardous. To ally oneself with an existing group necessitated the suppression of such personal inclinations as might run counter to the disposition of the majority, while to inaugurate an independent movement might mean early disaster and ultimate oblivion. Well-established rival movements were bidding for popular favor, and an ever enlarging number of interests had become stereotyped and labeled as the possession of definite parties whose proprietary rights must not be infringed upon by an outsider.

IV

The existence of clearly drawn party lines within the social fabric is not always the most serious barrier to the work of a reformer. Frequently he must cope with established institutions sanctified by long usage and popularly regarded as a sacred machinery whose undisturbed operations are thought indispensable to the well-being of mankind. By the beginning of the present era Judaism was equipped with elaborate institutions that were older and more deeply rooted in the social structure than even the most ancient of the party movements. They provided an intricate mechanism for insuring proper conduct in all the varied relationships of life. Individuals might differ in their interests and opinions without seriously disturbing public welfare so long as the ancient institutions were kept in orderly operation. They were the real safeguards against disaster and the guaranties of ultimate prosperity.

Until its final destruction in the year 70 A.D. the temple at Jerusalem was, for the Jews, uniquely the symbol and surety of God's presence. Although the magnificent structure reared by Solomon had been destroyed by the Babylonians, the returned captives had loyally struggled to rebuild a suitable successor. But it was Herod the Great who effected its reconstruction in really worthy fashion. In the time of Jesus this sanctuary was one of the most splendid religious edifices in the ancient world. It occupied a conspicuous position on the eastern hill of the city of Jerusalem, within a rectangular area surrounded on all sides by strong and high walls.

Various degrees of sanctity attached to different parts of this inclosure. While the outer court was accessible to both Jews and foreigners, where cattle dealers and money changers could be found particularly at the feast season, the inner court could be entered only by Jews. Nearer to the holy house, only male Jews could approach; and nearer still, only priests, except when a devout Israelite came to make his own offering. On higher ground rose the temple building proper, which none save priests might enter. In the first chamber stood the altar of incense with the seven-branched candlestick and the table of shew bread. In the rear was the chamber called the "Holy of Holies," which to every Jew was the most sacred spot on earth. Once it had contained the Ark of the Covenant, the symbol of God's own presence. While the temple still stood, preserving its sanctity and magnificence, it remained not only an object of unique admiration but also a very tangible assurance of the covenant between God and his people.

Not every Jew could attend the daily worship at the temple, but he remembered that its services were being maintained with fidelity at the morning and evening sacrifices. It meant much to him that the lamb was properly offered, that formal prayers were recited, that incense was burned, and that songs of praise and thanksgiving were rendered, all in accordance with instructions delivered by God in the distant past. The presence of numerous officials added to the impressiveness of the scene. The high priest in his gorgeous apparel participated in the ceremonies on the most notable occasions, but at all times a full quota of lesser priests and Levites, suitably robed, were on duty. In the time of Jesus the office of high priest was still regarded with the greatest veneration, even though the Romans had arrogated to themselves the right of appointment. Notwithstanding the defilement to which the office had been subjected by the foreign conqueror, it remained for the devout Israelite the highest and most sacred dignity in the Jewish religion.

Closely connected with the temple was the assembly known as the "Great Sanhedrin of Jerusalem." It convened in the "Hall of Hewn Stone" which is said to have been situated on the south side of the temple area. While the Sanhedrin might sit elsewhere, as is shown by its history in later times when the temple was no longer accessible, in Jesus' day the relation between the two institutions was intimate if not inseparable. This council of seventy elders, representing the quintessence of legal knowledge and experience, with its president, who might or might not be the high priest, was the supreme authority for the Jews in both civil and religious affairs. Beyond its judgments, in conventional Jewish opinion, there was no proper appeal on issues of either Church or State. The Roman procurator and his tribunal might by sheer force exalt them-

JESUS—A NEW BIOGRAPHY

selves above the Sanhedrin, but Jewish sentiment saw in this only a display of arrogance and injustice. And when Pilate had assured himself that Jesus stood condemned by this supreme court of the Jews, he knew that technically at least he could not be accused of irregularity in crucifying a member of their race. The prestige of the Great Sanhedrin was everywhere recognized by Jews, who regarded its activities with confidence and reverence.

The temple entered still more immediately into Jewish life through the observance of the three great yearly festivals, Passover, Pentecost, and Tabernacles. At these seasons everyone who could came to Jerusalem to participate in the ceremonies. Passover, celebrated in the spring, on the fifteenth of the month Nisan, was the principal feast and invariably brought together large numbers to commemorate the deliverance of the Hebrews from bondage in Egypt. The ceremonies were very carefully prescribed, and their proper execution was a matter of supreme moment. By this act the grateful Jew memorialized in the form of a sacred institution a unique manifestation of God's favor for his people in the hour of their dire distress; and the observance, scrupulously repeated from year to year, inevitably took on the character of a surety for present and future well-being.

So elaborate an institution as the temple with its varied activities could not be maintained without a substantial income. This support was gladly and faithfully rendered. Every male twenty or more years of age, whether living in Palestine or in the Diaspora, paid a tax of half a shekel yearly into the temple treasury. Wood for the altar fire was supplied by the people, different families taking turns in discharging this obligation. There was a levy upon agricultural products which was usually paid in kind. About one-fiftieth of the yield of all wheat, barley, fig trees, olives, pomegranates, vines, honey, and other less important products was taken up to the temple and presented to the priests. These contributions were supplemented by still another known as the "tithe," a gift of one-tenth of everything that grew. The fidelity with which these offerings were made by many of the people, even in the case of insignificant products like mint, anise, and cummin, is further evidence of the firm hold which the institution had taken upon the life of the Jews. In this respect it furnished them a highly prized opportunity to sur-

round themselves with the safeguard of proper
conduct in their dealings with Deity.

The architectural magnificence and elaborate
adornments of the temple, its array of gorgeously
robed officials, the pomp of its ceremonies, the
regularity and perpetuity of its daily sacrifices,
the glamor of its festival seasons, its great wealth
derived from both prescribed and voluntary offerings by the people, its antiquity and divine
authority as an institution, and its inseparable
connection with the history of the nation's struggle for freedom—all contributed to make the
central sanctuary a source of perpetual gratifi-
cation and satisfaction for every child of Abraham, whether he dwelt under its very shadow in
Jerusalem or in some remote corner of the Mediterranean world. While the temple still stood
and its ceremonies were regularly celebrated, it
continued to be an impressively concrete link in
the connection between the Jew and his God.
Should God again visit his people to effect for
them a new deliverance, these sacred precincts
would be the most appropriate spot on earth for
the display of his favor.

The needs of the local communities were
served more immediately by the institution
known as the synagogue. Even the smallest vil-

lages had at least one synagogue, and there were several in the larger places. Everywhere that Jesus went in the course of his public activity, he would be met by the conditions and interests which the synagogue and its activities had awakened and maintained. It was here that the local council of elders met to discharge the civic duties that fell to their care. It, too, was the courthouse where criminals were tried and where punishment was administered—sometimes scourging, sometimes excommunication, and sometimes condemnation to death. It also served as a place for the instruction of children, especially in the earlier stages of their education before they entered the school proper. But its chief function was to provide religious edification and an opportunity for public worship. Here the people met regularly on Sabbaths and festivals to pray and to hear the reading and exposition of scripture.

The synagogue services were comparatively simple and informal, yet the procedure was orderly and well regulated. Specified prayers were repeated, selections from scripture were read, and comments upon the scripture were made by any person present who might be thought worthy of a hearing. There was a presiding official who cared for the building and had general charge of the service. He selected persons to read, to offer the prayers, and to address the assembly. He was assisted by an attendant whose task it was to carry the sacred writings from the box in which they were kept to the reader, and afterward to return them to their place. Still others took care of the collection and distribution of alms. This institution was very close to the life of the people, and any reformer who would follow the method pursued by Jesus, of visiting the synagogue and giving expression to his opinions as opportunity offered, could thus be sure of obtaining at least an initial hearing. But should his message prove displeasing, the synagogue authorities had ample means at their disposal for resisting his innovations.

Of all the machinery that had been produced to control and direct Jewish life in a way pleasing to God, the sacred writings held the foremost place. Long before Christianity arose, the Jews had come to believe that certain portions of their literature had been given to their ancestors directly out of heaven. Greatest reverence was paid to the Law, which embraced the first five books in the Old Testament. Josephus expressed a long popular and generally accepted opinion when he affirmed that Moses had obtained these laws by divine revelation and had left them in writing as he had learned them from God. Next in authority came the collection called "Prophets," while slightly less sanctity attached to the remaining group, called "Writings." These sacred books had been composed in the ancient Hebrew language, no longer understood by the people at large. But in the synagogue they were read in Hebrew and orally translated section by section into Aramaic, now the language of daily life.

It was supremely important that the Law in particular, since it had been the very word of God given to Israel for guidance in all ages, should be properly taught to the people. Long before the time of Jesus a class of professional interpreters, commonly known as scribes, had attained wide recognition within Jewish society. They were mainly of the sect of the Pharisees, although there were also professional teachers among the Sadducees and the Zadokites. But it was the pious Pharisee who devoted himself most earnestly to the study and exposition of the Law. This work was carried on chiefly in connection with the synagogue, as occasion arose for expounding the lesson read from the Law and the Prophets or for rendering decisions on civil and religious questions.

Jesus was following the custom of the scribes when he chose the synagogue as a place in which to teach. But they also taught in the schools, and outstanding teachers were resorted to by young men preparing themselves to enter upon the profession of scribe. As the educators of the day, the scribes thus gave to Jewish society its particular cultural direction. Sometimes recognized teachers differed among themselves on specific points of interpretation, as was the case with Hillel and Shammai, two famous Jewish teachers in the time of Jesus' youth. But in its fundamentals Jewish education was a unit and was wholly scriptural. The sacred book was the basis of all instruction, whether in history, science, or religion. Sons of the more liberal families might supplement their Jewish training by study abroad, even at the university of Tarsus, Alexandria, or Athens, but they were not disposed to discover any new wisdom among the foreigners. Josephus, notwithstanding his favorable attitude toward Roman culture, affirmed that all the wisdom of the ancients had been derived originally from Moses; and his more scholarly predecessor Philo held the same opinion.

JEWISH LIFE IN PALESTINE

As time went on, the scribes produced a large body of instruction, passed down orally from generation to generation. Much attention was given to the formulation of detailed prescriptions for the regulation of conduct. Frequently the Law was not sufficiently specific to meet the more complicated problems of life in the Palestine of a later day. The Law required that the seventh day, for example, should be kept holy, but it did not specify exactly how far one might travel on the Sabbath or what things might be classed as works of necessity. It was the business of the diligent scribe, by careful study of scriptural texts and faithful rehearsal of the teaching of his predecessors, to find the answer to every practical ethical problem that might present itself to his own generation. For his devotion to this honorable task he was highly respected by many of his contemporaries, and over wide areas of Jewish society his decisions were received with almost as much reverence as was accorded the Law itself.

Notwithstanding the existence of these elaborate and influential institutions among the Jews, there was one area of interest, the political, where they had as yet been unable to surround life with a satisfactory institutional protection.

This ideal still remained the fleeing goal of popular desire. Surely God's people were entitled ultimately to citizenship in a genuine kingdom of God. But a would-be reformer, advocating a new line of conduct or a new phrasing of the familiar longing, might find it exceedingly difficult to break through the thick crust of institutionalized procedure that had already formed over Jewish society. In their efforts to live pleasing to God, were not the people already amply supplied with authoritative guides? Possessing their temple, their synagogues, their scriptures, their priests and their scribes, what more did they need? And in the event of a desire for greater specialization in righteousness, they might attach themselves to one or another of the established party movements, selecting its ideals as the object of their heightened loyalties. Even were a new teacher successful in finding a place for himself within this crowded area, he had still to reckon with the divergent demands of a society that now embraced in its complex personnel a wide variety of tastes and interests.

In this Jewish setting Jesus lived and worked. He was a Hebrew of the Hebrews and a Palestinian of the Palestinians. In so far as he refused to conform to current modes of thought and conduct, they supplied an inescapable environment and an immediate stimulus for his own course of action. The gravest problems to engage his attention were bequeathed to him by the people of this land in which he was born, and the hope of bringing his ideals to realization lay in a successful appeal to his contemporaries.

CHAPTER IV
THE HOME LIFE OF JESUS

JESUS was about thirty years of age, says one of his ancient biographers, when he left his carpentry to assume the responsibilities of a religious reformer. Half an average lifetime had passed before this momentous decision was reached. Infancy, childhood, youth, and mature manhood had all contributed their several quotas of experience to the making of the new preacher. Life under the parental roof had imposed on him its inescapable heritages, both physical and cultural. Year after year, as he grew to maturity, intimate contact with kindred, playmates, teachers, and fellow-toilers in the workaday world had been exerting a continuous influence on his personal development. True, these peaceful years now stand in sharp contrast to the hectic months of later public activity that terminated in the crucifixion. But only when viewed from the vantage ground of the previous decades spent in the home of his youth can the subsequent career of the martyr-prophet be seen in true perspective.

I

Unfortunately for modern curiosity, the first Christian preachers seem to have had no interest in recounting the story of Jesus' home life. Paul does speak of his birth, but in quite doctrinaire fashion. It had been the moment when a pre-existent heavenly creature had voluntarily dropped down to the humble level of mankind by taking on mortal flesh born of a human parent, descended from David, and subject to the Jewish law (Gal. 4:4; Rom. 1:3 f.; 8:3; Phil. 2:7 f.). There are no other allusions in the Pauline letters to events connected with the childhood and youth of Jesus. Also in Mark and in John there is an almost absolute silence on this subject. Not until the work of John the Baptist was well under way does Jesus come upon the scene (Mark 1:9; John 1:29). Incidental references to the later astonishment felt by kindred and former neighbors when they learned of his public activities may be meant to indicate that his previous manner of life had been entirely conventional and provocative of no comment (Mark 3:

21, 31–34; 6:2–4; John 7:3–5). But all particulars are lacking. Similarly, in the so-called "Logia" tradition, surviving in Matthew and Luke, the narrative begins with an account of Jesus' temptation, immediately following his baptism by John (Matt. 4:1–11; Luke 4:1–13).

In the course of time, reverent disciples endeavor to pierce the silence that previously had enveloped the earlier years of Jesus' private life. The author of Matthew prefaces his book with a list of Jesus' ancestors (1:1–17). He is shown to have been of the royal line descended from Abraham through David. Although this pedigree is called "the genealogy of Jesus Christ," immediately it proves to have been only that of Joseph, who was not in reality the father of Jesus. His mother had been "found with child of the Holy Spirit" before her marriage to Joseph (1:18–25).

The Gospel of Luke also traces the ancestry of Joseph back to David and Abraham, and ultimately to God through Adam (3:23–38). Only remotely does the Lucan genealogy coincide with that in Matthew. Yet the two most important links, David and Abraham, are prominently displayed in both tables. But in Luke, as in Matthew, the accrediting significance of this ancestral evidence is quite vitiated by asserting that

Jesus was not actually, but was only "supposed" to be, the son of Joseph. Not because Joseph was descended from God through Adam, as delineated in the Lucan family tree, but because the child of Mary had been "begotten" by the Holy Spirit, was he called the "Son of God" (1:35).

How did it happen that two of the evangelists, in accounts evidently independent of one another, were betrayed into the apparent inconsistency of defending the Davidic descent of Jesus, by reference to Joseph's ancestors, and the divine descent, by denying parenthood to Joseph? The social environment that conditioned the gospel-making process readily explains the dilemma. The Christian preachers were primarily concerned with the problem of presenting Jesus in worthy fashion to prospective converts. Their crucial task was to awaken in their hearers a saving faith in the crucified and heaven-exalted Christ. Paul could state the conditions of Christian salvation in a single sentence: "If thou shalt confess with thy mouth Jesus as Lord and shalt believe in thy heart that God raised him from the dead thou shalt be saved" (Rom. 10:9). This "gospel" was, again in Paul's phrase, "the power of God unto salvation to every one that

believeth; to the Jew first and also to the Greek"
(Rom. 1:16).

An effective presentation of Jesus to the
Jews called for one technique, while a successful
appeal to Gentiles required a somewhat different
procedure. At the outset, in their Palestinian
environment, the first disciples stressed their belief in Jesus' resurrection and elevation to the
right hand of God in heaven, as confirmed by his
appearance to them on different occasions. Paul,
too, accepted this experience as proof of Jesus'
lordship and traced his missionary commission
to this same heavenly source (I Cor. 15:5–11;
Gal. 1:11–16). Through his triumph over death,
Jesus had entered upon a new official dignity.
He was now the divinely appointed Jewish messianic deliverer of the future who would descend
from heaven with his conquering angelic host
when the time should arrive for the "restoration
of all things" (Acts 3:21). As Messiah, Jesus'
vindication still lay in the future. His earthly
life had been only a prelude to the great drama
upon which the curtain was soon to rise.

The presence of strong Jewish influences in
this type of early Christian thinking about Jesus
is self-evident. But those Jews who themselves
had not experienced visions of the risen Jesus

needed to be given additional reasons for belief in his messiahship. Outside the circle of those who had followed him previous to his death, Jesus had reappeared to only a few persons. Conspicuous among them were his own brother James and Saul of Tarsus. Others were dependent on second-hand testimony. To amass this evidence in a manner suitable to the requirements of the new cause at successive periods in the course of its progress was the first duty of the Christian preacher.

The task was undertaken with zeal and executed with skill by different individuals on various occasions. But all work in this field moved in the same general direction. Incidents and teachings from the life of the earthly Jesus were brought forward to demonstrate that he was worthy of the disciples' confidence in his present and future official dignity. The passing of the years gradually dulled the vivid messianic expectations of earlier times, but the prestige of Jesus suffered no serious consequences. In the meantime evidences of his official saviorhood had been so successfully associated with one or another feature of his earthly career that any further display of his redemptive significance became unnecessary.

The rise of traditions about Jesus' birth, as told in Matthew and Luke, can now be readily understood. They reflect two clearly distinguishable efforts to officialize the earthly Jesus at the very beginning of his career. First, the attempt to discover his lineage belongs to a Jewish setting. Not merely evidence that pure Jewish blood flowed in Jesus' veins, but also his descent from ancient worthies, particularly from David, was an important consideration when Jews were urged to recognize his messiahship. Many Jews believed membership in the Davidic house to be an essential qualification of the Messiah. Even though Jesus had not yet restored national supremacy after the Davidic model, hopeful Christian missionaries thought it worth while to indicate that he stood in direct line of descent from Israel's two great national heroes, David and Abraham. At least two different attempts at this demonstration had been made before Matthew and Luke were composed. Each evangelist found a genealogy among the traditions at his disposal. But the same original incentive had prompted the construction of these two family trees. By this means Christian missionaries had hoped to convince Jews that Jesus by blood descent was entitled to rank as the Jewish Messiah.

THE HOME LIFE OF JESUS

It goes without saying that originally this line of argument rested on the assumption that Joseph was the actual father of Jesus. Otherwise the appeal to a Davidic-Abrahamic ancestry would have been utterly futile. Indeed, within a strictly Jewish setting the fatherhood of Joseph never could have been called in question, at least by any friend and admirer of Jesus. While God might intervene to make fruitful those who had normally passed the age for childbearing, or might cherish unusual designs with reference to a particular child, for pure Jewish thinking direct parenthood on God's part was inconceivable. To be sure, he had given life to Adam and thus had become the father of all men. But his fatherhood rested in an act of creation, not in an act of procreation.

Even Paul, influenced though he often was by his gentile environment, still remained partially true to Jewish scruples in depicting the genesis of Jesus as Son of God. The relation of the earthly Jesus to the divine father had not affected the physical constitution of the son. He had appeared "in the likeness of sinful flesh" (Rom. 8:3). Yet Paul conceded something to the Gentiles' demand for the presence of actual deity in any savior on whom they were to place their trust. The spirit that tabernacled in the human flesh of Jesus had, according to Paul, pre-existed in heaven. After passing through the shadow of its earthly humility, it had been "declared to be the Son of God with power. . . . by the resurrection from the dead" (Rom. 1:3 f.). When preaching the supreme lordship of Jesus among Greeks, Paul might have won a readier hearing had he been willing also to affirm that the earthly Jesus had come into being by a pro-creative act of deity—at the time a favorite means of accrediting the heroes of different popular heathen cults. But Paul, while adopting the concept of a divine incarnation, never went so far as to admit divine generation for the physical body of the savior whose name he heralded among the nations.

When the Gentiles were first invited to accept Jesus as their savior, his qualifications for the rôle became to them a matter of keen interest. Characteristically Jewish arguments, such as his present position of messianic authority in heaven and the fulfilment of Old Testament prophecy in the course of his earthly career, were not without weight. That he had been the incarnation of a pre-existent being, as preached by Paul, and still more explicitly by the Johannine evangelist, was also a congenial form of imagery for depicting his worth. But those Christian interpreters who first informed Gentiles that Jesus was entitled to their esteem on the ground of his generation by the Holy Spirit rendered the expanding missionary enterprise a noteworthy service.

The full value of this new feature in the Christian apologetic on behalf of Jesus may be missed by one who fails to appreciate the genuine religious significance that was now attached to the notion of divine parentage among the adherents of contemporary heathen cults. The amours of Greek gods recounted in the ancient myths and the Gentile's thought of a supernatural generation for the god of his favorite religion were often as wide apart in their practical and moral value for humanity as were the biblical story of sons of God cohabiting with the daughters of men (Gen. 6:2) and the Christian account of Mary's impregnation by the Holy Spirit. The devotees saw in the divine increment of a savior's being an evidence of competency that would have been quite beyond his reach had he stood upon the common human level of natural generation. And even Gentiles of culture, though unable to take seriously the more naïve

[169]

imagery of popular fancy, still thought God operating indirectly as a spirit might beget children of mortal mothers.[1]

The authors of Matthew and Luke took a long stride forward in the direction of making Jesus more completely at home in a gentile environment when they eliminated the literal fatherhood of Joseph and ascribed the generation of Jesus directly to the Holy Spirit. Jesus could now be given the full credentials of a divine descent superior to that of all other claimants to the reverence of men in proportion as the Christians' god transcended all heathen deities. The satisfaction that Greeks derived from this type of appeal is indicated by the early and widespread persistence of the notion among gentile Christians. How tenaciously they held to belief in the dogma known as the "Virgin Birth," though it might more properly be termed "Supernatural Generation"! And how soon and persistently Christians of Semitic strain, or any others who hesitated to adopt this imagery, were consigned to the outer darkness of heretical oblivion by their zealous brethren! A savior of Gentiles had to be of more than mortal frame.

[1] Plutarch *Numa* 4: γυναικὶ μὲν οὐκ ἀδύνατον πνεῦμα πλησιάσαι θεοῦ καί τινας ἐντεκεῖν ἀρχὰς γενέσεως.

THE HOME LIFE OF JESUS

Our two evangelists may not have been the first Christians to evaluate the significance of Jesus in the coinage of supernatural generation, just as they certainly were not the first to frame for him an Abrahamic-Davidic pedigree. Indeed, the Old Testament style of the first two chapters in Luke—their peculiarities are apparent even in an English rendering — strongly favors the assumption that here this evangelist is drawing upon a block of earlier tradition. Whoever it was that first framed the new interpretation, he had no thought of abandoning the Jewish heritages of Christendom. A full scriptural authorization was summoned in support of this, as well as of the earlier effort to officialize the historical Jesus. Both accounts, although the evangelists are clearly independent of one another, deliberately aim to preserve the apologetic value attaching to the older notion of Jesus' right to the throne of David.

Taken literally, of course, the genealogies lose all meaning if fatherhood is denied to Joseph. But earlier tradition had unequivocally declared Jesus to be physically descended from David, and had rested his title to messiahship on this affirmation. The new interpretation gives him the additional advantage of divine parentage, yet without wishing to sacrifice his title to David's kingdom. The psychology of apologetic takes its usual course. Along with new features, it preserves the old, regardless of logical consistency. The momentum of past tradition is not to be sacrificed; the old "truth" has merely to be stated in new words. Jesus can still be called David's son, if not literally at least figuratively, because Joseph was popularly known as the father of Jesus. Formally, though not really, Jesus was a member of the Davidic family and so was entitled to claim its inheritance. Thus the new teaching about his supernatural generation is not allowed to annul his right to the Davidic throne.

II

The place of Jesus' birth was another theme apparently of slight interest to the earliest Christians. According to common gospel testimony the family lived at Nazareth in Galilee (Matt. 13:54; Mark 6:1; Luke 4:16; John 1:45 f.; 7:41 f.). The fact that this village was never mentioned in the Old Testament and played no rôle in messianic prophecy naturally occasioned no trouble for the first Christian preachers who looked mainly to the future for manifestations of Jesus' messianic prerogatives.

THE HOME LIFE OF JESUS

But when Matthew and Luke were written, conditions had changed. The past career of Jesus
was now being rehearsed especially for evidence
in support of belief in his messiahship, and the
Old Testament was being searched so diligently
for predictions about him that it had now become virtually a source-document for the story
of his life on earth.

With these new tools in hand it was possible
to relieve Jesus of any stigma attaching to the
assumption that the insignificant village of Nazareth had been his birthplace. Christian missionaries had demonstrated by genealogy his
royal descent and confidently proclaimed him to
be the prophesied savior descended from David.
They implicitly believed that the crucified Jesus
of Nazareth had met all the requirements of God
with reference to the promised messianic deliverer of Israel. Where ought this royal child to have
been born? The place of his nativity should
have been "the city of David," in "Bethlehem of
Judea."

The authors of Matthew and Luke are the
first evangelists to report the birth of Jesus at
Bethlehem, but they preserve this tradition in
two quite different versions (Matt. 2:1–6; Luke
2:1–20). Undoubtedly it arose in a Jewish en-

vironment and was of a piece with the interest in
Jesus' family tree. But in the present records
the story has been freely adapted to the tastes of
gentile converts. The place of the birth is itself
no longer the item of supreme importance. It
serves now as a focus about which to assemble
numerous decorative features, like the visit of
the Magi, the flight to Egypt, the slaughter of
the innocents, and the adoration of the shep-
herds. The legendary motif dominating these
stories, while not entirely out of place among
Jews, was nevertheless very pleasing to Gentiles.

Bethlehem was the ideal place for Jesus to
have been born. Yet the current tradition of his
residence in Nazareth was too firmly fixed to be
set aside. It is retained even in Matthew and
Luke. According to Luke, Nazareth had been
the abode of Joseph and Mary before their visit
to Bethlehem (1:26 f.; 2:4), and they returned
to their Galilean home immediately after the
presentation in the Temple (2:39). Since this
ceremony had taken place "when the days of
their purification according to the law of Moses
were fulfilled" (2:22), forty days after the birth
(Lev. 12:1–4), they will have been away from
their home in Nazareth at the most perhaps two
months.

THE HOME LIFE OF JESUS

In Matthew the troublesome Nazareth is disposed of in slightly different fashion. It is not mentioned as the previous abode of Joseph and Mary, nor do they take up residence there until Jesus is at least two years of age. From Bethlehem they journey to Egypt, where they dwell during the two remaining years of Herod's reign. Even then they would have returned to Judea had they not been warned by an angel to avoid these regions, now under the control of Herod's son Archelaus. Their wanderings come to an end at Nazareth. Although it is an inconspicuous place, the evangelist finds what seems to him good scriptural justification for assuming that the Messiah should come from this obscure Galilean village (2:23).

Shall we, then, picture Jesus passing his youth and early manhood in Nazareth? Of late years some scholars of repute—and some others —have contended that Nazareth is only a fictitious name invented to account for the fact that Jesus had first been known as "the Nazarene." The epithet originally had a class or a cult meaning, so the argument runs, but early Christian tradition converted it into a local designation and accordingly invented the town of Nazareth. The fact that it does not appear in the Old Testament or in any other pre-Christian Jewish writings, not even in Josephus, seems at first sight to lend an air of verisimilitude to this hypothesis. In the event of its truth, nothing could be said with respect to the particular section of Palestine in which Jesus had spent his early life.

On the other hand, the references to Nazareth in the earliest of the gospel records are of so incidental and unstudied a character that they prompt not the faintest suspicion of the presence of an apologetic motive in the narrative. Moreover, the failure of the name in contemporary Jewish literature is of relatively slight significance. There is no Jewish work of this period that can be called in any sense a geography of Palestine. No writer professed to mention all towns and villages in the Holy Land at the beginning of the Christian Era. Incidentally, one or another author specified certain places that were of immediate interest to him, but no one attempted a complete topographical catalogue. Josephus gives fullest particulars, but even he is often content to refer to the larger places and to pass by their neighboring villages, mentioning merely the fact of their existence but not citing them by name.

THE HOME LIFE OF JESUS

The very insignificance of Nazareth, and the absence of any pragmatic motive for making it the home of Jesus, sufficiently attest the historical accuracy of this feature in the gospels. Of quite a different sort are the references to Bethlehem. They are inspired by the exigencies of the growing missionary enterprise. Just as Davidic descent needed to be proved by a genealogical tree in order to furnish Jesus with new messianic credentials, so too the place of his birth needed to be the royal city. But doubtful as may be the tradition about Bethlehem, there is no occasion to question that Nazareth had always been the family residence. The conditions of life enveloping a Jewish youth in this Galilean village provide the specific environment within which to visualize the real home life of Jesus.

III

The experiences of Jesus in Nazareth will have been conditioned more definitely by the date of his birth. During this general period of Jewish history momentous happenings were in progress. The death of Herod the Great in 4 B.C. had shaken Palestinian society almost to its foundations, and the subsequent restoration of order under the administration of Herod's sons had been only partially effective. In the vicinity of Nazareth, particularly at Sepphoris, events of unusual importance had transpired. It would be particularly helpful for an understanding of the influences that may have shaped the life of Jesus in his formative years to be able to fix the time of his birth.

Again one observes the utter absence of interest on the part of early Christian preachers in the chronology of Jesus' life. They were far more concerned to determine the moment of his return from heaven to inaugurate a new régime that would mean the end of the present evil world. They said little about times and seasons that had already passed. They failed to record the date of Jesus' birth, the exact length of his public ministry, and even the year of his crucifixion. If only they had possessed more of the feeling for dates shown by their Jewish contemporary Josephus, the different evangelists would undoubtedly have provided a much larger body of materials suitable for the manufacture of chronological tables. Only among the latest of them does this interest begin to emerge.

Such chronological data as now stand in the gospels sometimes raise as many problems as they solve. Particularly is this true with reference to the time of Jesus' birth. According to Matthew, the event fell at least two years before the death of Herod the Great (2:16), which we know from other sources to have occurred in the year 4 B.C. Jesus would then have been not less than six years old at the beginning of the present era, and twelve or thirteen when Judas of Galilee raised his revolution following the deposition of Archelaus in Judea. When Pontius Pilate became procurator in the year 26 A.D., Jesus would have been fully thirty-two years of age; and by the time of his crucifixion he would have passed at least his thirty-fifth birthday.

Pilate held office until the year 36, and in the meantime, at a Passover season, Jesus had been crucified. Passover always fell on the fifteenth of the Jewish month Nisan. Christian tradition uniformly places the crucifixion on a Friday, but varies as to the day of the month. According to John it had occurred on the fourteenth of Nisan, that is, the day before Passover (19:14–16, 31, 42; cf. Luke 22:15 f.), but other evangelists place it on the fifteenth (Mark 14:12–17; Matt. 26:17–20; Luke 22:7–14). In which year during the procuratorship of Pontius Pilate would Nisan 14 fall on a Friday? The most probable calendar reckoning gives 29 A.D. Or, if the execution took

place on Nisan 15, the year will have been 30
A.D. These are the most certain dates available
for any event of Jesus' career. And if the Matthean tradition regarding the time of his birth is
correct, he will have been between thirty-five
and forty years of age when crucified.

The Gospel of Luke fixes a different date for
the birth of Jesus. This evangelist observes that
Jesus was "about thirty years of age" (3:1, 23)
when he entered upon his public ministry. Also
John the Baptist is said to have begun preaching
"in the fifteenth year of the reign of Tiberius
Caesar," which we know from Roman history to
have been the year 28 or 29 of our present era.
Soon afterward Jesus himself began public work.
Thus he was about thirty years old in the year 30
A.D., which would mean that he had not been
born until four years after the death of Herod the
Great. Of course the author of Luke does not report the visit of the Wise Men from the East and
Herod's attempt to slay the son of Mary by
ordering an indiscriminate assassination of male
children under two years of age. This distinctively Matthean tradition probably was unknown to the writer of Luke. His Jesus was
some six years younger than the Jesus of Matthew.

THE HOME LIFE OF JESUS

In still another Lucan context the birth of Jesus is again linked with contemporary history to explain why it was necessary for his parents to leave their home in Nazareth and journey to Bethlehem (2:1–7). They had gone up to the ancestral city to be enrolled in accordance with recent orders issued by the Roman government. Augustus was the reigning emperor, and Quirinius was the governor of Syria. This imperial decree is said to have called for a census of the whole Roman world, Palestine included. In his second treatise, the Book of Acts, this same author remarks that Judas of Galilee had raised a revolution "in the days of the enrolment" (5:37). Evidently the same census is referred to in both contexts.

From contemporary Jewish history it is a simple matter to date the Roman census taken while Quirinius was governor of Syria, and resulting in the Jewish outbreak led by Judas of Galilee. This uprising had been the direct outcome of the change of government in Palestine when Samaria and Judea were taken away from Archelaus and placed under a Roman procurator. Although Herod Antipas was still left in control of Galilee and Perea, his territory also was included in the census. This deposition of

Archelaus, and the succeeding events, cannot have occurred before the year 6 A.D. If not born until the time of the enrolment, in the "fifteenth year of the reign of Tiberius," Jesus would have been not more than twenty-three years old, instead of "about thirty" as Lucan tradition elsewhere affirms (3:1).

In order to obviate the difficulty, some interpreters have attempted to discover an earlier Roman census that would better harmonize the variant data in Luke. But any such effort flies in the face of facts too well known from contemporary Roman and Jewish history. We must allow that our evangelist was content to find a plausible motive for taking Jesus' parents from Nazareth to Bethlehem, without raising problems of critical research in the field of chronology. He was not writing a statistical chronicle, he was narrating a religious legend. Not only is his chronology at fault, but his assumption that it was necessary for Jews to travel to the residence of their ancestors for the enrolment is also unwarranted. In justice to the evangelist it should be remarked that he was dealing with events that had transpired nearly a century ago in a land and among a people of whom he had no first-hand knowledge.

THE HOME LIFE OF JESUS

The Fourth Gospel permits the supposition of still another date for the birth of Jesus. In John 2:20 an incident at the beginning of his public activity is placed in the forty-sixth year of the reconstruction work on the temple, which we learn from Josephus had been begun by Herod in 20–19 B.C. Hence it was now 27 A.D. It is also the Fourth Gospel that places the death of Jesus on the fourteenth of the month Nisan, from which we derive 29 A.D. as the date of the crucifixion. And since in John 'three Passover seasons are mentioned during the course of Jesus' ministry, one may quite properly infer that Jesus was already engaged in public work in the year 27 A.D. How old was he at this time? To this question no exact answer is given. But on a certain occasion the Jews are made to say of Jesus, "You are not yet fifty years old" (8:57). Had he been only in the thirties would not his questioners have said "not yet forty," granting of course that in any case they were speaking in round numbers? Apparently Jesus is assumed by the fourth evangelist to have been between forty and fifty years of age during the period of his public ministry. Since the date of his death in 29 A.D. is so definitely determinable by statements in this gospel, the time of his birth would have to be pushed back perhaps to the year 15 B.C. There is, really, no intrinsic reason why this should not have been the fact. The Johannine date is as adequately— and as inadequately—substantiated as any one of the varying Synoptic dates.

No absolutely certain dating of Jesus' birth is possible. The earliest documents made no reference to the subject. Christians writing in the last quarter of the first century were themselves imperfectly informed. Even within a single book, like the Gospel of Luke, conflicting data were recorded. But in spite of Luke's reference to the census of Quirinius in 6 A.D., it is once implied that this evangelist also knew a tradition which placed these events "in the days of Herod, king of Judea" (1:5). All that one may infer with any degree of probability is that Jesus grew to manhood in the Galilean village of Nazareth during that significant period in Jewish history which followed upon the death of Herod the Great in 4 B.C.

IV

The manner of Jesus' life during the silent years spent in his home at Nazareth has often tempted flights of fancy. Lack of information in the older records left this period an open field for speculation. The motives prompting these legendary growths have already been illustrated by the infancy stories of Matthew and Luke. Writers who attempted to fill in the previously unrecorded years sought thereby to adduce new proofs of Jesus' official significance. They would establish his royal descent, his divine parentage, his supernatural equipment, and his fulfilment of Old Testament prophecies that were thought to demonstrate God's choice of him to be the savior of mankind.

At first, narrators are content to describe the circumstances of Jesus' birth. In Matthew, after the parents reach Nazareth complete silence settles down upon his career until he appears among the people seeking baptism at the hands of John. The Lucan narrative is slightly more detailed. Things happen to Jesus that presumably would have occurred in the normal career of any other Jewish child of devout parents. He is circumcised on the eighth day, the appropriate offering for the purification of the mother is made on the fortieth day, and he goes up to Passover at Jerusalem when twelve years old. But these items of information are cited not primarily for the purpose of giving readers a set of unadorned vital statistics. Rather, the events recorded provide the evangelist an apologetic

[185]

opportunity. With each incident as a text, he would tell his readers how they should appraise the person of Jesus. Circumcision is mentioned in order to remind us that an angel had given the child his name. Among Jews of Palestine, Joshua—spelled "Jesus" in Greek—was an exceedingly common designation. It was as if one were to be called "Karl" among Germans, "Louis" among Frenchmen, or "George" in England. The historic fact that the new savior preached by Christians had been known by an ordinary Jewish name was too well established to be denied, but, happily for the evangelist, its commonplace character could be redeemed by angelic mediation. The child should be christened "Joshua" because heaven had so ordained (1:31; 2:21; cf. Matt. 1:21).

Similarly, the visit to the temple on the fortieth day serves to introduce the aged Simeon and Anna the prophetess, who hail Jesus as Israel's promised deliverer (Luke 2:25–38). The second visit, when Jesus is twelve years of age, would itself call for no exceptional comment. But the evangelist finds in it an opportunity to note that on this occasion Jesus had displayed a wisdom that astonished even the most learned teachers in Israel (Luke 2:41–50).

THE HOME LIFE OF JESUS

The process of filling in the story of Jesus' early years with incidents primarily to demonstrate his equipment for later work went on unabated in subsequent Christian literature. The canonical gospels of Matthew and Luke represent only a beginning in this direction. Certain apocryphal books developed the theme at great length. As a boy in his play, among his companions, and in his life at home Jesus showed himself to be a veritable incarnation of divine power. He was superior to all the laws of nature, and his wisdom transcended all the knowledge of men.[1]

This entire area of interest, from the earliest story in the canonical gospels down through the whole course of later literature, conceived of Jesus' childhood in strictly official and formal imagery. No account was taken of the normal career of a growing boy. There was no thought of his acquiring education by the same process of drill and application to study that would have been necessary for his companions. The experiences of family life, the consciousness of responsibilities awakened by adolescence, the sense of obligation felt by the youth confronted with the duty of earning a livelihood, the reaction of the

[1] See above, pp. 54 f.

individual to the stimuli of his social environment, and the solution of personal problems in terms of one's own emotions and aspirations, were no part of this story.

To visualize the real home life of Jesus, one needs an imagery quite different from that exhibited in the usual Christian accounts. If his experiences prior to his public career are to be recovered with any degree of historical probability, our quest must begin with the characteristic activities of a Jewish youth at the time and in the land of Jesus' nativity. Available data from contemporary Palestinian life are sufficient to give one a much more real picture of Jesus during his childhood and later youth than can be derived from the idealized portraits that are displayed in the later Christian records.

During the first three decades of the Christian Era life in Nazareth was not essentially different from life in Palestine at large. While still at home with other members of the family, Jesus would have been intimately bound up with the activities and interests characteristic of contemporary Palestinian Judaism. He shared with others the thrilling memories of a revered past when God's own people had been politically independent. He was buffeted by the same waves of emotion that tended to sweep other young men of the Jewish race into groups of revolutionaries. The established institutions of Judaism were operating in his native village, and the pious hopes of the suppressed nation were a possession of its inhabitants. At the same time Jewish life was sufficiently fluid to permit the individual to cherish his own distinctive interests and to register his own reactions toward the issues of the hour. In the case of Jesus, the influences of the home where he dwelt with parents, brothers, and sisters, the life of the village in its different phases of activity, and the extent of its contacts with the outside world are matters of primary significance. Only within this setting can his youth and early manhood be portrayed in terms of real life.

Jesus belonged to a family circle including four other brothers and at least two sisters. The names of the brothers were known to the author of Mark (6:3). They were Jacob (rendered "James" in English), Joseph, Judah, and Simon, but neither the names of the sisters nor their exact number can now be determined. It is commonly assumed that Jesus (Joshua) was the oldest of the children and that the father, Joseph, had died before Jesus took up public work. Had the father been living, there is no reason why he should not have been included in the family group mentioned on two different occasions in Mark (3:31–35; 6:3). This gospel, unlike its successors Matthew and Luke, made no allusion to the supernatural generation of Jesus; and the evangelist had no apparent motive for omitting reference to Joseph had he been still alive.

A few scattered items of information about other members of the family emerge in the history of Christianity after the death of Jesus. From these one may catch stray glimpses of the probable conditions in the family home. At the outset the mother and brothers had not been sympathetic with Jesus in his new activity. In fact they had desired to take him back to Nazareth (Mark 3:21). That they thought him "beside himself" may be quite true, and doubtless they also missed his much-needed help in the support of the family. But in later years they attached themselves to the group of disciples. In Paul's day there were married brothers of Jesus among the professional missionaries of the new religion (I Cor. 9:5), and by the year 44 A.D. James (Jacob) the oldest of the brothers was the recognized leader of the Christian community in Jerusalem (Gal. 2:12; Acts 12:17).

Still later tradition brought the whole household, including also the mother, into the bosom of the new Christian family (Acts 1:14; John 19:26 f.).

If the two brothers, Jesus (Joshua) and James (Jacob), resembled one another in temperament and attitudes, one might deduce from the conduct of James some inferences as to the upbringing of the family. But close similarity in brothers is not at all inevitable, and between these two in particular there are evident points of contrast. Yet James himself and his Christian associates must have believed that he was closely enough in harmony with the attitudes and purposes of his martyred brother to be the fitting head of the society that now existed to perpetuate the memory of Jesus. Evidently James had been well disciplined in Jewish piety, and even as a Christian he loyally retained his respect for the religious practices of his ancestors. He was offended by the action of Paul and Peter in eating with Gentiles (Gal. 2:12). Also, Josephus bears testimony to the esteem in which he was held by contemporary Jewish religionists (*Ant.* XX, 201). Perhaps Jesus never could have gained the same reputation, but certainly he had grown up under the same type of influences.

JESUS—A NEW BIOGRAPHY

It may be that Jesus was more truly a child of the Law than any of his ancient biographers cared to admit. They represented gentile interests and were writing at a time when the breach between Jews and Christians, even between Jew and Gentile within Christendom, had widened into an impassable gulf. Naturally it was no part of their purpose to seek in Jesus' upbringing under the Law any cue to the determination of his character. They might be much concerned, as was the author of Matthew, to note the obedience of Jesus to the Law as a formal decree of heaven to be complied with in order that thereby it might be supplemented with the new Christian law promulgated by Jesus. But one could hardly expect any of the writers of our present gospels to give Jewish religion credit for producing in Jesus a vital and praiseworthy piety. Yet it was under the discipline of Judaism that he became equipped with such religious heritages as he carried over into his public work.

In the time of Jesus, the education of a Jewish youth was a simple but effective process. The sacred Scriptures were his only textbooks. The ordinances of Moses, the admonitions of the prophets, the wisdom of the sages, and the meditations of the psalmist were his sources of inspiration. In the home, in the school, and at the services in the synagogue this scriptural wisdom was taught to every member of the community. Long before he reached manhood, the boy was thoroughly acquainted with the story of the nation's past. He was made familiar with those rigorous ethical ideals that Judaism had so diligently cultivated. He learned his duty both toward God and toward his fellow men, and on the strength of this instruction took his own position of responsibility in the life of his generation. The Jews knew no distinction between secular and religious in their system of education. The single aim was essentially a training for worthy membership in a society of God's chosen people.

The zeal displayed by Jews in teaching their sacred wisdom to their children needs no reiteration. From youth up, says Philo in his appeal to the Emperor Gaius (210 f.), the Jew bears stamped on his soul the image of his god-given oracles. And Josephus, with characteristic hyperbole, alleges that a Jew will more readily recall his sacred laws than he will his own name, because he learned them with the very dawning of his consciousness (*Apion* II, 178, 204). The Christian missionaries knew, and profited not a little by the fact, that "Moses from generations of old has in every city them that preach him, being read in the synagogues every sabbath" (Acts 15:21). The Jewish child, whether brought up in Palestine or in the Dispersion, received instruction in religion almost from the moment of birth.

Parents were the first teachers, and home was the school. But only the most elementary stages of instruction were entrusted to these agencies. Not all parents had the leisure or the equipment necessary for the adequate education of the child. In this connection the synagogue rendered indispensable service. In even so small a village as Nazareth there was at least one synagogue. Here Jesus in the course of every three and a half years would hear the first five books of the Bible (the "Law") read through from beginning to end. At the same time supplementary portions of the Prophets also were read. The prayers, responses, and hymns were likewise passages from the sacred writings, or were so shot through with its thought and diction as to be virtually an additional tutor in the Scriptures.

Jewish education, scriptural though it was in bone and sinew, embraced more than a mere memorizing of the laws. When Jesus attended the services in the synagogue at Nazareth, he heard not only selections read from the Law and the Prophets, but also those who "preached Moses." This exposition of Scripture made him familiar with the traditions of the scribes, who through successive generations passed on their accumulated wisdom to the people in their audiences. Whether these discourses dwelt on rules of conduct (*halakah*) or were entertaining and edifying expositions of some scene or character in Hebrew history (*haggadah*), they must often have left lasting impressions on the youth.

Had there been no more specifically educational institution than the regular synagogue service held every Sabbath in Nazareth, Jesus could hardly have avoided acquiring not only a familiarity with the general content of the Scriptures but also a knowledge of the scribal traditions in both their halakic and their haggadic form. But one would like to know whether the education of Jesus went beyond these limits reached by every Jewish boy. That he was not an educated person, in the current professional sense of the word, was stressed by Christians themselves—perhaps indeed overstressed to magnify their view of his native superiority to all human wisdom. Viewing education in its more secular aspects, to what extent had Jesus

received formal cultural discipline and how far had such education progressed?

If Josephus is to be trusted, it was a general custom among Jews of that time to maintain schools where children could learn "letters." Certainly in Jesus' day there were separate elementary schools where boys acquired a knowledge of reading and writing, and perhaps some instruction of this sort was carried on in connection with the synagogue. But we cannot be certain that every village in Galilee had such a school at the beginning of the present era; and when parents were unable to send their child to the larger centers to be educated, his attainment in "letters" is likely to have been rather meager.

The educational problem was complicated by the language situation. One might be able to read and write the Aramaic spoken in daily life and still be quite uneducated from the religious point of view. The language of learning was Hebrew, in which the Scriptures were written. It is altogether probable that very few of the peasants, laborers, and artisans, particularly of Galilee, could read or understand Hebrew. They knew some phrases of course, and on the Sabbath they heard the scripture lesson read in the original, but this reading in Hebrew was always accompanied by a faithful rendering in the Aramaic. The prevalence of this custom of translation shows how little the populace understood "letters."

It is true that if Jesus on occasion "read" Scripture in the synagogue, as is once represented in the Gospel of Luke (4:16), he must have been at home in Hebrew. But the author of Luke could hardly have doubted that Jesus possessed this knowledge, since already when only twelve years old his wisdom had amazed the learned doctors of Jerusalem. On the other hand, in general the evangelists restrict Jesus' activities at the synagogues to teaching and preaching, certainly in the Aramaic speech of the populace. And his alleged cry from the cross, though repeating words from a familiar psalm, is uttered in Aramaic rather than Hebrew. It is quite improbable that a carpenter of Nazareth would have had adequate opportunity to acquire any thorough knowledge of the Hebrew language. The Aramaic of daily life was sufficient for his purposes in youth, save as he may have picked up a few Greek phrases through contact with foreigners.

Had Jesus been set apart by his parents for the profession of scribe, then he would have been instructed in the sacred language, much as a modern Roman Catholic youth designed for the priesthood early seeks proficiency in Latin. Such elementary education would have been followed by further study in a more advanced school, and might have terminated in attendance upon the lectures of some famous teacher like Hillel or Shammai. Then Jesus would have become a true "disciple of the wise," skilled in the exposition of the Law according to recognized rules of exegesis. And in that event he might have remained quite unknown to fame.

Instead of becoming a scribe versed in knowledge of the Law, Jesus had learned the trade of carpenter, probably from his father. He, like the other "people of the land" among whom he must be classed, has to be counted "ignorant of the Law" in the technical sense. He knew little about the casuistic refinements that had become the stock in trade of the schools and professional scribes. Moreover, the *'Am ha-'aretz* was not only unacquainted with many decisions of the specialists but he lacked the time and means necessary for the attainment of the legalist's goal of perfection. While in the eyes of a zealous scribe one ignorant of the Law was inferior before God, the "man of the land" might himself be thor-

oughly devout in his own area of experience.
Some harsh things were occasionally said of such
people, yet they constituted a large element in
the population, and certainly they believed
themselves to be genuine Israelites.

V

Jesus had grown up in the village of Nazareth
a member of the artisan class. Through parental
training and synagogue attendance he had
acquired the common man's knowledge of
Jewish religion. To this he added a further discipline in the practical school of real life. Here
he made various contacts with different types of
people, as the circles of his activity gradually
widened. First.in the home, then in the immediate vicinity, then in the life of Palestine at large
he was disciplined in the school of experience.
Even during the "hidden" years of his career he
was not merely a citizen of Nazareth; he was
also a resident in the Holy Land.

The significance of Jesus' wider contacts with
the life of his day has not always been fully appreciated. Nazareth has commonly been assigned the rôle of a secluded village, almost lost
behind the surrounding hills. It is assumed to
have been so cut off from the rest of the country

that its inhabitants had no intimate contact with the varied interests of contemporary Galilean society in the larger centers of population. Sometimes Jesus is permitted a wider outlook as he makes imagined ascents to the top of the encircling hills where the panorama might refresh his memory of Old Testament history. Or his imagination might have been stirred by sight of the peoples and caravans moving along the busy highways of Galilee. But even so he remains detached, an individual apart, contemplating the passing scene from a position of isolation. That he himself actively participated in the life of a going society, which included in its maelstrom many diverse currents, is rarely or never imagined.

That the village of Nazareth was a bare hour's walk from Galilee's largest city, Sepphoris, and but a half-hour from its largest village, Japha, are facts whose import in this connection may be far greater than has ordinarily been supposed.[1] With the freedom of movement

[1] The physical fact of Nazareth's proximity to important centers of population is recognized clearly by G. Dalman (*Orte und Wege Jesu*, 3. Aufl. [Gütersloh, 1924], pp. 68 f.), but the question of its social significance for the experience of Jesus is not broached. In G. A. Smith's *The Historical Geography of the Holy Land*, the whole matter is ignored, and in the Index neither Japha nor Sep-

characteristic of Palestinian society in the time of Jesus, it is very doubtful whether the inhabitants of even a small village so near to two comparatively large centers of population could have maintained anything like the seclusion that has been commonly assumed for Jesus prior to his public activity. The modern traveler, approaching Nazareth from the south by way of Japha, cannot imagine that there ever was any serious barrier separating the two places. And if he approaches Nazareth from the north, by way of the modern village marking the site of the ancient Sepphoris, he will realize how easily accessible it was to the people of Nazareth when travel by foot was the ordinary means of locomotion.

Certainly Nazareth was not so isolated that the villagers were not within easy reach of both Japha and Sepphoris. Even had they not been impelled by business or curiosity to visit these

---

phoris is listed, although the latter is mentioned at least once in a footnote (p. 414, note 4). Data about Japha are given by Josephus in *War* II, 289 ff., 573; *Life* 188, 230, 233, 269. References to Sepphoris are numerous, e.g., *War* I, 170, 304; II, 56, 68; *Ant.* XIII, 338; XIV, 91, 414; XVII, 271, 289; XVIII, 27. Talmudic references may be found in literature cited by E. Schürer in *Geschichte des jüdischen Volkes*, 4. Aufl. (Leipzig, 1907), II, 209, note 489.

neighboring communities, it is still improbable
that they could have remained completely immune from urban influences. Travel between
these centers would have touched at least the out-
skirts of Nazareth. Since Japha lay on the short-
est road from Galilee to Judea, leading through
Samaria, undoubtedly much of the intercourse
between Sepphoris and Jerusalem would follow
this route. Not every Jew, it must be remembered, would carry religious scruples to the limit
of avoiding the more convenient road through
Samaria, and for non-Jews it would be a matter
of indifference.

The proximity of Nazareth to two important
centers of population, and particularly to Sepphoris, suggests the possibility of significant social contacts for Jesus during his youth and early
manhood. From early in the first century B.C.
Sepphoris had figured conspicuously in Jewish
history. In the time of Alexander Jannaeus it
had been so strong a fortress that his enemy,
Ptolemy, was unable to take it. A generation
later, when the Romans divided Palestine into
five administrative regions, Sepphoris was chosen as the capital of Galilee. When Herod the
Great was struggling for possession of his kingdom, this city offered him no resistance, but he

found here much-needed supplies for his army. Evidently it remained under Herod an important military post where arms and provisions were stored, for after his death the revolutionary leader Judas equipped his followers with weapons from the royal palace in Sepphoris and made this region the center of his operations. Presently its citizens were to pay dearly for their seditious inclinations. When the Romans, assisted by Aretas of Arabia, fell upon the city, they burned it and made slaves of its inhabitants.

Later a new and more brilliant city arose from the ruins. It was so splendidly restored by Herod Antipas that it became the "ornament of all Galilee." Until the founding of Tiberias, Sepphoris was the royal residence, but not even the loss of this distinction seriously impaired its standing. Its prominence in the time of the revolution of 66 A.D.,[1] and in still later Jewish history, is further testimony to its prestige. In Jesus' day its population included both Jews and foreigners, although it passed for a Jewish rather than a Greek city. It was not reckoned among the cities of the Decapolis. In its neighborhood

[1] This is much stressed by Josephus. See *War* II, 511, 574, 629, 645 f.; III, 30 ff., 59, 61, 129; *Life* 30, 37 ff., 64, 82, 103, 123 f., 188, 203, 232 f., 346, 373 f., 379 f., 384, 394–96, 411.

there were, according to Josephus, also many villages. Had he listed them by name, likely enough Nazareth would have been included in the group. It would not be from lack of opportunity if the young men of these adjacent villages did not become familiar with the many-sided life in a commercial and political center ranking in importance second only to Jerusalem. All the varied interests characteristic of Galilean society in the early Imperial age were present in the cosmopolitan atmosphere of Sepphoris.

Jesus was a lad perhaps between five and ten years of age when the Romans wreaked on Sepphoris their vengeance for its connection with the revolution of Judas. Apparently Antipas began the work of reconstruction about ten years later, but at what date it was completed is unknown. A heap of ruins could not be converted into the "ornament of all Galilee" in a single day. One may surmise that the task was not finished until about the year 25 A.D. and that its completion, and the accomplishment of a similar rebuilding program at Betharamatha,[1] released laborers

[1] Josephus *War* II, 59, 168; *Ant.* XVIII, 27; but written Ἀμμάθα in the usual text of *Ant.* XVII, 277. Elsewhere in Josephus it is called "Julias" (*War* IV, 438, 454). This Perean city had perished also in the seditions following the death of Herod the Great. Its reconstruction would seem to have gone on contempo-

who could now be employed upon the new foundation at Tiberias.[1]

That a vigorous building enterprise was in progress at Sepphoris while Jesus was still a youth, and at the same time the main support of a family of at least six younger children and a widowed mother, suggests the probability that he may have plied his carpenter's trade in the city. Very likely "carpenter" as applied to Jesus meant not simply a worker in wood but one who labored at the building-trade in general, and it requires no very daring flight of the imagination to picture the youthful Jesus seeking and finding employment in the neighboring city of Sep-

---

raneously with that of Sepphoris (*Ant.* XVIII, 27). The parallel reference in *War* II, 168, which mentions Julias after Tiberias, probably is in the nature of an afterthought and should not be taken to imply chronological sequence. That the city when first rebuilt had been rechristened "Livias"—it is so called by Eusebius and Jerome—in honor of the empress, shows that it was rebuilt before the death of Augustus (14 A.D.), after which his widow acquired the right to membership in the *gens Julia* (Ovid *Fasti* i. 536; Tacitus *Annals* i. 8; Cassius Dio lvi. 46). From the order of events listed in Josephus *Ant.* XVIII, 26-28 it would appear that the work on Sepphoris and Betharamatha was not begun before the year 7 A.D.

[1] One infers from the context in Josephus, *Ant.* XVIII, 35 f., that this work was begun early in the procuratorship of Pilate (26-36 A.D.).

phoris. But whether or not he actually labored there, his presence in the city on various occasions can scarcely be doubted; and the fact of such contacts during the formative years of his young manhood may account for attitudes and opinions that show themselves conspicuously during his public ministry. Had his earlier experience been confined within the narrow limits of a secluded village, certain traits of his character are exceedingly difficult to explain. They become more readily understandable when we assume that in his youth and early manhood his outlook had been shaped by wider contacts with a more varied environment.

The unconventionality of Jesus in mingling freely with the common people, his generosity toward the stranger and the outcast, and his conviction of the equality of all classes before God, perhaps owe their origin in no slight degree to the proximity of Nazareth to Sepphoris. Had Jesus spent his youth exclusively in a small village amid strictly Jewish surroundings, he would have been less likely to acquire the generous attitudes which later characterized his public career. But if in Sepphoris he had come into contact not only with Jewish fellow-laborers but also with artisans of other nationalities, or if only on brief but numerous visits to the city he frequently encountered a mixed population on the streets and in the shops, and thus grew accustomed to freedom of intercourse, one can a little better understand the genesis of that spirit of toleration which caused him to be called the friend of publicans and sinners.

Still another distinctive feature about the career of Jesus was his method of procedure. He quite reversed the program of the contemporary Jewish reformer, such as one meets in the Zadokite sectary, the Essene, a Bannus, or a John the Baptist. The representatives of these movements summoned people to separate themselves from their customary pursuits as a condition for realizing a better righteousness. In order to be especially pleasing to God, one must withdraw from the ordinary contacts of daily life. Jesus, on the other hand, did not call upon his followers to sever relations with their fellows, nor did he perpetuate in his own practice even the distinguishing mark of the Johannine baptismal rite. In his view religion was something that could function to the full while people were engaged in their normal activities. His ideals of righteousness were realizable and to be realized in close contact with society in the actual process of everyday living. Had he arrived at his convictions in the seclusion of a small village, from which occasionally he withdrew to the quiet of the surrounding hills to perfect his meditations, probably he would have demanded of his disciples a similar isolation as the condition necessary for attaining true righteousness. If, on the contrary, his own deepest religious experiences had been evolved amid the multifarious contacts of a complex society, such as residence in the neighborhood of Sepphoris provided, one can the more readily understand why he was no voice crying in the wilderness, but was the companionable teacher equally at home in the crowded streets of Capernaum, among the fishermen on the shore of the lake, among the laborers in the fields, or with the travelers on the highways. They had all been a part of his earlier experiences, and nothing about these relations seemed strange or unnatural to him now or inconsistent with genuine piety.

Perhaps the influence of Sepphoris is to be seen even more effectively in the shaping of Jesus' attitude toward the Roman government. The people of Sepphoris and its vicinity were three-quarters of a century earlier than the people of Jerusalem in learning by sad experience

THE HOME LIFE OF JESUS

the utter futility of a revolution against Rome. When at the time of his first insurrection Judas had taken possession of the royal treasures and arms at Sepphoris, evidently the citizens were not unsympathetic with his action, for when the Romans suppressed the revolution they burned the city and enslaved the inhabitants. But the residents of the new city were distinctly opposed to all revolutionary movements. Not even its Jewish population could be persuaded to take up arms against Rome. When at the time of the census Judas instigated a fresh revolt, he had to find a new center for his operations.[1] Again, during the early stages of the uprising of 66 A.D., when Josephus was busy fortifying Galilee to resist the Roman armies, he found the citizens of Sepphoris entirely out of sympathy with his enterprise, although the city was recognized by all concerned as quite properly a part of the Jewish

[1] That this Judas, "a Galilean from the city of Gamala" (Josephus *Ant.* XVIII, 4), was the same Judas, "son of Hezekiah," who had got Sepphoris into trouble a decade earlier is not to be doubted. The family had a very persistent revolution-complex, if Josephus is correct. The father himself had been an "arch-robber," Judas' sons, James and Simon, were crucified for sedition during the procuratorship of Tiberius Alexander; their brother, Manahem, was a martyr-leader in the revolt of 66 A.D.; and still another relative, Eleazar, was commander of the Sicarii (*Ant.* XVII, 27; XX, 102; *War* II, 433 ff.; VII, 253).

domains. Notwithstanding the fact that it was strategically situated and could have offered formidable resistance, when the Romans appeared upon the scene, Sepphoris, with its surrounding villages, immediately declared itself opposed to the policy of revolution. The citizens pledged fidelity to the Romans and were given a Roman garrison for their protection.

That shortly before the year 30 A.D. a carpenter from the neighboring village of Nazareth should have had his own attitude toward the Roman government influenced by this characteristic psychology of the people of Sepphoris is, of course, only conjecture. But the attitude which this city and its outlying villages took in the year 66 A.D. had been in force for over half a century. After the restoration by Antipas, the inhabitants realized how futile had been the attempt of their predecessors to wrest independence from the Romans by force of arms. Those persons who participated in the work of restoration, whether laborers, merchants, or residents in general, had no desire that history should repeat itself. It required no very extraordinary powers of foresight on their part to perceive that further revolution would issue only in a new disaster to life and property. But in holding to this attitude, they were entirely out of harmony with other sections of Galilee, where Judas and his kinsmen continued the agitation that issued in the uprising of 66 A.D.

Similarly, Jesus, living in the environment of Sepphoris and facing life's problems in the light of its experiences, shared the conviction that the Kingdom of God was not to be established by the use of the sword. Deliverance for the chosen people was to come in some other way. Throughout his career he maintained this attitude of nonresistance toward Rome. But this was not the characteristic psychology of other parts of the country. When his enemies induced him to admit the propriety of paying tribute to Caesar, they executed a skilful maneuver for undermining the loyalty of his followers from Galilee (Mark 12:13 ff.). His state of mind was hard even for his most devoted followers to comprehend. Up to the very end they were expecting him to restore the Kingdom of David and give them positions of honor in his cabinet. The hope that Jesus would ultimately effect Israel's deliverance by assuming the rôle of a new and more successful revolutionist clung to his disciples until the crucifixion. When this took place, they fled from Jerusalem with the conviction

[211]

that God had forsaken him. But Peter, James, and John were from that region of Galilee where the psychology of revolution still flourished. As yet they had not learned the lesson that had been taught Sepphoris and its neighborhood a generation earlier, and had not appreciated the full measure of Jesus' inherited conviction that God had no intention of asking his people to initiate their own desired redemption by a revolt against Rome.[1]

[1] The previous half-dozen pages repeat statements published in a paper on "Jesus and Sepphoris," *Journal of Biblical Literature*, XLV (1926), 14–22.

CHAPTER V
JESUS' CHOICE OF A TASK

JESUS had arrived at mature manhood before he laid aside hammer and trowel to enter upon a public career. He abandoned his customary means of earning a livelihood, left his native village, and severed even the more intimate ties of family life. Henceforth he would seek new friends among persons who might respond to his preaching, and would rely on new sources of supply for food and shelter. This was indeed a radical move. His previous activities had afforded him no social prestige. Without either technical equipment or professional experience the relatively unknown artisan of Nazareth undertook the task of religious leadership for all Israel. It must have been a significant combination of circumstances that induced him to make so revolutionary a change in his course of life.

At first the attention of Jesus had been arrested by the activity of John the Baptist. One day the Nazarene carpenter joined a band of pilgrims on their way to the Jordan Valley to hear the new prophet. This, so far as we are aware, was the initial move toward the choice of a new life-work for Jesus himself. His favorable response to John's message was followed by the acceptance of baptism and ultimately by the inauguration of a vigorous preaching activity on Jesus' own part. Contact with the Baptist is fundamental to an understanding of what Jesus at first conceived to be his new task.

I

That Jesus had been baptized by John was a well-remembered fact. Had Christians been prone to forget it, there were still disciples of John who would gladly have stimulated faltering Christian memories. Later, Jesus left John's company to go his own way and may have taken along with him some of his new acquaintances, but there were others who remained loyal to the cause of the Baptist and continued after his death to perpetuate the movement he had begun. While he was in prison, his disciples were still active (Matt. 11:2; Luke 7:18), and after his execution they were on hand to care for the corpse (Mark 6:29). It was commonly known that they maintained their own distinctive customs, which in respect to fasting, at least, contrasted sharply with the practices of the group about Jesus (Mark 2.18; Matt. 9:14; Luke 5:33; cf. Matt. 11:16; Luke 7:33). In Paul's day the Johannine movement had developed a missionary propaganda, even among the Jews of the Dispersion. Apollos of Alexandria had come under its influence, and a dozen of its adherents furnished the nucleus for the Pauline church at Ephesus (Acts 18:24 f.; 19:1–7).

From the Christian point of view, the continuation of "Johanninism" was, to say the least, unideal. All disciples of the Baptist should have transferred their allegiance to Jesus. But that had not been done, as Christians themselves were well aware. Moreover, in the original relation between the two reformers, whose respective followers were now advocating rival movements, John had appeared to be the master, and Jesus the disciple. This situation presented a serious problem for Christians, in that it reflected upon the validity of their contention that trust in Jesus offered the only sure hope of deliverance for mankind. The fact of his contact with John was too well known to be ignored, consequently it had to be interpreted in the light of later Christian conviction regarding the supremacy and official dignity of Jesus. It was no longer sufficient simply to describe interests, attitudes, and activities of John and Jesus that would have been apposite to their original Jewish environment. The account of their relations with one another had now to be recast in accordance with the needs of the Christian propaganda. Gradually the story of John's deeds and words was woven into the fabric of expanding Christian tradition.

One early Christian portrait of John makes him a preacher of judgment admonishing his hearers to "flee from the wrath to come." The crisis was imminent; the axe was already lying at the base of the tree. Only by a new attainment in righteousness secured through repentance and cleansing was escape from the fiery anger of the Almighty to be insured (Matt. 3:7-10; Luke 3: 7-9). John warned his hearers of judgment and summoned them to repentance. This imagery was characteristically Jewish and biblical. The novel features in John's activity were merely his specific program for effecting immediate reform and his interpretation of current events as indicative of God's early action. Both points of emphasis—judgment and repentance—were entirely congenial to the thinking of early Christian preachers, if only John's message could be squared with the course of events that had transpired since the Baptist's death.

As had been the case with many an earlier prophet in Israel, John's zeal had outrun God's purposes. The day of Jehovah had not come, judgment had not been enacted, the restoration of the kingdom to Israel still awaited realization, and the present order of the universe continued to run its course without catastrophic interference. In the meantime Christians dwelt on their story of Jesus' career. He had preached and wrought miracles, had died on the cross, had arisen and appeared to some of his disciples, had ascended into heaven, had been declared God's chosen agent for accomplishing man's salvation, and had inspired the formation of a new religious society to maintain his cause and his dignity. Between the repentance and the judgment as preached by John, Christians now inserted the work of Jesus and the rise of their own new religious movement. John had stood on the threshold of this series of memorable events. The hope that he had held out to the men of his own generation had now to be harmonized with the Christian interpretation of intervening history.

Above all else, John was called upon by Christian interpreters to support the contention that Jesus had been the Messiah promised to the Jews. But at first John's testimony to this important Christian tenet was still vague and faltering. One of the older sections of gospel tradition represents that when in prison he had heard about the growing popularity of Jesus and had sent messengers to ask whether he was "the coming one" (Matt. 11:2 f.; Luke 7:18 f.). John was not yet a witness-bearer to Christian dogma, he was only an interested inquirer. Nor is it clear that he was expected to approve the reply of Jesus. Indeed the implication seems to be that he would reject the evidence. A display of messianic credentials culminating in the assertion that "the poor have the gospel preached to them" might well cause John, the Jew, to "stumble" (Matt. 11:6; Luke 7:23). Any messiah that would appear in connection with the day of Jehovah and the scenes of the final judgment, as preached by John, would have been portrayed in very different imagery. He must have been, not an earthly preacher of righteousness and healing, but an angelic avenger of wickedness who would gather the wheat into the garner and burn up the chaff. The earliest Christians seem to have been aware of this fact, and they did not force John the Baptist into the incongruous position of identifying one of his own former disciples with any God-sent messenger from the upper world who might be commissioned to inaugurate the new age.

From the later Christian point of view John's shortsightedness had been his misfortune. He had expected judgment too soon and so was unable to appraise Jesus at his true official value. In the light of their present belief in his resurrection and exaltation to heaven, the followers of Jesus during the gospel-making period were able to correct, as it seemed to them, John's faulty perspective. The risen Jesus—John had known only the earthly Jesus—was now in a position to serve as God's representative when the day of Jehovah should dawn. The exalted Christ descending from heaven would himself be both judge and redeemer. In the meantime Christian preachers were busy with the work of preparation that had been initiated by John and accelerated by Jesus during his public ministry.

Judgment was still impending, but Christians had discovered new standards to be applied in the final day of testing. Naturally they made one's attitude toward Jesus, about whom the new religion now centered, the determinative consideration (Matt. 10:32 f.; Luke 12:8 f.). Those who accepted his teaching and remained faithful in their allegiance to him would be suitably rewarded, while those who had rejected his ministrations were doomed. Sweeping condemnation threatened cities like Chorazin, Bethsaida, and Capernaum, whose inhabitants refused to respond favorably to the appeals of Jesus and his followers (Matt. 11:21–23; Luke 10:13–15). The Ninevites who heeded the preaching of Jonah, and the queen of the south who came from afar to hear the wisdom of Solomon, would stand up on the day of judgment to condemn the contemporaries of Jesus for their failure to appreciate his greatness (Matt. 12:41 f.; Luke 11:31 f.).

Christians of this temper were still firm in their expectations of judgment and stressed the necessity of repentance in preparation for the dreadful day. They were highly appreciative of John's earlier activity in this same area of religious interest. His main defect had been failure to recognize that approbation of Jesus and his work was the true criterion of righteousness.

JESUS' CHOICE OF A TASK

Yet John had performed a great service, particularly in urging upon his hearers the necessity of repentance. Thus Christian preachers made him an essential link between the old order, represented by Judaism, and the new order, of which they now were the heralds. They reported that Jesus himself had picturesquely affirmed John's superiority to the prophets and his unsurpassed status among the sons of men. This honor was his because, in fulfilment of prophecy, he had prepared the way for Jesus. Yet John remained outside the Christian fold; he was less than the least in the Kingdom of Heaven. And his ascetic practices were not adopted by the followers of Jesus. But it was a praiseworthy thing to have been a disciple of the Baptist. Even the most sinful in Israel who had heeded this reformer's call were better prepared to enter Christianity than were the most respectable Jews who had refused him a hearing (Matt. 11:7–19; Luke 7: 24–35).

In Mark the difficulty of connecting John with Christianity is relieved by the complete omission of John's references to impending judgment. He calls upon his hearers to repent and be baptized with a view to release from their sins, that they may be ready, not for the fire of judgment, but for John's more worthy successor who is to supplement the Johannine baptism in water with a new baptism by the Holy Spirit (Mark 1:4, 7 f.). Thus John's activity is made to fit perfectly into the Marcan scheme of Christian origins. People were to repent in order to be ready for the first public appearance of Jesus. This event would usher in a new order. He was the "stronger one," since it was he who, by binding Satan and plundering his house, was to inaugurate the age of good news, the Christian "gospel." During Jesus' lifetime the Holy Spirit received at baptism was his peculiar possession, but after his death the disciples were to experience their own Pentecostal endowment, as John had predicted.

In Mark there is perfect harmony and understanding between John and Jesus. Each is dutifully performing the specific task assigned him in God's prearranged scheme of things. John figures in the rôle of official forerunner, after the model of the prophet Elijah whose return to earth in the last times had been forecast in the Book of Malachi. But Mark conveniently forgot that the work of this Elijah *redivivus* was to culminate in the advent of "the great and terrible day of Jehovah," when God would suddenly

descend to the temple to destroy the enemies of
Israel and purge his chosen people with the re-
fining fire of judgment (Mal. 3:1–6; 4:5). As
Mark re-read Scripture, the new Elijah fulfilled
his mission simply by announcing Jesus and preparing the way for the rise of Christianity.

Jesus also was fitted neatly into the Marcan
scheme. He delayed his first public appearance
until John's work had closed, for the preparer
and the fulfiller must not be contemporaries and
must not be rivals (Mark 1:14). Also the message of the Baptist is reiterated by Jesus, who
opens his ministry by announcing the nearness
of the Kingdom of God and calling upon men to
repent—not, however, in preparation for judgment, but as a prelude to belief in the Christian
"gospel." For the author of Mark, the content
of this "good news" was, above everything else,
the fact that Jesus, spirit-endowed from the
moment of baptism and supremely powerful to
overcome all the forces of evil, had now set out
upon his triumphant career of miracle-working
and preaching to issue in victory over death and
the founding of a new Christian society.

According to Mark, on more than one occasion Jesus had deliberately placed the stamp of
approval on John and his work. The later fol-

lowers of the Baptist had erred in their continued attachment to Judaism. They had not yet
learned the futility of sewing new cloth on an old
garment or of pouring new wine into old wine-
skins (Mark 2:18–22). But such disciples of
John were robbing their master of his rightful
honor. His reform found its proper consummation in the growing Christian movement. Jesus
himself was made to corroborate the Marcan
identification of John with Elijah (Mark 9:11–
13) and to cite the authority of John's baptism
against those who called in question his own
qualifications (Mark 11:27–33). In the act of
baptism the Holy Spirit had descended on Jesus
and the voice of God had declared its choice of
him as the one who should bring to realization
the kingdom of which John was the forerunner.
Thus both reformers operated under the one authority from heaven.

The readers of Mark were also to understand
that John enjoyed a goodly measure of popular
esteem, by which Jesus—not the continuing
Johannine movement—rightfully profited. Even
Herod Antipas, it is said, had stood in awe of
John and was impressed by the similarly unusual activity of Jesus (Mark 6:14 ff.). In Marcan
opinion it was complimentary to Jesus, though

not an adequate appreciation of him, to call him a second John the Baptist (Mark 8:28). And it seemed entirely proper for Jesus, when pressed by the questions of his opponents, to take refuge behind the name of John, whom the populace still revered so highly that the religious authorities dared not call in question the validity of that reformer's baptismal rite (Mark 11:31 f.). For the author of Mark, it was entirely appropriate to admit, or even to magnify, the success of John, since by so doing the preparation for Christianity becomes all the more apparent and adequate.

In the Fourth Gospel the Baptist is no longer a mere preparer and announcer of Jesus and Christianity. He is virtually the first Christian believer. Although it is his mission to "make straight the way of the Lord," he explicitly denies that he is the expected Elijah (John 1:21). His preaching is neither an announcement of impending judgment nor a call to repentance in preparation for the work of his successor. Rather, it is his function to identify Jesus when the latter appears on the scene, and to bear witness to his supremacy. This task is accomplished by John's affirming the pre-existence of Jesus, his messiahship, his saviorhood, his ability to baptize his followers with the Holy Spirit, and his right to be hailed as Son of God (John 1:6–35; 5:33–36; 10:41). Here Jesus and John are allowed to carry on public work side by side, but not in any spirit of rivalry. John clearly indicates to his own disciples that his popularity is due to wane as that of Jesus grows; and Jesus, with similar generosity, transfers his activity to the more remote territory of Galilee when it becomes evident that he is attracting more followers than John (John 3:22—4:3).

By gradual stages in the evolution of Christian tradition John, the prophet of judgment, who had summoned his Jewish contemporaries to a baptism of repentance in preparation for the great and terrible day of Jehovah, was transformed into the official herald, and even the admiring disciple, of a new preacher, Jesus, whose more numerous followers had come to constitute an independent and increasingly self-conscious religious community. In the eyes of the second and third generation of Christians, who composed the gospel records, the Baptist was, above all else, the harbinger of the new Christian era. But in actual fact it is improbable that he had visualized himself in any such rôle, or that Jesus had heard words of such import from his lips.

JESUS' CHOICE OF A TASK

The veil of early Christian interpretation must be drawn aside before one may correctly determine how far contact with John had influenced Jesus' decision to enter upon a public career. To answer this question one must return to the distinctively Jewish setting within which both reformers had originally worked.[1]

II

According to Luke, it was in the fifteenth year of the reign of the emperor Tiberius that John began preaching. At the time, Jewish society in Palestine was athrob with desire for liberation from the yoke of Rome. The feeling of

[1] Modern studies on John are relatively scanty and usually follow the gospel model. In English, A. Blakiston in *John the Baptist and His Relation to Jesus* (London, 1912) does little more than reproduce the traditional view, although professing a desire to rescue John from the position of entire subordination to Jesus. Of similar type is P. A. E. Sillevis Smitt's *Johannes de dooper, de wegbereider des heeren* (Amsterdam, 1908). For erudition the work of the Roman Catholic scholar, T. Innitzer, *Johannes der Täufer* (Wien, 1908), is notable. Reversing the usual bias, C. A. Bernoulli in *Johannes der Täufer und die Urgemeinde* (Leipzig, 1918) would make the first Palestinian Christians disciples of John. There is a dependable critical monograph by M. Dibelius, *Die urchristliche Überlieferung von Johannes dem Täufer* (Göttingen, 1911). Of late new interest in the significance of John's movement has been aroused by study of the Mandean literature. See W. Bauer, *Das Johannesevangelium*, 2. Aufl. (Tübingen, 1925), pp. 15 f.

discontent had not been appreciably checked either by the outbreaks that had followed the death of Herod the Great or by the uprising of Judas in the days of the enrolment. This desire for deliverance was not merely a political ambition: it was an overmastering religious aspiration.

Outwardly the status of Palestine under Tiberius might seem tolerably stable. The Romans had suppressed incipient revolutions almost before they were launched. In Galilee and Perea, Herod Antipas had the situation well in hand. For two decades Judea and Samaria had been ruled by procurators who were amply equipped with Roman soldiers to police Jerusalem and its neighborhood. During this period the strong hand of Rome rested so heavily upon Palestinian society that its surface was not conspicuously ruffled by the powerful revolutionary undercurrents already gathering momentum for the great upheaval to come in 66 A.D. But in the meantime the oppressed people could turn more directly to God for help. The efficient government of Tiberius might discourage attempts to secure national freedom by the ordinary processes of political revolution, but this situation only led many a pious Jew to a firmer belief that God would deliver the chosen people by some more effective means.

For hundreds of years before the days of John the Baptist the political experiences of the Jewish nation had been seriously undermining popular faith in earthly princes, even though they might be thought chosen and anointed by God to administer the government. The kings of Israel and Judah had been unable to avert conquest and captivity by the Assyrians and Babylonians. Even under the more favorable domination of the Persians, the returned exiles' faith in Zerubbabel as the "Servant of Jehovah" and the "Branch" whom God had chosen to restore the national fortunes proved vain. During a brief period in the latter part of the second century B.C. the successful Maccabeans had temporarily rehabilitated the monarchical institutions of the Jews. John Hyrcanus had indeed combined in his person both the royal and the priestly functions, but within half a century his descendants lost their kingdom to the Romans, and even before John's death his glory had passed for many of his subjects.

Formally, to be sure, reverence for the Maccabean line and the picture of a future king descended from David and anointed by God to rule his people remained prominent in Jewish thinking even under the Romans. But perhaps this ideal of royalty owed not a little of its perpetuity to the very fact that it had been put so far beyond the possibilit, of realization by the might of the foreign oppressor. In reality, as a practical institution, Jewish monarchy had quite lost its prestige as a ground of popular hope for national deliverance. More and more the people had turned directly to God himself for the fulfilment of their desire, and in those moments when their temporal power was least in evidence their reliance on divine intervention was strongest.

In the history of the Hebrews the hour of dire calamity had often been hope's golden opportunity. The trying experiences of the Babylonian exile had stimulated prophets to predict a glorious future restoration to the land of their fathers. Thanks to Ezekiel and his successors, the unfortunate captives were encouraged to visualize a triumphant deliverance through God's own action on their behalf. The hope of return to Palestine was heightened by an extravagant portrayal of attendant miraculous events. The land itself would be transformed into a veritable garden of the Lord. The Holy

City would rise in new splendor and become the very dwelling place of Jehovah. The nature of men and beasts would undergo a remarkable change in character. All evil would disappear, and no enemy of Israel would survive. Ferocious animals would perish or be rendered harmless and kindly under the new conditions. Even devout Jews would be changed, as God gave them new hearts and poured out his spirit upon all flesh.

Trust in God was put to the crucial test again in the second century B.C. Under the persecution of the Syrian ruler Antiochus IV, Jewish religion was temporarily threatened with extinction. The destruction of the temple and captivity in Babylonia had not been a greater calamity than that which now menaced the Jews. They were ordered to abandon all their traditional religious customs; they might not even read or possess a copy of their Scriptures; their holy temple was defiled by the introduction of an altar of Zeus within its sacred precincts and upon which a swine was sacrificed; their priests were commanded to eat the defiling flesh of the swine; and the people throughout the country were required to worship after the manner of their conquerors.[1]

[1] I Macc. 1:41-64; Josephus *Ant.* XII. 248-56.

This crisis inspired that new outburst of faith portrayed in the Book of Daniel.

Exilic prophets, in consequence of knowledge that had been disclosed to them in visions and revelations, had pictured a restored Palestine as the goal of ardent desire; but the Danielic seer depicted the new estate of God's people in more transcendental fashion. Their future welfare was bound up less closely with the fortunes of the Holy Land, even though miraculously restored to prosperity; and hope centered upon the inauguration of a quite new age. God was seen seated in judgment on a flaming throne and ministered unto by a heavenly host numbering "thousands of thousands." After this vision of judgment, the final redemption of the Jewish people was witnessed in the portrayal of "one like a son of man" coming with the clouds of heaven and endowed directly by God with a new and eternal glory—"his dominion is an everlasting dominion which shall not pass away, and his kingdom that which shall not be destroyed" (Dan. 7:9–14). This hope is distinctly "apocalyptic" and "eschatological"—it is a matter of supernatural revelation and its realization will mark the end of the present world-order.

From the early days of the Maccabean struggle against Syrian oppression on down to the final overthrow of the Jewish nation by Rome in the second century A.D., apocalyptic visions and eschatological expectations were frequently invoked to strengthen Jewish confidence in ultimate deliverance from misfortune. From time to time new spokesmen of this type of hope appeared, until it had become for John the Baptist and his followers a well-established form of imagery. It even produced a literature, portions of which have survived to the present day. Apparently no season of distress lacked its apocalyptic prophet of a new and better day and perhaps at no period since the time of Antiochus had the need for fresh assurances of heaven's protection been more keenly felt than in the days of protracted subjugation by the Romans, particularly during the first century of the present era.[1]

In those circles where the apocalyptic type of expectation prevailed, the very imagery of a kingdom to be established after the Davidic model was abandoned outright. Redemption was to come directly from God. Suddenly from his position of supremacy in the heavens he

[1] A more extended account of this form of Jewish thinking will be found in the chapter on "Hebrew and Jewish Hopes" in S. J. Case's *The Millennial Hope* (Chicago, 1918), where additional literature is cited on pp. 243 ff.

would intervene anew in the affairs of mankind. By his own might, or through an appropriate angelic intermediary, he would utterly destroy the enemies of his people. Judgment would overtake sinners even though they might be found among the children of Israel, and the new kingdom would be no mere recrudescence of the Jewish monarchical institution. Hope of deliverance lay not in any political maneuvering to restore the Maccabean line of princes whom Herod had supplanted, not even in the re-establishment of an idealized national existence under a God-anointed scion of the house of David, but in a sudden act of Deity to destroy all evil and miraculously constitute the Jewish people into a blessed theocratic nation.

An advocate of the apocalyptic hope was, in the nature of the case, destined to be in some measure a prophet of warning. Preparation for God's impending action was a matter of supreme concern. Whether his delay thus far had been due merely to the working of his own inscrutable purposes, or had been occasioned by displeasure with the conduct of his people, his advent would be a crucial moment in their history. From days of old, preachers in Israel had admonished their hearers to beware the day of Jehovah when he

would come as was popularly supposed to destroy the enemies of his people, and also, the
prophets added, to punish the sins of the chosen
race. It was of the very genius of Judaism to assume that winning the favor of God depended
upon one or another type of specialization in
righteousness on the part of man. A Gentile
might buy the favor of his Deity with a generous
offering, or might control divine actions by
means of magical rites, but Jews knew no method of coercing God. His will was absolute and
supreme; but the doing of that will, especially as
it had been made known to men in the sacred
Scriptures, was essential to human welfare. And
at a moment when the need of divine assistance
was felt most keenly, the call to a new attainment in righteousness could be counted upon to
meet with a ready response.

This social and psychological situation provided the setting in which John found his task.
Judas of Galilee had urged that the people reconsecrate themselves to military efforts as a
means of showing God that they were worthy of
his favor. Thus they would make a bid for
divine assistance in the struggle to throw off
Roman domination and effect a restoration of
national autonomy. God would deliver his op-

pressed people when they were ready to demonstrate their willingness to sacrifice everything in his service. But John measured devotion to Deity by a different set of standards and summoned his hearers to another type of reconsecration. They were advised to withdraw from the distracting activities of the time and in the quiet of the less frequented wilderness to dedicate themselves anew to ideals of individual righteousness.

John would hardly imagine that such conduct as he prescribed could materially affect the predetermined purposes of the Almighty. But in the distresses of the time the new preacher saw evidences of the rapidly approaching day when God would intervene to inaugurate the new age by a sudden act of destruction and restoration. Now that the long-awaited day of Jehovah was thought to be at hand, it was tremendously important that the Jewish people themselves should be prepared for this event. With great zeal John devoted himself to the task of persuading his kinsmen that by personal effort they should seek escape from their sins and renew their allegiance to God. As a distinctive mark of their new devotion, his disciples received at the reformer's hands the rite of baptism, thus constituting themselves into a more consecrated society, a worthier Israel, especially prepared to meet their God on the imminent judgment day.

John's preaching seems to have been received with favor by many of his contemporaries. Even Josephus bears witness to the new prophet's reputation for piety. Almost a decade after John's death there were still some Jews who thought the destruction of Herod Antipas' army by the Arabians was a divine punishment inflicted on Herod because of his execution of the reformer. Naturally, Josephus gives his readers no hint of the political significance of John's propaganda. It would have been quite out of place to inform the Romans, under whose protection Josephus was now living comfortably at the capital, that this stormy prophet of the desert had announced an early end of all existing governmental institutions, both the imperial and the Herodian, by the catastrophic intervention of God. John had to be painted in the image of a gentile philosopher whose primary concern was to inculcate "virtue."[1]

[1] Josephus says: "To some of the Jews it seemed that Herod's army had perished by the vengeance of God, and that very justly, as retribution for the death of John called the Baptist. For Herod

That John stressed righteousness in men's dealings with one another and the cultivation of genuine piety toward God, as Josephus affirms, is undoubtedly true. Unquestionably, also, this ethical emphasis was capable of making a strong appeal to contemporary Jews. But the pursuit of virtue for its own sake can hardly have been regarded as the chief end of life by the disciples of John. Within Palestinian society as constituted in the age of Tiberius the sense of crisis was too keen and the psychology of revolution too overpowering to permit the thoughts of men to rest short of a more ultimate goal. Reforms, to make an appeal, must direct the gaze toward the future when present distress would find relief in specific action, either by man or by God.

The power of John's appeal to his hearers lay

---

killed him, though he was a good man and exhorted the Jews to cultivate virtue, practising both righteousness in their dealings with one another and piety toward God, and to come to baptism. For thus only would the baptism be acceptable to God, if used not to secure forgiveness for specific sins but for the purpose of bodily purification when the soul had been previously purified by righteousness. When men rallied about him, for they were exceedingly pleased on hearing his words, Herod feared lest John should instigate a revolt, so very persuasive was he with men, for they seemed to do everything he advised. So Herod thought it much better by putting him to death to anticipate any new agitation that might proceed from him than to repent afterwards of any

[238]

fundamentally in his announcement that special divine action was imminent. As John viewed his task, and as his audiences appraised his significance, his first duty was to warn men that a new age was at hand. Preparation for its approach was a pressing necessity. Repentance, cleansing, and reconsecration were in order; and haste in accomplishing these preparatory measures was highly advisable. But the change in the existing social order would be far greater than the change in the individual. The imperial régime, the tetrarchy of Herod Antipas, the Davidic line of royalty, and even the Abrahamic compact with the Jewish race, would all be supplanted by the new kingdom to be set up miraculously by God in the near future.

That John's preaching had a distinctly po-

---

disturbance that might occur. So, on account of Herod's suspicion John was sent to Machaerus, the fortress previously mentioned, and there he was killed. The Jews were of the opinion that the destruction of his army was in accordance with the will of God to afflict Herod" (*Ant.* XVIII, 116-19). The actual fact probably is that in popular opinion the prophet was sacrosanct. His enthusiasm, his unusual dress and his strange conduct marked him as God's man regardless of whether his message was acceptable to his hearers, and it was assumed that violence done to his person would inevitably be attended by disaster. Similarly in the gospels both John and Jesus are objects of popular reverence (Mark 11:32; Matt. 14:5; 21:26, 46; Luke 20:6).

litical bearing Josephus himself incidentally reveals when he says that Herod executed John out of fear lest the new movement should develop revolutionary tendencies. Perhaps Herod well knew that its leader was no Zealot agitator like Judas, and had no disposition to force God's hand by an appeal to the sword. The new régime announced by John was to be established suddenly by the power of heaven. But the unstable crowds that assembled to hear a new herald of approaching judgment might not remain content to await the divine good pleasure in bringing their hopes to realization. At any moment, especially if a favorable opportunity offered, they might suddenly grow impatient. The ideals of passive apocalypticism and aggressive zealotism were easily interchangeable in the popular mind. The logical inconsistency involved in vacillating between them is more evident on paper than in the heat of real life. Each program counted ultimately on divine support for its effective realization, and each pictured final victory in terms of violence, a violence to be initiated in one case by God and in the other case by man as the servant of God. Whether man or God would strike the first blow must have been, for many Jews in these agitated times, mainly a

question of expediency. It was quite possible
that the prophet of a new order might be transformed over night by his enthusiastic admirers
into its divinely appointed inaugurator. With
true political sagacity Herod realized the menace
in this situation and cut short John's career.[1]

Although zealot and apocalyptic ideals of deliverance were in some respects closely akin,
there is no reason to suppose that John himself
agitated revolution. His task, as he saw it, was
to summon his contemporaries to repentance in
preparation for the speedily approaching judgment. Ancient prophecies regarding Israel's deliverance through the intervention of God were
thought to be on the verge of fulfilment, and the
new prophet found in this impending crisis an

[1] The gospel writers chose a different, but not at all inconsistent, item in John's work to account for Herod's antipathy
(Mark 6:14–29; Matt. 14:1–12; Luke 9:7–9). Their readers would
not have been interested in the political implications of John's
conduct, just as Josephus' audience would have found Herod's
marital irregularities rather tame, save as his actions affected
political relations with his former father-in-law, Aretas of Arabia.
Among the Jews the matrimonial aberrations of their princes had
always been regarded by prophetic reformers as a proper subject
for criticism, and it is altogether likely that John had made no
exception of Herod when calling upon sinners to repent. This
would not please either Herod or his new wife, but probably
Josephus has perceived more accurately than the author of Mark
the real motive behind the arrest and execution of the Baptist.

opportunity to serve both his God and his fellow
men by a vigorous propaganda on behalf of a
fresh specialization in righteousness. It was entirely consonant with the characteristic psychology of the prophet that John should feel God-
driven to his task, but the distress of the times
furnished the immediate occasion for the divine
voice to utter its imperious summons.

III

It was John the preacher of reform, calling
upon the people of Palestine to reconsecrate
themselves to God in preparation for the day of
judgment, who had first aroused the interest of
Jesus and to whose appeal he had responded.
His very presence among those baptized by John
is ample proof that he was heartily in sympathy
with the Baptist's message and shared his concern for the welfare of the Jews. Their distresses
called for alleviation. Their political institutions
had failed to bring desired relief, while sporadic
outbursts of revolutionary zeal had merely aggravated their misfortunes. But the group of
sympathetic hearers that gathered about the
new preacher of repentance looked more directly
to God for deliverance. By an early display of
supernatural power he would suddenly bring to

realization the final age of blessedness. The day of Jehovah was at hand.

Among Palestinian Jews in the time of Jesus an advocate of eschatology was no monstrosity. For upward of two centuries this form of thinking had been gaining popularity and had served in more than one crisis to inspire confidence in the power and protection of God. Just how extensively apocalypticism was in vogue, or whether its adherents could ever have been properly called a "school," may remain a matter of doubt. Moreover, its representatives sometimes deviated more or less widely from one another on points of detail, according to personal inclination or in response to the demands of a particular situation. In the very nature of the case, eschatological thinking was more fluid in character than were, for example, the tenets of scribism, and people who looked for deliverance through catastrophic establishment of the Kingdom could hardly have constituted so well-defined a social group as were Pharisees or Sadducees. Yet, unquestionably, the eschatological hope was an attitude of mind thoroughly familiar in Jesus' environment. It was not only entirely respectable, but in some circles very highly esteemed.

That Jesus believed judgment to be at hand,

[243]

and was impelled by this conviction to take up
the preaching of repentance, is one of the most
certain conclusions to be deduced from his early
association with John. Jesus was not content
simply to insure safety for himself; he would also
save his neighbors. This impulse transformed
him into an aggressive preacher who presently
was to become even more effective than John
had been in demanding preparation for the impending Kingdom of Heaven.[1] He strove to con-

[1] In Mark and Luke, Jesus says "Kingdom of God." But
among Jews it was customary to avoid direct reference to the
Deity and to employ a surrogate like "Heaven(s)," "Place" or
"Name." Kingdom of Heaven (*malkuth shamajim*) was familiar
terminology among the Jews (see Strack and Billerbeck, *Kommentar zum Neuen Testament aus Talmud und Midrasch* [München,
1922], I, 172–84). The author of Matthew imitates the Semitic
idiom, even to the extent of retaining the plural "Heavens." But
his usage is not the result of literal translation from his sources. As
a matter of fact, in his sources he uniformly found "Kingdom of
God," which he studiously altered. Only on two or three occasions
has he nodded. He was fond of the more awkward expression,
perhaps just because it had an archaic flavor and would seem a
novelty to his Greek-speaking readers. Probably this same sort of
feeling helped to preserve in Christian circles other unusual locu-
tions like ὁ υἱὸς τοῦ ἀνθρώπου and ἀμὴν λέγω ὑμῖν that were intelligible only to the initiated. Probably it had been Jesus' custom to say
"Kingdom of Heaven," either the Hebrew *malkuth shamajim* or
the Aramaic *malkutha dishmaja*, the sense of which is, however,
quite properly rendered by the Greek "Kingdom of God." About

vince his kinsmen of their sins and to lead them out into an experience of more perfect accord with the will of their God before the arrival of the judgment day. This attempt to effect in his hearers a religious renewal was an interest that from time to time had been championed by a noble succession of preachers in Israel. In giving himself to this endeavor the carpenter of Nazareth proved to be morally and spiritually a lineal descendant of the Hebrew prophets.

Notwithstanding the prevailing disposition of the disciples after his death to employ messianic categories in their efforts to officialize Jesus, they did not completely obscure the fact

---

the year 70 A.D. the rabbis spoke of the government of Rome as simply the "Kingdom" (*Aboth* III, 2 and 6), with which the eschatological notion of a Kingdom of Heaven would stand in striking and agreeable contrast for Jews of Jesus' day who were chafing under the dominion of the Romans. In rabbinical literature the new age of expected blessedness was also designated "the coming age" (*ha-'olam habba*) in contrast with "this age" (*ha-'olam hazzeh*). Probably these expressions were known and used by Jesus, although their equivalents are not of common occurrence in the Greek gospels (Matt. 12:32; Mark 10:30; Luke 16:8; 20:34. Cf. J. Klausner, *Die messianischen Vorstellungen des jüdischen Volkes im Zeitalter der Tannaiten* [Berlin, 1904], pp. 17 ff.). Paul retained this Semitic idiom to describe the present order of existence (I Cor. 1:20; 2:6; 3:18; II Cor. 4:4; Rom. 12:2), but referred to the coming age by the more easy Greek expression "Kingdom of God."

that his contemporaries had regarded him a prophet, although this had been an entirely inadequate classification from the later Christians' point of view. They reported occasions when it had been definitely affirmed that Jesus was the prophet whose coming had been foretold by Moses (Acts 3:22–26; 7:37; cf. Luke 24:19). Jesus was said to have likened the rejection of himself and his cause to the similar treatment accorded ancient preachers of reform (Matt. 5:12; 23:29–34; Luke 6:22; 11:47–50). His experience at Nazareth, where he was reputed to have been refused a hearing on the ground of an inadequate display of mighty works, had been typical of the prophet (Mark 6:4; Matt. 13:57; Luke 4:24, 27). Receiving Jesus paralleled receiving a prophet (Matt. 10:41), and his death at Jerusalem followed the prophetic pattern (Matt. 23:37; Luke 13:33 f.).

It was said that on various occasions Jesus had been called a prophet by both friends and enemies. The epithet had been used by Herod, as well as by the Jewish populace in Jerusalem (Mark 6:15; Luke 9:8; Matt. 21:11, 46). On the occasion of Jesus' raising the widow's son the crowd had hailed him as a prophet, and it was with this thought in mind that the Pharisee had

[246]

invited him to dine (Luke 7:16, 39). The same popular notion served the disciples as a foil against which to display the new messianic confession of Peter (Mark 8:28; Matt. 16:14; Luke 9:19). The woman of Samaria, the multitude that witnessed the miraculous increase of food, an audience when impressed by a striking discourse, and a blind man who had been healed, all were said to have employed the word "prophet" to express their estimate of Jesus (John 4:19; 6:14; 7:40; 9:17). This designation, so eminently appropriate in Jesus' own environment, had not been entirely lost from view in later tradition, even though it now seemed quite inadequate according to the new standards of appreciation possessed by the gospel writers.

Had Jesus been called upon for self-classification in the interests of indicating the type of task to which he had set himself, undoubtedly the word "prophet" would have been the first to spring to his lips.[1] The prophet, it is true, can

[1] See the brief but suggestive discussion by H. J. Cadbury, "Jesus and the Prophets," *Journal of Religion*, V (1925), 607–22. The gulf separating prophecy from apocalyptic, once thought by some scholars to be virtually impassable, has been gradually narrowing. In fact, the newer interpretation of prophecy, which finds ecstasy and visions to have been a fundamental experience in the making of even an Amos, a Hosea, an Isaiah or a Jeremiah, renders

scarcely be said to have thought that he was choosing his own task. He performed a duty that seemed to him superimposed by the decrees of heaven. Not on his own authority, but equipped by divine inspiration, he delivered the word of God to the men of his own generation. It was no mere literary device, but was a declaration of the prophet's sincerest conviction, when he prefaced his utterances with the typical phrase "Thus saith Jehovah." The prophets commonly make it plain that they pursued their

---

it possible to see in the apocalyptic seer of later Judaism the natural successor to the national prophet of earlier times. Consult, for example, G. Hölscher, *Die Profeten* (Leipzig, 1914), p. 358; T. H. Robinson, *Prophecy and the Prophets in Ancient Israel* (New York, 1923), pp. 195 f. Ecstasy is still denied to the greater prophets by M. Buttenwieser, *The Prophets of Israel* (New York, 1914); and N. Micklem, *Prophecy and Eschatology* (London, 1926). But an ever increasing number of interpreters recognizes a more or less extensive display of religious emotions, even in the most noted of the literary prophets. In addition to Hölscher and Robinson, cited above, one may refer to H. P. Smith, *The Religion of Israel* (New York, 1914); J. M. Powis Smith, *The Prophet and His Problems* (New York, 1914), and *The Prophet and His Times* (Chicago, 1925); J. Skinner, *Prophecy and Religion: Studies in the Life of Jeremiah* (Cambridge, 1922); H. W. Robinson, "Hebrew Psychology" in *The People and the Book*, edited by A. S. Peake (Oxford, 1926), pp. 353–82; B. Duhm, *Israels Propheten* (Tübingen, 1916); H. Gunkel, *Die Propheten* (Göttingen, 1917); A. Allwohn, *Die Ehe des Propheten Hosea in psychoanalytischer Beleuchtung* (Giessen, 1926).

work at the behest of a compelling force from without and not merely in compliance with their normal inclinations.

An arresting religious experience seems to have been the necessary antecedent to a prophetic career. Sometimes the prophets spoke of the stirring incidents that had transformed them from ordinary citizens into chosen messengers of God. The summons had come to Isaiah in a vision of Deity enthroned in the temple (Isa. 6:1 ff). The seer was overcome with the sense of his imperfection in the presence of the holy God. Not until cleansed by the purifying touch of a coal from the altar was he fit to undertake a prophetic career. Similarly, Jeremiah had been changed from a timid village youth into one of the most effective of the prophets through the touch of God's hand upon his mouth and the accompanying commission to address himself not only to Israel but to the nations and the kingdoms (Jer. 1:4–10). Although the Scriptures did not always describe the initial experience that had constituted a prophet's call, it must have been commonly apparent to Jews of later times that he had been a man wholly motivated by a sense of divine commission.

In the early days of Hebrew history the divine afflatus had proved so overwhelming that the prophets were a class of men virtually maddened by religious enthusiasm. The sanity of the greater prophets of later times stands in sharp contrast to that extravagant ecstasy characteristic of a more primitive stage of culture. But these saner men of God were no less conscious than their predecessors had been of an experience which had changed them from ordinary people into the inspired heralds of the divine will and purposes. Nothing short of such impulsion could have induced an Amos to leave the Judean countryside to become a spokesman for Jehovah at the very center of Jeroboam's kingdom. The new preacher lacked even the professional standing of the conventional prophet, but he had a superior equipment. It was none other than God who had called him away from his flocks and fig trees and had commanded him to "go prophesy unto my people Israel" (3:8; 7:15). So sure was the prophet that his task was no mere accidental undertaking of his own, but was a God-assigned obligation, that sometimes he projected the divine purpose back to his very infancy (Isa. 49:1; cf. Gal. 1:15).

God's special equipment of his chosen spokesmen is a pervasive phenomenon throughout the

Jewish Scriptures from the time of Moses down to the days of the apocalyptic seer of Maccabean times. Not only was it true of Moses, Samuel, Elijah, and Elisha that their effectiveness was a result of unique endowment, but the prophets of later days often bore testimony to their own sense of a compelling inspiration. Jeremiah felt within himself the impulsion of a force that burned like a fire in his bones, intoxicating him with the very words of Jehovah (20:9; 23:9). So completely had the prophet been infused with the message from above that he was a marked man who might fittingly be called by the name of "Jehovah, God of hosts" (15:16). When opponents taunted him he fell back upon the conviction that the words he had spoken had come directly from the presence of Deity (17:16). Notwithstanding the insuperable difficulties that often confronted them, the prophets moved forward in the confidence that they were God's chosen messengers. Their work was to be done, not in their own strength, but by the operation of that supernatural power with which they had been equipped. Rejection of their message was never taken to mean that their call had been spurious or that they had not been genuinely inspired.

The great prophets were men of strong character and mighty emotions. The specific content
of their sermons might vary with the age and
the circumstances under which they severally
lived, but all of them were devoted to the same
lofty enterprise of effecting religious reform and
renewal among their contemporaries. Whether
they were heralds of disaster or messengers of
hope, threats and promises were alike employed
for the accomplishment of moral ends. They
boldly pronounced the scathing verdict of conscience upon the sins and sinners of their day,
justifying their boldness on the sincere conviction that they were spokesmen for God himself.
They felt that they had been irresistibly impelled to surrender their own wills to the higher
will of heaven. This had been their consistent
self-representation. A later Christian was entirely true to the prophets' own mind when he
affirmed that prophecy was never of human origin but had been a message delivered by men
equipped with power from heaven to utter the
very words of God (II Pet. 1:21).

IV

The memory of the prophets and their work
constituted one of the most picturesque and

stimulating religious heritages that antiquity had bequeathed to later Judaism. The story of their lives had been familiar to Jesus from early youth and it is not surprising that he should in a measure have duplicated their experiences and interpreted his own emotional life in similar fashion. Those were days when feeling ran high and when religion often expressed itself most effectively in forms of activity that might seem in later times to border dangerously on fanaticism. Jesus would have been quite out of place in the life of his day had he chosen his new task with utter calmness and deliberation. When he forsook his handicraft to become a preacher of repentance to his kinsmen, he made a change in his career as radical as that made by an Amos, a Jeremiah, or any other of the ancient prophets. For him, as for them, the new obligation was God-given, and the individual felt conscious of unusual divine equipment for his mission. Like the prophets, he justified his new course of action by reference to stirring initial experiences, the memory of which has been perpetuated by his followers in the gospel stories of his baptism and temptation.

Christian preachers in the first century were not always of one opinion regarding what had actually happened in connection with the baptism of Jesus. Mark's readers were informed that on coming up from the baptismal waters Jesus had seen the Spirit in dove-like form descend upon him through a cleft in the sky and had heard a heavenly voice declare "Thou art my beloved son, in thee I am well pleased" (1:11). In Luke this statement is reproduced, with the added note that Jesus was in prayer when he experienced his vision.[1] In Matthew the most significant change in the Marcan narrative consists in making the voice speak in the third person: "This is my beloved son, in whom I am well pleased" (3:17). According to Mark, the baptism had been the moment when Jesus attained the consciousness of divine sonship that constituted his commission to found Christianity. The voice addressed itself directly to him and for his own personal instruction. On the other hand, one who had been miraculously born and set apart for his task from childhood, as Jesus was already represented to have been in Matthew, hardly needed to be told that he was the

---

[1] Mention of Jesus in prayer is a peculiar feature of this gospel (3:21; 5:16; 6:12; 9:18, 29; 11:1; 23:34, 46). Whether the author had reliable sources of information for these incidents can hardly be determined, but undoubtedly the other evangelists slighted this aspect of Jesus' religious experience.

official Son of God. Quite fittingly, the voice now spoke, not to Jesus, but to the assembled people informing them of his high status. He was still permitted to witness the descent of the Spirit, but even this part of the experience lost not a little of its vitality in consequence of the earlier statement that he had submitted to the rite simply for the purpose of setting an example in righteousness (Matt. 3:14 f.). In the Fourth Gospel the baptism was still further deprived of essential significance in Jesus' own experience. The Spirit had exhibited itself for John the Baptist's benefit; it was the sign by which he had been able to discover the Son of God (John 1: 33 f.).

The gospel-writers, and the Christians of their day, were far more interested to find meaning for themselves in the story of Jesus' baptism than they were to discover its meaning for him. In their environment the incident seemed especially valuable as a means of classifying officially the founder of the new religion and authenticating its rite of initiation. But neither of these interests had been a part of the situation in which Jesus lived. The voice that could transform a Nazarene carpenter into an ardent prophetic preacher must have spoken in accents of far greater reality. Officialdom and ritualism, as areas for self-interpretation, had made no appeal to Amos and his successors. Prophets as a class were prophets at their worst, in the eyes of those Hebrew reformers who appeared from time to time summoning their kinsmen to higher living. The true spokesmen of God were those who had heard his voice in their own souls revealing to them the message that was to be passed on to their contemporaries. These men were confident that they had been chosen for their task by the decree and favor of heaven, but they neither demanded nor expected self-exaltation and hardly claimed even that measure of honor that would seem to have been their just due. Inspiration—not installation—was the essence of the prophetic experience.

John the Baptist had summoned his audiences to repentance. The persons who heeded his call sealed their determination to attain higher standards of personal righteousness by submitting to the new rite of purification practiced by John. Baptism as a token of cleansing was entirely appropriate to the Judaism of that age.[1]

[1] For the significance of baptism and kindred rites of cleansing in later Judaism, one may consult W. Brandt, *Die jüdischen Baptismen* (Giessen, 1910) and *Jüdische Reinheitslehre* (Giessen,

JESUS' CHOICE OF A TASK

In the experience of Jesus the act was attended by a heightening of emotion that impelled him to assume the responsibilities of a new life-work. As an Isaiah and a Jeremiah had been purged by the touch of God, not simply for their own sakes, but that they might become messengers of righteousness to the men of their time, so Jesus heard the call of God summoning him to a similar service.

Heaven never sent forth its messengers unaccoutered for their appointed tasks. Very commonly in the Scriptures the endowment of men especially favored and chosen by God to perform unusual duties was expressed in terms of the outpouring of the Spirit. In later Judaism this way of thinking became more and more prevalent.[1] Prophecy, above all else, was the characteristic work of the Spirit. It is true that the older preachers of reform had not been accustomed to use this language, perhaps because their professional rivals had universally claimed

---

1910); I. Abrahams, *Studies in Pharisaism and the Gospels* (1st ser., Cambridge, 1917), pp. 36–46; H. L. Strack and P. Billerbeck, *op. cit.* I, 102–13.

[1] See P. Volz, *Der Geist Gottes* (Tübingen, 1910), particularly pp. 78 ff.; I. Abrahams, *Studies in Pharisaism and the Gospels* (2d ser., Cambridge, 1923), pp. 120–28.

to be thus endowed. But Amos, Hosea, Isaiah, and Jeremiah were none the less conscious of possessing the divine presence which they depicted in other imagery. Endowment by the Spirit, however, was the most appropriate terminology that could be found for the description of such experiences among Jews. Micah affirmed that he felt "full of power by the spirit of Jehovah" and therefore was commissioned "to declare unto Jacob his transgression and to Israel his sin" (3:8). In a more kindly vein, another prophet declared himself anointed by the Spirit to preach a message of good tidings to the unfortunate in Israel (Isa. 61:1). In later times the Spirit was referred to with increasing frequency as a means of describing the operation of God in the life of his chosen representatives. This overmastering presence fell upon Ezekiel, it lifted him up, it transported him from place to place, and it commissioned him to speak the will of God.[1] In moments of high emotion the prophet was completely Spirit-possessed.

In the Judaism of Jesus' day endowment by the Spirit was characteristic terminology for describing the way in which God made choice of individuals and prepared them for special tasks.

[1] Ezek. 2:2; 3:12, 14, 24; 8:3, 14, 16; 11:1, 5, 24; 37:1; 43:5.

JESUS' CHOICE OF A TASK

That Jesus would feel himself empowered by the Spirit for the new work to which God had called him would be but to repeat in his experience the favor which heaven had shown in the past to a Moses, a David, and a long line of prophets. One possessed by the Spirit was lifted quite above the plane of ordinary living, at least on all critical occasions. The driving force for life's work now came from without and from above. Impulses and emotions were sanctified, convictions were made doubly strong, and the whole area of moral and spiritual ideals was transported into the regions of the absolute by the certainty that the individual no longer pursued simply the dictates of his own will but was directed in his activities by the very Spirit of God.

Confident though Spirit-filled men were that God himself had chosen and equipped them for their tasks, they were not unaware of the difficulties that lay in the way of realizing their ideals. The Scriptures told of prophets who would, if possible, have resisted the divine impulsion. They shrank from the responsibilities laid upon them and felt personally quite unequal to their new calling. They expected opposition from their audiences, an opposition that might at any moment cost them their lives. Rarely

were they rewarded with the crown of martyrdom, but frequently it was their fate to find
themselves without a following, while their message was unappreciated and their hopes were
thwarted. A new teacher well acquainted with
the story of the prophet's career among the Hebrews would hardly choose on his own initiative
to enter a profession that offered so little prospect of success. But the great prophets had
never taken up their duties because they thought
the calling promised them a brilliant career.
They, like their Christian successor Paul,
preached because they must. Necessity was upon
them; to resist would have been worse than
death.

Yet had prophets no right to expect, or even
to demand, success? Having been called to their
work by God and endowed by the Spirit, these
new messengers of righteousness occupied a position of favor with heaven that surely deserved
to be recognized and honored. It was not inconsistent with their sense of authority to ask of
God on their behalf continued displays of approval and protection. But to have indulged
themselves in this respect would have menaced
the prophets' characteristic moral integrity and
their ideal of absolute devotion to the will of

God. History had shown that they must be prepared to meet rejection and defeat, even persecution and death, without losing confidence in the sanctity of their mission. Nevertheless, it might well seem incongruous that chosen spokesmen of heaven could not ask special privileges for themselves in the prosecution of their God-assigned duties. It was in some such area of conflicting emotions, when, in the presence of a mighty task, the sense of a divine summons momentarily stood in sharp conflict with the feeling of personal limitations, that the so-called "temptation" of Jesus had its original setting.

The gospel writers, true to the interests that were uppermost in their age, saw in the temptation of Jesus a demonstration of his authority rather than a crisis in his own religious experience. In his official capacity as Son of God and founder of a new religious régime it was to be expected that he would display his superiority over the satanic prince of evil. In the older form of the story, as preserved in Matthew and Luke (Matt. 4:3-10; Luke 4:3-12), the supremacy of Jesus is shown by his very refusal to make any exhibition of miracles. Presumably it lay within his power to perform these proposed wonders, but as suggestions of the tempter they must be rejected. For the circle of Christians where this form of the tradition first crystallized, miracles as a test of Jesus' authority were less highly esteemed than was his prophetic equipment to speak the word of God. With this disposition Jesus himself probably would have been in hearty sympathy. But other Christians saw in the temptation what appeared to them a more significant triumph for Jesus. In Mark's version (1:12 f.) no mention was made of Jesus' refusal to perform miracles. On the contrary, the whole performance was transported into the sphere of supernaturalism. Jesus was with the wild beasts, who, contrary to all their natural impulses, did him no harm. And instead of declining angelic assistance, as in the older tradition, it was now affirmed that during the temptation he had actually been attended by ministering angels.

It was entirely natural that Christian interpretation of the temptation should move farther and farther away from the picture of a realistic struggle in the personal experience of Jesus. As in the case of the baptism, the incident demanded explanation. There was no slight incongruity in the very notion that the Son of God could be tempted at all, unless it were for the purpose of setting his later disciples a worthy ex-

ample of resistance (Luke 4:13; Heb. 2:18; 4:
15), or of demonstrating his poise, dignity, and
authority. But for Jesus the immediate issue
had not been how the Christian Son of God
should conduct himself in the presence of the
prince of demons. Rather, it was a question of
how an unschooled artisan, with a summons to
religious leadership suddenly thrust upon him
from above, should proceed toward the accomplishment of his task.

Jesus could not lightly abandon his customary occupation and ignore the problem of securing food and other necessities of life that would
still be required in his new work. He knew the
strength of the current desire among the people
for unusual displays of God's favor. The revolutionary psychology of the day invited the activity of leaders who would demonstrate miraculously their divine equipment to instigate a successful revolt against the Roman government.[1]

[1] Judas of Galilee in 6 A.D. was well aware of the popular belief
that an uprising could not be successful without the assistance of
"the divine" (Josephus, *Ant.* XVIII. 5), but he urged the necessity
of human action as a preliminary condition of intervention by
Deity. The failure of Judas would only strengthen the common
feeling that initial displays of divine approval were in order for
one who would be a successful leader. In the years that followed,
until the great revolt of 66 A.D. was ultimately launched, several
adventurers capitalized this popular credulity—if, indeed, they

But for Jesus the path of duty lay in a different direction. He would make no claim upon heaven for ravens to bring him his bread, he would ask no assistance from ministering angels, and he would trust God himself to abolish the rule of Rome. The duties that had been imposed upon him called for a different program of action. His response to John's preaching had culminated in a keen sense of new consecration to righteous living before God and among men. This attainment in his own life had been accompanied by a conviction of divine impulsion to lead others in a similar quest. The times were evil and the long-awaited day of reckoning was at hand. The supreme need of the hour was to summon the Jewish people to a life in more perfect accord with the will of their God. Without reserve Jesus now gave himself to the pursuit of this new-found prophetic task.

---

were not actually deceived regarding themselves. But Josephus, adopting the Roman point of view, represented these agitators as base charlatans. About the year 45 A.D. a certain Theudas, claiming to be a prophet, had led astray many persons by his promise to conduct them through the Jordan river on dry land (*Ant.* XX. 97). While Felix was procurator (52–60 A.D.), similar "imposters and deceivers" appeared who promised to perform wonders and signs in proof of their claims to be authoritative leaders. Also, one who called himself a "prophet" came from Egypt and gathered followers by promising that the walls of Jerusalem would be thrown down at his command (*War* II. 259–65; *Ant.* XX. 167–70).

CHAPTER VI
JESUS' PURSUIT OF HIS TASK

IT MIGHT seem to have been a simple undertaking for Jesus to urge his contemporaries
to seek worthier attainments in religious living. The reformer in Israel had long since become a familiar, and not always an unwelcome,
figure. The older prophets had set a distinguished example for later generations, and the
social unrest of more recent times had inspired
new propagandists to offer their several programs for alleviating current ills. The age was
ripe for preachers of reform.

Sometimes agitators were political revolutionists of the type of Judas of Galilee. Sometimes they were solitary figures like Josephus'
teacher Bannus, who in the quiet of the desert
strove to perfect himself by means of ascetic discipline. Others were strange creatures who
moved about among their fellows proclaiming in
half-demented fashion messages of doom. Such

was that other Jesus whom Josephus describes.[1] He was a peasant, an *'Am ha-'aretz*, who at the feast of tabernacles four years before the revolt of 66 A.D. suddenly cried aloud in the temple: "A voice from the east, a voice from the west, a voice from the four winds, a voice against Jerusalem and the temple, a voice against the bridegrooms and the brides, a voice against the whole people." Though whipped until the flesh fell away from the bone, he refused to cease his cry of lamentation, "Woe to Jerusalem." Inspired, as Josephus says, by a kind of divine frenzy, he kept up his activity until slain in the siege when Jerusalem fell in the year 70.

When Jesus from Nazareth undertook his public work, he too had to decide upon a mode of procedure. Would he rail against the Roman oppressor? Would he attack the established institutions of Judaism? What should be the range of his operations? Would he be content to gather about him a coterie of sympathetic friends in the wilds of the desert, as John the Baptist had done; or would he visit the chief centers of population, even the city of Jerusalem, and there publicly declare himself to be the one who could safely lead Israel in this time of distress? Would

[1] *War* VI. 300–309.

JESUS' PURSUIT OF HIS TASK

he attempt to assemble disciples and form a
school, thus founding a new religious society within Judaism; or would he endeavor to accomplish
his purposes in more individualistic fashion?

I

A noteworthy step in Jesus' pursuit of his
task was his decision to break with the movement of John and inaugurate an independent
work along new lines. Those who would benefit
by John's call to repentance must have been sufficiently interested in preparing themselves for
the advent of the Kingdom to leave their homes
and travel to the Jordan valley where they
might join the company of the newly baptized.
Jesus, on the other hand, would carry his message to the people, seeking them out in the common walks of life. As occasion offered, he
preached in the synagogues, talked with laborers
on the countryside, conversed with travelers on
the public highway, associated with fishermen
on the shore of the lake, or addressed people who
assembled at the house where he sojourned with
friends in the city. Jesus was himself a man of
the people who sought his audiences wherever
they were to be found amid the varied activities
of daily living.

Throughout his entire public career Jesus was conspicuously an itinerant prophet. According to the Marcan outline of his life, he confined his labors mainly to the northern section of Palestine, particularly the regions about the Sea of Galilee; but the course of his movements is only vaguely outlined. First he is in Capernaum, then he is journeying among the synagogues "throughout all Galilee," then he is in desert places, and again he returns to Capernaum. Mark needs only a column or two of space for this catalogue of activities. Subsequent references to times and places are similarly sporadic and incidental. Jesus is beside the sea, he enters the synagogue, he withdraws to the sea, he ascends the mountain, he comes into the house, he is by the seaside, he crosses the sea to the country of the Gerasenes, he returns across the sea and journeys over to Nazareth. Immediately he goes on a speaking tour through the villages, he withdraws to a desert place, he goes to the mountains to pray, at night he crosses over to Gennesaret, and afterwards makes his way through villages, cities, and the country on a tour of miscellaneous healings.

The range of his activities widened when Jesus paid a visit to "the borders of Tyre and Si-

don," which provided a setting for the story of
his generous attitude toward the Syrophoenician woman. But immediately he returned to the
Sea of Galilee, passing through "the midst of the
borders of Decapolis." Again there is further
zigzagging back and forth across the sea, with
the mention of Dalmanutha and Bethsaida, followed by a journey northward to villages lying
within the jurisdiction of the city of Caesarea
Philippi. From this point on, statements become more definite. The narrative specifies that
"after six days" Jesus and three of his disciples
went up "into a high mountain," where the
transfiguration scene was enacted. Thence he
returned through Galilee to Capernaum and began a journey to Jerusalem, entering Judea from
the region beyond the Jordan. He ascended to
the Mount of Olives by way of Jericho, Beth-
phage, and Bethany, and arrived in Jerusalem
accompanied by a band of zealous followers.

The remainder of Mark, with a much greater
show of exactitude than in the earlier part of the
narrative, catalogues the events of the closing
week of Jesus' career. At the end of the day on
which he arrived in Jerusalem, he and the
Twelve went out to Bethany to spend the night.
The next morning they visited the temple court

where Jesus ejected the money-changers. In the evening they returned to Bethany, but on the third day they came again to Jerusalem, where Jesus continued teaching. The same evening, while sitting with his disciples on the Mount of Olives, he delivered his famous discourse relative to the destruction of the temple and the end of the present world. The events of the next day are left unrecorded, but "after two days" came the time of the preparation for the Passover, when Jesus made the necessary arrangements and ate the meal with his disciples at the regular time for its observance. During the night there followed the scene in Gethsemane, the betrayal of Judas, the arrest of Jesus, and his arraignment before the chief priest. In the morning he was delivered to Pilate, at nine o'clock he was nailed to the cross, and at three o'clock in the afternoon with a loud shout his spirit left his body. Further, it is noted that this Passover fell on a Friday, that is, "the day before the sabbath."

The author of Matthew finds little to alter in the Marcan itinerary, nor is he able to supplement it at all extensively by data derived from non-Marcan sources. Minor changes are introduced, but in no important respect does Mat-

thew add either to the topographical or to the
chronological information of Mark.[1]

Luke is similarly dependent on his predecessor, Mark. There is one conspicuous deviation.
The visit to Nazareth is placed earlier in the life
of Jesus and is omitted from the parallel Marcan
setting.[2] But even the Lucan account, by making Jesus refer to works already done in Capernaum (4:23), shows that the Marcan narrative has
been forced at this point. Later in Luke,[3] where
a lengthy interpolation is introduced into the
Marcan sequence of events, some rather vague
additional data are supplied. But they are of
the usual accidental type. At a certain unspeci-
fied moment Jesus and his disciples are in southern Galilee on the Samaritan border, planning a
journey to Jerusalem. Later, when on their way,
they are in "a certain village," where Jesus visits
at the home of Martha and Mary. Still later, he
is praying "in a certain place." Various unlocated occurrences follow, as when Jesus teaches
"in one of the synagogues on the sabbath day."

---

[1] This fact will be evident on consulting any standard "Introduction" to the Synoptic Gospels. One of the most recent and
elaborate tabulations of the pertinent data is that of M. Goguel,
Les évangiles synoptiques (Paris, 1923), pp. 150 ff.

[2] Luke 4:16–30; Mark 6:1–6.   [3] 9:51—18:14.

He continues preaching while passing through "cities and villages" on his way up to Jerusalem. On a certain Sabbath, he goes to eat in the house of one of the rulers of the Pharisees. There is no further allocation of events, except for a puzzling reference to his passing "along the borders of Samaria and Galilee," until the Marcan series is resumed at the point where Jesus and his disciples arrive in the vicinity of Jericho.

In the main, the events of Passion Week follow the order of Mark, although Luke contains fragments of a tradition that does not always harmonize with its Marcan setting.[1] Perhaps the most conspicuous example is a reference to the last meal eaten with the disciples. In two supplementary verses of the Lucan account it is clearly implied that Jesus had expressed regret at being unable to partake of the Passover (22: 15 f). Were this intimation historical, it would imply that disaster overtook him on the day pre-

---

[1] The use of non-Marcan tradition in the Lucan Passion narrative is no longer open to reasonable doubt, however divergent may be the attempts thus far made to isolate the specific document or documents. See A. Wautier d'Aygalliers, *Les sources du récit de la passion chez Luc* (Alençon, 1920); A. M. Perry, *The Sources of Luke's Passion-Narrative* (Chicago, 1920); B. H. Streeter, *The Four Gospels* (New York, 1925); Vincent Taylor, *Behind the Third Gospel* (Oxford, 1926), pp. 33-47.

ceding Passover rather than, as Mark represents, though not with entire consistency (Mark 14: 1 f), on the day of the feast. But such phenomena are all too scanty to satisfy one's biographical curiosity. Of Luke, as of Matthew, it must be said that this gospel offers almost no new information concerning the course of Jesus' public ministry.

In the Fourth Gospel, as compared with the Synoptics, the movements of Jesus are usually connected with new sites and are arranged in a new order.[1] Whether the fourth evangelist deliberately aims at a studied sequence of events or whether his references to time and place are merely incidental cannot always be determined. But in the early portion of his narrative he lists occurrences day by day in such fashion as to make clear that this part of the record is intended to catalogue incidents in their chronological order. On the first day of public activity Jesus is present among the people gathered at "Bethany beyond the Jordan," where John was preaching. The occurrences of the two following days belong in the same region, but on the fourth day Jesus makes plans to go into Galilee. On the third day—if the author has deliberately

[1] See above, pp. 34 ff.

used the expression, it must be the third day after the departure from Bethany—Jesus is present at the marriage feast in the Galilean town of Cana, where he performs his first public miracle.

Later, Jesus with all the members of his family pays a short visit to Capernaum, but almost immediately he goes up to Jerusalem to the Passover, at which time he comes conspicuously before the public by his purgation of the temple. Nothing is said of his departure from Jerusalem; but, following the account of his conversation with Nicodemus, one reads that "after these things Jesus and his disciples came into the land of Judea." At once he leaves again for Galilee, taking the route through Samaria. He tarries in this region two days, and then goes a second time to Cana. But he is back again in Jerusalem for the Feast of Tabernacles. Then suddenly the scene of his activity is transferred to the Sea of Galilee and it is remarked that the Passover feast "was at hand." Here he engages in a series of activities, and it would seem that he does not leave Galilee to visit Jerusalem at the time of this Passover. But in the autumn he journeys thither for the next Feast of Tabernacles. Apparently he spends the winter in southern Perea and Judea. On one occasion he is "beyond the

[274]

Jordan," where John had originally baptized. Again he is in Bethany at the home of Lazarus. Afterwards he is in hiding in a "country near to the wilderness," in a city called "Ephraim." But six days before the Passover, he comes to Bethany and is entertained at the home of Lazarus.

In the story of Passion Week the Fourth Gospel more nearly approximates the narrative of the Synoptics. Jesus is in Bethany six days before the feast. Later he is in conference with his disciples in Jerusalem. He is arrested in the garden, is hailed before the priestly authorities, and subsequently is executed by Pilate. But in this connection there are also significant chronological variations as compared with the other accounts. There is no reference to any preparations made by Jesus and his disciples to celebrate the Passover, and the supper at which he taught his great lesson of humility is represented neither as the celebration of the Jewish feast nor as the institution of the Christian Eucharist (13:1–30). It is about noon on the day preceding Passover that Pilate delivers Jesus up to be crucified. He is led to Golgotha, and there executed. This is the day of "preparation," and the next day is not only a Sabbath but is also the day of the feast (18:28; 19:31, 42).

From the present records it is quite impossible to reconstruct a full itinerary of Jesus' career. Just how widely he traveled, the time consumed in his preaching tours, and the exact course of his several journeys are matters now very difficult, if not impossible, to determine. The available information is too meager in content and of too divergent a character. One cannot hope to recover the complete story of his movements, although likely enough the disciples remembered that they had been with him at many of the times and places mentioned in the gospels. But when the tradition first began to be collected, they were interested in what he had said or done rather than in the dates of events or scenes of operation. In citing one or another incident, a narrator might introduce his remarks with the stereotyped phrase "in a certain place," "at a certain time," or "after these things"; but he made no effort to provide a complete sequence of events or a comprehensive topographical record. His interests were not biographical in any formal sense of the term.[1]

On the other hand, the incidental character of the gospel references to Jesus' itinerary may itself be a blessing in disguise. Lack of design in

[1] See above, pp. 95 ff.

an ancient document is a great virtue in the eyes of the historian. Whenever reference is made to times and places without any evident apologetic motive on the part of a gospel-writer, there is no serious occasion for doubting the dependability of the information. Unfortunately, however, one's peace of mind is often disturbed by contradictory items in the tradition. Sometimes these divergences are very pronounced. In Mark the scenes of Jesus' activity up to the last week of his career are laid exclusively in Galilee and its environs. But, according to John, Jesus began his work in southern Perea and made Judea the principal area of his operations, with only brief and occasional visits to Galilean territory. There are likewise some arresting chronological divergences. The mention of three Passover seasons in the Johannine narrative would imply that Jesus' public ministry had continued for upward of two years (2:23; 6:4; 19:14); but in Mark only one Passover is noted, and apparently this evangelist had thought a period of less than twelve months sufficient for the story of his hero's career.

Sometimes the interpretative character of contradictory statements is self-evident, as when the author of Luke brings Jesus to Nazareth for the first sermon in his ministry (4:16 ff.), or when in John, Judea is called Jesus' own country (4:44). Each of these evangelists saw in Jesus' program of action a model to justify the course of procedure that had been adopted by the early Christian preachers in the prosecution of their missionary enterprise. They had begun work with their own kinsmen and when their efforts met with failure in that quarter they had turned to gentile fields. Similarly in Luke, Jesus went to his boyhood home in Nazareth to make his first public announcement of his mission. In John it was in Judea at the very temple, where dwelt those who religiously were his nearest of kin, that he made his initial exhibition of authority. As Christian preachers, in pursuing their task, had gone first to Jewish congregations, so Jesus at the outset "came unto his own" (John 1:11).

The disposition of early Christians to make Jerusalem the center from which the new religion sprang, accounts for the tendency so apparent in John to let Judea supplant Galilee as the scene of Jesus' operations. For Jesus himself Galilee undoubtedly offered the most promising opportunities for pursuing the task upon which he was engaged. Here he could easily reach

large numbers of the people. There was a throng-
ing life about the shores of the lake and tours
into the country among the villages numerous in
the territory were easily accomplished. But it is
also quite inconceivable that a reformer concerned with the religious welfare of the Jewish
race should not be greatly interested in Judea.
Certainly if he felt convinced that he had a message for the children of Israel at large, Jerusalem
must have been included in his purview. Probably we should grant that Jesus spent more time
in southern Palestine than the Synoptic Gospels
would lead us to infer, and likewise that his activity in Galilee was much more extensive than
is represented in the Fourth Gospel.

The period of Jesus' activity is exceedingly
brief in the Marcan account, but this representation may be accidental rather than deliberate.
It is noteworthy that the closing week of his career is narrated with much greater fulness than
any other period of his activity. It embraces
more than a third of the entire Gospel of Mark.
Evidently the Passion story had been the earliest
considerable section of gospel tradition to take
fixed form. When the present books were composed, the process of standardization had gone
so far that even the account in the Fourth Gos-

pel followed, in its main features, the Synoptic narrative. The outstanding incidents in this short period must already have become the common property of Christendom. The story would be rehearsed in connection with the celebration of the Lord's Supper, at the time of the Passover festival, and on every occasion when the triumph of Christ and the efficacy of his death might appropriately be recalled. For these Christian congregations Jesus' ministry scarcely needed to have been of more than six days' duration. The crucial events insuring the validity of the new religion were sufficiently demonstrated by reference to the last week of their revered martyr's life.

When interest in the earlier stages of Jesus' activity first arose, considerations of time and place evidently were not fundamental. The sum total of events recorded in the Synoptic Gospels, from the first public appearance until Jesus' arrival in Jerusalem, requires the assumption of a period not exceeding six or eight months. But whether, in view of the conditions under which he labored, so short a time would have made possible the significant results attending his efforts, is certainly a fair question. Disciples had been associated with him for a sufficient period to acquire an impression of his personality that even the crucifixion could not eradicate, and the effect upon his enemies was hardly less impressive. He had worked long enough and persistently enough to produce in those who were offended at his activities not merely a sporadic outburst of hostility, but a set determination to rid themselves of the disturber. Even the suspicions of the political authorities—Herod Antipas and Pilate—had been awakened. This situation would hardly have resulted from only a few short weeks' activity on the part of Jesus.

A period of more than two years, allowed by the Gospel of John for Jesus' public career, is not inconsistent with probability. But one must guard against assuming that the mention of three Passovers in the Fourth Gospel is really valid documentary evidence for the longer ministry. This author's habit of associating Jesus' various discourses with one or another feast made it easy for him to mention a Passover or a Feast of Tabernacles or a Feast of Dedication without very much attention to accurate chronology. Yet the evangelist seems to display no particular apologetic interest in the actual length of Jesus' ministry, and the belief that it covered upward of two years may well be derived from a reliable source. Perhaps in Luke also there is a reflection of an early belief that Jesus had attained martyrdom on the third year of his activity. This may be the meaning of the enigmatical remark about his casting out demons and performing cures "today" and "tomorrow" and on the third day being perfected (Luke 13:33). The assumption that Jesus had met his death in the third year of his public career, rather than within the first year as the Synoptic record implies, better suits all the demands of the situation.

The most puzzling chronological datum of the gospels is that pertaining to the time of Jesus' death. Here the Synoptic narrative—which is really only the Marcan—and the Johannine are in flat contradiction. The former represents that Jesus expired on the cross at three o'clock on the afternoon of Passover day, having eaten the regular paschal meal with his disciples at the usual time on the previous evening. That is, all of these events fell on the fifteenth of the Jewish month Nisan. According to John, on the other hand, the crucifixion must have occurred on the afternoon of the preceding day. Not only is the Johannine account of the supper which Jesus ate with his followers on the night before his death entirely lacking in the festal significance so prominent in the Synoptic Gospels, but it is def-. initely affirmed that at the time of Jesus' trial the Jews refrained from entering the Praetorium "that they might not be defiled, but might eat the passover" (18:28). The feast had not yet been celebrated, and the events that were now in progress belonged to the day of "the preparation of the passover" (19:14). The language of John is explicit and its meaning is unmistakable. Jesus had been crucified on the afternoon of Nisan fourteen, which was the day when the Jews were making their preparations, including the slaughter of the paschal lamb, for the Passover feast to occur later in the evening. But the feast itself, according to the Jewish method of reckoning the new day from sunset, fell early on Nisan fifteenth. On that year the fifteenth was also a Sabbath (19:31).

At this distance it is impossible to know positively whether Jesus was put to death on the fourteenth of Nisan, as represented in the Fourth Gospel, or whether the Synoptists were correct in placing his crucifixion on the fifteenth.[1] In

[1] Among the more recent advocates of the Johannine dating is E. Meyer, *Ursprung und Anfänge des Christentums* (Berlin, 1921), I, 167–72. On the other hand, the Synoptists' date is vigorously

each case it is easy to surmise a practical motive
that might have determined the choice of date.
The Marcan chronology enabled Christians to
think of their sacred meal, the Lord's Supper, as
a continuation and transformation of one of the
most highly revered ceremonies in Judaism.
This association with the Passover feast might,
in some Christian circles, have been an influential consideration in determining opinion as to
the date of the last meal eaten together by Jesus
and his disciples. On the other hand, the Johannine dating synchronized the death of Jesus with
the slaughter of the paschal lamb. In circles
where stress fell upon the saving significance of
Jesus' martyrdom it might have seemed especially desirable to think of the crucifixion in this

---

defended by G. Dalman, *Jesus-Joshua* (Leipzig, 1922), pp. 80–98.
A mediating solution of the difficulty is to accept the Johannine
date and make the supper, that would then fall early on Nisan
fourteen, an actual Passover celebration. This procedure would
have been in accordance with a custom, assumed to have been
current at this time among some Jews, of keeping the feast one
day early when Nisan fifteen came on a Sabbath. So D. Chwol-
sohn, *Das letzte Passamahl Christi und der Tag seines Todes*
(Leipzig, 1908), who is followed by J. Klausner, *Jesus of Nazareth*,
translated from the original Hebrew by H. Danby (New York,
1925), pp. 326 f. H. L. Strack and P. Billerbeck (*Kommentar zum
Neuen Testament aus Talmud und Midrasch*, Bd. II [München,
1924], pp. 812–52), would effect a more complete harmonization

close association with the preparation of the paschal sacrifice.[1] Yet, when tested by suitability to the situation in which Jesus himself actually moved, preference must be given to the Johannine representation. The part assigned to the Jewish authorities in connection with the apprehension and trial of Jesus is altogether unsuited to the type of conduct befitting the sacred day of the Passover. The usual explanations for their irregular procedure required by the Synoptic accounts are quite insufficient. However much the enemies of Jesus may have desired to rid themselves of him, he can hardly have seemed so important to them as he did to his

---

by assuming that the Synoptists follow one and John another of two different modes of fixing the first day of Nisan. A narrator using one calendar would specify the fourteenth as the date of the crucifixion. If the other calendar were used the same event would fall on the fifteenth. But this interpretation does not carry conviction. It is not adequately substantiated and it seems motivated too strongly by the assumption that in the period of gospel composition Christians could not have been of two opinions regarding so important a matter as the date of Jesus' death: *"Ein wirklicher Zwiespalt in der Tradition über Jesu Todestag innerhalb der ältesten Christenheit will uns undenkbar scheinen. Es muss sich eine Lösung finden lassen mit dem Ergebnis: nicht ist Johannes nach den Synoptikern und nicht sind die Synoptiker nach Johannes zu deuten, sondern die Synoptiker haben recht und Johannes hat recht"* (p. 845).

[1] See John 1:29, 36; I Cor. 5:7; Rev. 5:6 ff.

own followers. The Jews would scarcely have fared forth on their most holy day of the year to participate in a public execution. Nor would Pilate have been likely to force on them this indignity. Probably Jesus met his death on the afternoon of Nisan fourteen, the day before the Jewish Passover, in the year 29 of the present era.[1]

II

Early in his public activity Jesus had attracted to himself a few personal friends who became his traveling companions. Their association with him is one of the best attested facts of his career. Not only are these men figures of note for all the gospel writers, but the letters of Paul bear ample witness to the esteem in which they were held by him and his Christian contemporaries. Their claim to have been companions of Jesus was never questioned, embarrassing though this fact was for Paul when his enemies charged him with inferiority. On the strength of his vision of the risen Christ he aspired to equal authority with them, yet he was well aware of the popular disposition to assign him a subordinate place because he had never seen the earthly Jesus. On the other hand, everyone knew that

[1] See above, pp. 179 f.

they had been with the Master in the flesh. It was also a commonly accepted opinion that there had been twelve of these special disciples, among whom Peter, James, and John had been outstanding figures.

The "Twelve," although now only eleven of the original group were left, could hardly have been so highly revered in Paul's day had they not been unusually close to Jesus during his lifetime. Yet undoubtedly their new prominence in the Christian movement in the years following his death has added greatly to their prestige in the present gospel narratives. Here from the very outset they enjoy a distinctly official dignity. They are regarded not merely as helpers of Jesus in the pursuit of his own task, but as prospective leaders whom he had deliberately chosen and prepared for their subsequent duties in the early church. This ecclesiastical interest comes to the surface time and again in the different gospels.

There is a manifest formality in the selection of the Twelve, as though in the first instance they had not spontaneously attached themselves to the new prophet, but had been arbitrarily chosen by him with a view to their later functions. Readers of Mark might readily assume that it was entirely on Jesus' own initiative, and apart from any previous acquaintance with him, that the sons of Zebedee had been induced to abandon their fishing for a career of discipleship to the new teacher (Mark 1:16–20). In Luke, and here only, a story of a miraculous draft of fishes is introduced to account for the readiness of Peter, James, and John to "leave all" (Luke 5:1–11). According to the Fourth Gospel, John the Baptist had taken the initiative in directing the attention of his followers to the "Son of God." The first to respond had been an unnamed individual—possibly John the son of Zebedee is meant—and a certain Andrew. Presently Peter, Philip, and Nathaniel join the group in consequence of the testimony of their predecessors to Jesus' fulfilment of Old Testament prophecy (John 1:35–51). In these incidents each of the gospel stories is more or less highly dramatized and is altogether lacking in the elements of realism essential to the actual experience of any disciple who would abandon his present occupation to become the permanent companion of a new teacher.

Also, the relations of mutual friendship between master and disciple, that would normally prevail among fellow-workers in a common cause, are quite generally lost from view in the gospels.

[288]

Instead, the Twelve are pre-eminently a class of individuals in training for the leadership of a new religious movement at a subsequent date when it will need efficiently equipped and duly authorized missionaries, organizers, and directors. Viewed from the standpoint of later times the outstanding task of an apostolic preacher was to persuade his hearers that Jesus was worthy of their full confidence. Accordingly, emphasis fell upon this aspect of the disciples' own training, as though Jesus himself had been chiefly concerned to effect in them a proper appreciation of his dignity and personality. They confessed that this alleged effort of his had not been eminently successful, but even their failure was now thought to have been a valuable phase of their missionary equipment. The stupidity of their present audiences seemed less discouraging in the light of their own earlier shortcomings in this respect. Probably it was not so much for the purpose of disparaging the memory of Jesus' companions as it was for the encouragement of contemporary Christian teachers that gospel-writers so frequently recalled the failure of the Twelve during Jesus' lifetime to appreciate his official status. This temporary stupidity on their part now seemed to have been in reality a providential feature in their training for future labors as apostolic missionaries.

It was similarly appropriate to recall specific words of installation and commission that Jesus was supposed to have spoken. Strictly in accordance with his own independent will he had gathered the group together and had appointed "Twelve" (Mark 3:13–19)—had even named them "Apostles," some Christians alleged (Luke 6:13). Their duties at the outset were specified; they had a threefold function. They were to be companions of Jesus, they were to go out on formal preaching expeditions, and they were to exorcise demons (Mark 3:14 f.). They were to follow prescribed rules of procedure. They were to travel in companies of two, simply clad and free from anxiety regarding food and shelter. All this was to be done in accordance with Jesus' orders (Mark 6:7–10; Matt. 10:1–11; Luke 9:2–5; 10:1–9). In some quarters it was thought that the disciples had been instructed to labor exclusively among Jews (Matt. 10:5–8), while other Christians believed that Jesus had had definitely in mind the training of leaders for the world-wide missionary enterprise that was already in progress when the gospels arose (Mark 13:9 f.; Matt. 10:17 f.; Luke 21:12). In their attempts to turn to practical account the well-remembered fact that Jesus in pursuing his purposes had gathered about himself a group of close personal friends, early Christians could scarcely avoid distorting the actual history. Too many vital interests in their own present situation were involved. As the years passed they were under an ever increasing temptation to adorn the Twelve with a more complete equipment of apostolic regalia. This disposition led farther and farther away from the less formal but more real situation that had obtained in the lifetime of Jesus.

It was characteristic procedure in Jewish society for teachers to draw to themselves groups of especially devoted disciples. These companies were composed of individuals who had been especially attracted by the message and personality of the teacher and who were so deeply moved by their contact with him that they abandoned their former course of life in order to remain constantly in his presence. Sometimes pupils attached themselves to noted interpreters of the Law, like the great scholars Hillel and Shammai. The so-called "Zadokite" movement had been founded on loyalty to a teacher and his message. Many persons had joined the ascetic company of the Essenes. John the Baptist had won a distinct following, and probably Josephus was not the only Jewish youth who had been drawn to the desert hermit Bannus. When followers gathered about Jesus, they were acting in accordance with a genuinely Jewish custom.

Jesus' disciples were from among the common people. Some fishermen of Capernaum were the earliest and most influential members of the company. Peter, the most prominent individual in the group, was destined to play an important rôle within Christianity after Jesus' death, and presumably he possessed similar qualities of leadership in earlier days. His partners in the fishing business, James and John, also were forceful personalities who subsequently proved their loyalty to the teacher's memory by suffering martyrdom for his cause. The Twelve seem all to have been Galileans except Judas Iscariot, who was the treasurer of the company.

Preparation for the introduction of the Kingdom of God was the professional interest that held Jesus and his disciples together and inspired their common activity. They had been stirred by Jesus' call to repentance in preparation for future events. Now they sought safety not alone for themselves. They left their earlier occupations to become his helpers in summoning their kinsmen to a new attainment in righteousness. Had Jesus followed the example of John in gathering disciples together in the quiet of the desert, they might have thought themselves a select society whose chief duty was to maintain their present state of holiness unendangered by contact with the outside world until God should intervene to establish the Kingdom. But Jesus' own aggressive manner of life left little opportunity for his followers to assume the inactive attitude of calmly awaiting the divine initiative. Although they were firmly confident, as was Jesus, that the favor of God would ultimately be demonstrated through the establishment of the eschatological Kingdom, in their present relations they could hardly escape a sense of responsibility for helping to create the specific qualities of life stressed by their leader. From the start they were virtually a corps of assistants who, like Jesus, announced the advent of the Kingdom and urged their contemporaries to prepare for its coming.

On the more material side of existence, the disciples had an important responsibility. Food must be secured; certain obligations, like the payment of the temple tax and the imperial tribute, had to be met; clothing also was necessary; and sometimes it would be desirable to secure lodging in the course of their travels. Had they reverted to the more primitive conditions of life in the desert, their physical needs would have been reduced to a minimum. But when they carried on their work amid the ordinary contacts of daily life there were numerous social demands that had to be satisfied. We have no means of knowing to what extent Jesus was able personally to finance his enterprise, but undoubtedly he needed the help of his new-made friends. In this respect probably the fishermen of Galilee could render him important aid. Although the Twelve had "left all" to follow him, at those times when their funds were running low they were able to turn aside temporarily to their former occupations. Perhaps more than once they found a needed coin in the fish's mouth. It is quite possible that they stuck more closely to business than subsequent Christian idealization in depicting the activity of the apostolic group would lead one to imagine.

The mind of the disciples is not easy to read. One suspects that their attachment to Jesus was based more on the attractiveness of his individuality than on allegiance to, or an understanding of, his teachings. Unschooled men from the common walks of life are much more susceptible to the power of personal contacts than they are to the more abstract influences of academic indoctrination. Jesus was a picturesque figure, who had stirred his followers with a desire for higher attainments in righteousness and had convinced them afresh that God was concerned with the welfare of his people. Their moral sensibilities had been quickened by contact with this sincere and earnest leader. He had not given them a new rabbinical rule for the guidance of conduct. He had not demanded of them even the baptismal bath practiced by John. They were bound to him not by rules which he had imposed, not even by new doctrines or rites, but by the ties of personal association and the attracting power of his own contagious zeal. Evidently he had inspired in them a new confidence in God and a vigorous expectation of early deliverance.

In the course of time, as Jesus became a more conspicuous figure, there gathered about him on different occasions larger crowds who expected of him some performance that would have ameliorating significance for the present unhappy state of the Jewish race. He himself had no cut-

and-dried program, other than that of declaring confidence in God and admonishing his contemporaries to heighten the quality of their religious living. God's power, and spiritual sincerity on the part of man, were the two foci about which Jesus' own hope revolved, and he wished others to share his confidence. But quite naturally his disciples soon added a third factor to their own hopes. This was trust in their teacher himself and an expectation that he might do much more for the situation than he had ever openly promised to effect, as they themselves afterward very freely admitted. During this restless period, when the psychology of revolt was so widely operative in Jewish society, no picturesque individual, however remote his own intentions were from any meddling in politics, could escape idealization and an expectation among his admirers that ultimately he would prove to be a successful revolutionary hero.

The gap between the eschatological program for realizing the Kingdom, and the program of immediate rebellion, was no wider in the thinking of the followers of Jesus than it had been in the case of the group that gathered about John. When the teacher talked of God's giving deliverance to his people, the audience readily nodded approval and visualized, perhaps without the slightest warrant, an early day when God would employ the teacher as an immediate instrument in accomplishing the desired results. But if God were to proceed in this fashion to throw off the domination of the Romans, and the teacher assented to this version of his task, it would only mean that he, like Judas of Galilee, would ultimately stake everything on the success of a revolt. It is highly probable that neither John nor Jesus ever sought any such rôle, but it is equally probable that many of their contemporaries, dazzled by the growing popularity of their leader and inspired by the mob spirit that the very presence of the crowd engendered, freely cherished revolutionary hopes. Even the inner circle of Jesus' followers, the Twelve themselves, had not been immune from this temptation; and they partially justified their frailty by assuming that Jesus himself had been compelled to fight off a similar satanic suggestion.

The admiration of Jesus' well-meaning friends easily became a danger to him and his cause. Popularity brought in its train misunderstanding and suspicion. During the first half of the first century A.D. it was not safe for anyone in either Galilee or Judea to be found surrounded by too many enthusiastic followers. The political authorities immediately suspected trouble. The statement that Herod Antipas feared Jesus, and would have put him to death had Jesus not left Galilee, accords perfectly with the situation (Luke 13:31–33). Just as Herod had acted to forestall any possible revolt by John, so probably he would have proceeded against Jesus, had the latter remained in the territory under Herod's jurisdiction. When Jesus arrived in Jerusalem it certainly was no kindness on the part of his friends, in view of the delicate political situation, for them to give him a welcome that bore any such revolutionary implications as would inevitably be associated with the scene of the so-called "triumphal entry."[1] Pilate and the temple police would have needed no further information to arouse them to action. The mere semblance of political criminality was sufficient in their eyes to justify the execution of a prospective culprit.

III

Not everyone who heard a prophet became his friend. The same qualities that attracted admirers inspired in others a correspondingly strong hatred. Jesus and his followers may not

[1] Mark 11:1–10; Matt. 21:1–9; Luke 19:28–38.

have fully anticipated the menace of the political opposition that so quickly accomplished his execution, but they cannot have been unaware of the religious hostility that had been gradually developing in the course of his public activities. When Jesus left the desert, where he had been with John, and went about among the people everywhere proclaiming the necessity of repentance, he placed himself in an even more precarious position than that occupied by the Baptist. Those who had taken the trouble to visit John, by that very act bore witness to a measure of sympathy with his cause. They had gone to him on their own initiative and generally would be in a receptive state of mind. But Jesus talked to less well selected audiences. He preached, as it were, in season and out of season, addressing himself to anyone who might be within range of his voice. It was never necessary to go out of one's way in order to hear this new prophet. It would be difficult to imagine a method of procedure that might more quickly awaken opposition, or convert potential into actual enemies.

Perhaps Jesus deliberately chose his program of action with a view to its effectiveness. Certainly it was not his design to make enemies, but he wished to proclaim his message over as exten-

sive a territory and in as short a time as possible.
He adopted a method of work well calculated to
accomplish this purpose. By making his presence felt throughout a wide range of contacts, he
was able to reach a greater variety of people and
to extend his activities over a larger area than
ever would have been possible had he followed
the example of John the Baptist. Jesus could
talk to men in the market place, or beside the
Sea of Galilee, or in the open country, or wherever they were to be found. Whether they liked
or disliked what he had to say, they could not
easily avoid hearing his words. This direct method of action was attended by significant consequences.

Jesus might have fared better had not Jewish
society been already so well stocked with religious institutions. It was a venturesome undertaking for a new preacher to set himself up as an
authoritative leader in the presence of the existing machinery that had long been operating to
provide guidance for the Jewish people.[1] There
was the ancient cultus perpetuated with great
ceremonial splendor in the temple at Jerusalem.
The Scriptures were read regularly at the synagogues and interpreted by well-trained scribes

[1] See above, pp. 146 ff.

whom the people highly revered. The oral tradition had been developed by successive generations of teachers until there was now no area of
life where one needed to be ignorant of what God
desired. And the hope that he would one day deliver his people in a manner suitable to his dignity and power was universally entertained.
What opportunity was there for a new teacher
with an unconventional program to win a hearing in this environment? It might have been different had he been satisfied to draw his audiences
from among such restless spirits and malcontents
as would wander off to some desert spot to hear
him preach. But what place was there for him
in the busy centers where religious interests
were already safeguarded by firmly intrenched
institutions?

In connection with the services in the synagogues Jesus at first found an opportunity to
make known to his kinsmen the interests that
were closest to his heart. When the presiding
officer gave permission for the stranger, or indeed
invited him, to address the assembly, Jesus undoubtedly welcomed the privilege. But he was
not the type of teacher who would confine
his activities to formal gatherings, and it is not
improbable that in the present gospel records

his connections with the synagogue have been somewhat magnified. The fact that the early Christian missionaries, particularly in their activities among the Jews of the Dispersion, found this institution so useful for launching their propaganda, may have led them to overemphasize the activities of Jesus among the synagogues of his day. On the other hand, it would be quite inconceivable that one whose interests were eminently religious should fail to avail himself on occasion of the opportunity to speak in these local assemblies. Presently it must have become apparent that he was virtually elevating himself to a position beside, if not above, the official teachers of Judaism, an attitude on his part that might readily cause offense.

It is easy to exaggerate the breach between Jesus and the scribes. In later years, when Christianity and Judaism existed side by side at all important points around the Mediterranean, the conflict between these two religions became constantly more pronounced. Their respective leaders saw in the work of their rivals little to approve and less to commend. And they found much to criticize. From the Christian side, the charges leveled against the Jews were scathingly condemnatory, and it was believed possible to discover in the stories of Jesus' controversies with his contemporaries the prototypes of these acrimonious discussions common in the later period between Christians and Jews. Gospel writers saw in Jesus the great champion of their own present attitude of freedom from the Jewish law —a problem that had first projected itself into Christianity in Paul's day. The sabbath customs of the Jews had often been ridiculed among the Gentiles, and Christian missionaries were now happy in believing that Jesus had been one of the severest critics of sabbath observance—had even declared himself master of the Sabbath (Mark 2:28). The woes that he was supposed to have pronounced upon scribes and Pharisees were thought to foreshadow the degradation of Judaism from the position of divine favor which it had held prior to the rise of Christianity. The fatal outcome of the revolution in 70 A.D. had been a God-ordained punishment for both the people and their religious leaders.

Undoubtedly Christians from an early date failed to appreciate the ideals and achievements of the Pharisees.[1] As a class they were conspicu-

[1] Jewish writers have often protested against the Christians' unfair treatment of the Pharisees. In recent times they have found defenders even outside the pale of Judaism, e.g., R. T. Herford,

ous for their devotion to the Law. Fidelity, sincerity, and great persistence in the quest for righteousness were eminent Pharisaic virtues. But these very qualities foreordained to failure the efforts of the Christian missionary to win disciples from among the religious leaders of the Jews. They were men with the rabbinic zeal of a Saul of Tarsus, who never were vouchsafed an experience like his on the Damascus road, and to whom the new movement continued to be as truly anathema as formerly it had been to him. This unswerving loyalty of devout Jews to their own distinctive religious traditions could hardly seem to a zealous Christian other than a display of sheer perversity. The formidable array of charges against "scribes and Pharisees" assembled in the twenty-third chapter of Matthew is typical of first-century Christianity's defiant answer to its stubborn Jewish opponents.

Pharisaism: Its Aim and Method (New York, 1912) and *The Pharisees* (New York, 1924); G. F. Moore, "Christian Writers on Judaism," *Harvard Theological Review*, XIV (1921), 197–254, and "The Rise of Normative Judaism," *ibid.*, XVII (1924), 307–73, and XVIII (1925), 1–38. Among Jewish authors, L. Baeck, *Das Wesen des Judentums*, 3. Aufl. (Frankfurt a. M., 1922), is especially to be commended; and also certain essays in I. Abrahams, *Studies in Pharisaism and the Gospels* (1st ser., Cambridge, 1917) and (2d ser., 1924); C. G. Montefiore, *Some Elements of the Religious Teaching of Jesus* (New York, 1910).

JESUS' PURSUIT OF HIS TASK

A judgment of Pharisaism, based on the observations of a native of Palestine, whose own religious life had matured under the fostering care of Judaism, very likely will have been of a somewhat different sort. Jesus must have realized something of the Jews' debt to these faithful guardians of Israel's religious well-being. Thanks mainly to them, the Scriptures had been made a possession of the people. They were the group who had done most to keep alive the ideal of devotion to the will of God in daily living, and it was among them that the hope of divine deliverance had been most ardently cherished. In his sympathies and aims Jesus had more in common with them than with any other Jewish party of his day. It is altogether improbable that a deliberate attack upon the character of the Pharisees, or even upon the scribal system of religious instruction, had been an original part of Jesus' intention. Ultimately the institutional machinery of Jewish religion proved a serious barrier in his pathway, and one which he did not hesitate to attack; but at the outset he had conceived of his task in more positive and constructive fashion. He would not remove scribism to make way for his message. He would supplement present endeavors and inject a new vitality

[305]

into religion in conformity with his own more recent experiences.

Probably it was more the method of Jesus than his message that first awakened hostility among the Pharisees. There was nothing necessarily offensive in a teacher's stressing the need for repentance. A summons to the realization of a more excellent morality was always in order within Judaism. When the scribe diligently worked out detailed instructions for conduct, he was motivated by a sincere desire, felt by him and by his audiences, to provide a means for attaining to better living. It was always appropriate for him to encourage his hearers to repent of their sins in the presence of a holy God, to strive for the realization of a worthier ethical standard, and to renew their hope of God's deliverance. In so far as these ideals were advocated by Jesus, he had no grounds for suspecting that his message would awaken enmity. Even when he phrased his hopes in eschatological imagery he would have found sympathetic hearers in many quarters. And those who might have differed with him at this point would not have felt any occasion for bitter hostility, unless at the moment they happened to be active propagandists for political revolution.

JESUS' PURSUIT OF HIS TASK

The cleft between Jesus and the Pharisees
was wider and deeper than it ever could have
been on the mere charge that he taught irregular
doctrines. In that social setting, conduct was
far more important than opinion, and practice
took precedence over theory.[1] For more than a
hundred years the Pharisees had been cherishing
the conviction that they in particular were the
guardians of Israel's spiritual treasures. That
they felt a keen sense of satisfaction in their position is not surprising, but their feeling of privilege did not result in any slackening of effort to
attain a more perfect understanding of the divine will, and they never shrank from any embarrassment that unswerving loyalty to the Law
might involve.[2] They possessed not only a zeal

[1] A famous rabbi who had lived in Arab in the vicinity of
Sepphoris before the revolt of 66 A.D. used to say that the performance of good works was a more enduring virtue than was the possession of wisdom (*Aboth* III, 12).

[2] Paul, the converted Pharisee, was similarly proud of his
achievements in Judaism (Gal. 1:14; Phil. 3:5 f.), as he was later
of his position in Christianity (I Cor. 9:1 f.; II Cor. 11:21 ff.;
12:1 ff.). Yet in the same breath he could with equal sincerity
declare that of himself he was nothing (I Cor. 9:16; II Cor. 12:11).
A contemporary Jewish rabbi is less self-assertive but is just as
submissive in his statement that no credit is due one for whatever
amount of the Law he may have kept, for in so doing one is only
fulfilling the purpose of his creation (*Aboth* II, 9).

[307]

for God, but an elaborate technique for the realization of their ideals. As a well-defined class in society, they bore distinctive marks recognized both by themselves and by outsiders. They were called by distinguishing epithets—the "associates" (*haberim*), the "separated" (*perushim*), the "wise" (*hakamim*), names which not only differentiated them from other strata of Jewish society but which were also descriptive of their own special interests.

As "associates," the Pharisees cultivated a strong feeling of solidarity and devotion to a common cause. They were companions in a great enterprise. Admission to the group required individual effort and was accomplished by appropriate rites of initiation. The term "separated," that seems to have given them the name "Pharisees," indicates more exactly the character of their ideals for conduct. It was an essential principle with the members to guard against ceremonial uncleanness. Especially were they concerned to secure strict observance of the laws regarding priests' dues and Levitical tithes.[1]

[1] The offerings from agricultural products should have been made before goods were placed on sale, but of this a conscientious purchaser might often be in doubt. A pious man would, therefore, seek to correct any possible neglect of the less scrupulous producer by separating the proper tithes from what he purchased, as is

They certainly would have been diligent in tithing "mint, anise, and cummin," but they would
have resented any charge of neglecting weightier
matters in the Law (Matt. 23:23; Luke 11:42).
They were intent upon keeping the whole Law,
from the least to the greatest. Although Paul's
teacher, Gamaliel, is said to have been liberally
disposed in his attitude toward the new Chris-

---

accurately represented in Luke 17:12. Various chapters of the
Mishnah give instructions about ways to avoid the impiety of
withholding these dues. The treatise called *"Demai"* is devoted
especially to the problem of the priests' tithes (*terumoth*). There
is also an entire treatise under the name *"Terumoth,"* another on
tithes for Levites (*ma'aseroth*), another on the dough to be set aside
for the priests (*hallah;* cf. Rom. 11:16), another on "second tithes"
(*ma'aser sheni*) to be eaten at the feast season in Jerusalem, another on the bringing of the first fruits (*bikkurim*) to the temple
and their relation to the *terumoth* and the *ma'aser sheni*. All these
are early chapters in the Mishnah (and Tosephta); and one is
surprised that the rabbis in codifying these materials a hundred
years and more after the temple had perished, when priests and
Levites and festivals in Jerusalem had passed away, should have
devoted so much space to these subjects. They would hardly have
manufactured these rules on the strength of a merely antiquarian
interest. Had these regulations been of vital practical concern at
the moment, free fabrication might be suspected, but they were not
crucial issues of Jewish life at this later date. Under the circumstances there is every reason to believe that for the most part these
sections of the Mishnah relate to customs that had been actually
in vogue and established by tradition prior to the destruction of
the temple, and probably also in the time of Jesus.

[309]

tian movement (Acts 5:34 ff.), he used to emphasize the importance of carefully observing
the requirements of the Law with reference to
tithing.[1] In addition to their carefulness in separating the tithes, the Pharisees were particular
in the observance of all rules pertaining to clean
and unclean, such as hand-washing before meals.
They were strict also in their attitude toward
"hallowed things"[2] that had been solemnly dedi-
cated to God. The holy thing might be property
of any sort, or food; and if the latter, it could be
eaten only by a priest. In the handling of such
food the hands were not only washed, as in the
case of ordinary food, but were plunged into the
water.[3]

The Pharisee's devotion to legal minutiae
could not have gone far without the assistance of
persons especially trained in the interpretation
of the Law. Every Pharisee was a purist, but
not everyone could become a scholar versed in
the technique of scriptural exegesis. Many did
engage in study and win for themselves the right
to be accounted "wise," but this was not possible for everybody. Yet every member of the
guild was exhorted to be diligent in study and to

[1] *Aboth* I, 16.

[2] *Kodesh*, Deut. 26:13.   [3] *Hagigah* II, 5; III, 1 ff.

seek out for himself a reliable teacher who could give him a thorough understanding of God's requirements.[1] Hillel, who had flourished while Jesus was a youth, had said that one who will not learn the Law is deserving of death and, on the other hand, he who has acquired such instruction has won for himself the life of the world to come.[2] People who complained of lack of time for study were not excused from the obligation.[3] This studious ideal of the Pharisees is tersely expressed in the oft-quoted saying attributed to the men of the Great Synagogue: "Be deliberate in judgment, raise up many disciples, and make a fence for the Law."[4]

As applied to the Pharisees, the designation "separated" also had a social significance. The members of the association were concerned not alone with their own status as a group, but gave

[1] *Aboth* I, 6.　　[2] *Aboth* I, 13; II, 8.　　[3] *Aboth* II, 5.

[4] *Aboth* I, 1. This ideal is also witnessed to by Paul in what he says of his own studies as a Pharisee (Gal. 1:14; Phil. 3:5 f.) and by Acts 22:3; 26:5. The testimony of Josephus bears the same import, *War* I, 648; II, 162; *Life* 191; *Ant.* XVII, 41. Rabbi Akiba, in the generation after Paul and Josephus, developed the figure of the fence more in detail. Not only did the formulation of an oral tradition safeguard the Law but, he added, tithes were a fence for riches, vows for separateness and silence for wisdom (*Aboth* III, 17). True to Pharisaic principles, good deeds were safeguards against the transgression of virtuous ideals.

much attention to their relations with outsiders. This was inevitable where ceremonial purity was a fundamental consideration. In contrast with the Pharisees, the rest of society, whether beggars, peasants, priests, or aristocrats, were the impure "people of the land" (*'Amme ha-'aretz*). These outsiders might be thoroughly religious so far as concerned their attachment to Judaism, their participation in the services of the synagogue, and their visits to the temple and its festivals. But they fell short when judged by the Pharisee's ideals of ceremonial purity, proper tithing, and rendering of priests' dues, correct treatment of "holy things," and devotion to study of the Law. Hillel, though reputed to have been more liberal than his contemporary Shammai, had said that no *'Am ha-'aretz* is pious,[1] and one of his successors, who was a younger contemporary of Jesus, affirmed that attendance upon a synagogue where people of this class predominated "drives a man out of the world."[2] Among Pharisees them-

[1] *Aboth* I, 13.

[2] *Aboth* III, 14. Probably the meaning is that this type of conduct brings on untimely death. Similarly Paul believed that attendance upon heathen feasts and unworthy participation in the Lord's Supper had hastened the death of some Christians in Corinth (I Cor. 10:20–22; 11:28 ff.).

selves there were different gradations of piety, but the garments of the '*Am ha-' aretz* defiled even the Pharisee of lowest station.[1] The Pharisaic way of salvation was open to everybody who wished to pursue it, or who could be won to it by missionary effort.[2] Far from being indifferent to the religious welfare of their neighbors, the leading Pharisees were enthusiastic guardians of society's well-being. The hope of Israel, they believed, lay in faithful observance of the Law as expounded in the oral teachings of the scribes.

The Pharisee loved his Law and thought it worthy of his meditation both by day and by night. When his social and economic status made possible the fullest observance of the rules laid down in the oral tradition of the schools of interpretation, he naturally felt no slight satisfaction with the result. The more elaborate the institutional machinery became, the more efficient it

[1] *Hagigah* II, 7. A Pharisee might invite an '*Am ha-'aretz* to dinner (cf. Luke 7:36) without incurring defilement if the latter shed his outer garment before entering the house. But a Pharisee might not be the guest of an '*Am ha-'aretz* lest the host should serve food from which the tithes had not been properly separated.

[2] So far as the Pharisees' desire to add new members to the society of the *haberim* is concerned, Matt. 23:15 is no misrepresentation.

was as an instrument for perfecting his living. The mechanism of religion, while not necessarily an end in itself, was thought to be the indispensable vehicle by which men might hope to rise higher and higher in God's esteem. This was an attitude not unlike that of a later Christian ecclesiastic who affirmed that one who will not have the church for a mother cannot have God for a father. Such is the distinctive trend of institutional piety in all ages.

The prophetic temperament cannot easily come to terms with institutional religion. For the prophet, the voice that speaks within his own soul is supreme. It may be the same divine voice that has spoken to good men in all ages, but its utterances in the past cannot overshadow its present and immediate summons to the emotions and conscience of the individual. Every institution of Judaism—the temple, the Law, the oral tradition—may at the outset have been thought by Jesus to possess an appropriate measure of divine sanction. But when these heritages were cited against him by opponents, his own prophet-like consciousness of inner certainty quickly transcended them all. Experientially, Jesus' sense of sudden and divine commission for his task was utterly irreconcilable with the scribe's feeling of religious responsibility acquired by a long preparatory discipline culminating in official recognition of his function. The scribe may have been no less certain than Jesus was of divine guidance, but neither of them was in a state of mind to grant the adequacy of the other's credentials.

Fundamentally, the difference between Jesus and the contemporary religious leaders of Judaism was one of personal and social experience. He and his followers were "people of the land" (*'Amme ha-'aretz*), unhabituated to the more meticulous demands of the scribal system. Their neglect of legal niceties was not the expression of a studied effort to undermine scribism. It was but the spontaneous pursuit of their former way of life, now sanctified by their leader's conviction of a new mission. Jesus was now confident that he had arisen to a higher level of religious attainments without attention to legalistic refinements, and he was inviting others to follow his example. Under these circumstances conflict with the guardians of institutional piety was inevitable. They might have been ready enough to concede that it was entirely proper for Jesus to summon people to repentance, but they could not conscientiously grant that the new teacher

offered a valid program for the realization of a
better life. He and his helpers had themselves
not kept the Law as faithfully as it had been kept
by many persons whom they exhorted to repent.
If they should succeed in winning large numbers
of followers, it would mean, from the Pharisees'
point of view, an undermining of the very foundations of Judaism. They had an ancient tradition which declared that the very stability of the
world hung upon the Law, the temple worship,
and acts of piety;[1] and one of their teachers of
note contemporary with Jesus was said to have
specified the fundamentals of the Law to be hallowed things (*kodesh*), priests' dues (*terumoth*),
and tithes (*ma'aseroth*).[2]

Apart from occasional instances of conflict
due to personal pique, where the professionalist
is irritated by the audacity of one who seems to
him a mere dilettante, the Pharisean scribes
would be entirely conscientious in their opposition to Jesus. He must have seemed to them
atrociously ignorant of many matters essential
for one who would set himself up as a religious
leader among the people. His education had
been altogether inadequate. He had attended no
professional school and had no institutional

[1] *Aboth* I, 2.   [2] *Shabbath* 32b.

[316]

standing. His lack of discipline in their technique, which had been so assiduously cultivated to insure the safety of the Jewish people, disqualified him in their eyes for the work of religious teacher. He was a non-conformist who was unwittingly, if not wilfully, encouraging the populace to neglect those duties that alone would insure their safety before God. It was incumbent upon the diligent scribe to resist this innovator and his irregularities. As one who was leading Israel astray, Jesus would seem to deserve those punishments which God had ordained in the Scripture for the transgressor among his people. Conscientious Pharisees could not avoid opposing Jesus, and those of more sensitive temperaments might feel impelled by stern duty to seek ways and means of delivering society from the dangers involved in his further activity.[1]

[1] Among the transgressions listed in the Mishnah (*Aboth* V, 11), as bringing down God's wrath upon the world, are carelessness in tithing, failure to execute the death penalty when it is required by the Law, lack of heed to the *halakah* of the scribes, and profanation of the Name by its too familiar use. Such sentiments, if not the actual language of the present Mishnah text, were undoubtedly current among Pharisees in the time of Jesus; and in view of his irregular conduct they might well have thought that failure to bring about his death would further incite the divine displeasure.

IV

When Jesus visited Jerusalem at the Passover season, his career came to a sudden and fatal climax. Possibly for two and a half years he
had been pursuing his task of prophetic preacher
with results not dissimilar to those that attended
the work of many of the ancient reformers. His
message had been heard and heeded by a few
faithful disciples. Others had temporarily gathered about him but had not become permanently
attached to his person. Others had rejected and
turned away with indifference, while still others
had been incensed by fear of the damage that
might come to the Jewish people if this agitator
continued his operations.

Jesus was now an object of suspicion and hatred in two quite different quarters. When he
went to Jerusalem, he had, to be sure, escaped
any embarrassment that might have resulted
from the political suspicions of Herod Antipas.
The possibility of a revolutionary disturbance in
consequence of the popular agitation attending
Jesus' activities could not have been permanently ignored by the tetrarch. But political suspicion was only further augmented by the visit to
Jerusalem. The Roman authorities were always
watchful, particularly at the feast seasons when

large crowds came together. This was a favorite time for adventurers to play upon the discontent felt by the people under Roman domination, and it was an exceedingly unpropitious moment for Jesus' friends to become vociferously enthusiastic in their admiration of him and in declarations of their hope that he would bring deliverance to the oppressed nation.

In the second place, the religious animosity which had been growing up against Jesus in Galilee became only the more acute in Jerusalem. Those religious leaders who were most influential and who had been most offended by his conduct were also in attendance at the feast. Their zeal for ceremonial piety would only be heightened by the approaching celebration of Passover. At the same time, Jesus had lost none of his fervor for proclaiming the need of Israel's repentance, and the realization of a new righteousness. When he came into the precincts of the temple, it was inevitable that his zeal should burn with new flame amid those sacred environs. He would have been no prophet had he refrained from lifting up his voice in protest against what seemed to him to be formalities, insincerities, and even desecrations, in the very shadow of God's holy house. Perhaps this is the first occasion on which the Sadducean aristocrats and the priestly class had come in contact with the Galilean reformer. But thereafter it would require no great urging to persuade them to join forces with the suspicious Romans and the offended scribes in the effort to rid society of the new trouble-maker.

One can easily imagine how bitterly Jesus' enemies must have felt against him and how very necessary it must have seemed to them that he be prevented from carrying on further work. But it seems entirely out of harmony with any modern sense of justice to learn that he should have been adjudged worthy of punishment by death. Would it not have been sufficient to arrest him, to cast him into prison, to impose a fine upon him, or even to have condemned him to exile? To raise such questions is simply to show one's self ignorant of the conditions of the times in which Jesus lived. Life then was exceedingly cheap from the point of view of the ruling classes, and capital punishment for what might in modern times be regarded as only slight offenses was of common occurrence. The Scriptures themselves prescribed the death penalty even for ritualistic transgressions. And the religious contemporaries of Jesus might very conscientiously have condemned him to be stoned because of his violations of the Sabbath, even if not for his laxity in the matter of clean and unclean foods. But when the operations of Jewish law were combined with the activities of the Roman procurator, the life of the individual was still further jeopardized. One who had come to be regarded as an undesirable citizen might take it for granted that in the natural course of events he would sooner or later lose his life perhaps by assassination, if not by some more dignified process in the regular administration of justice.

Jesus was well aware of the danger in which he and his disciples stood. Behind the dramatized form in which the gospel writers tell the story of his arrest, his trial, and his crucifixion, one is able still to perceive elements of stern reality. Not only did Jesus anticipate violence, but the form which he expected it to assume was that of assassination. It was the attempt to avoid this eventuality that gives meaning to his movements during the hours following the last supper with his disciples. The company disbanded, Jesus going quietly with three of them to the Garden of Gethsemane. He saw to it beforehand that they were equipped with daggers to protect themselves against attack. He sta-

[321]

tioned his companions at the gate to watch, while he himself withdrew apart to commune with God at this critical hour. Under the restrictions of Roman domination, zealous persons among the Jews had in many cases come to feel that it was necessary to take the administration of justice in their own hands and execute those penalties which righteous conduct demanded, but which they might not hope to effect with becoming speed in a Roman court. Even in more sober days, when the laws of the Mishnah were codified, it was noted that provision was made for "zealous people" to execute the death penalty in certain cases, even without the formality of a trial.[1] By the time of Josephus, assassins had become persons so well recognized in Jewish society that they constituted a distinct group, the Sicarii. They were condemned by Josephus, but were as a matter of course admired by their followers; and unquestionably they regarded their own course of action as approved by God.

When the temple police, who represented the political rather than the religious hostility against Jesus, appeared upon the scene, resistance was futile. The hiding-place had been disclosed by the traitorous disciple, Judas. While

[1] *Sanhedrin* IX, 6.

JESUS' PURSUIT OF HIS TASK

Jesus might have hoped to resist an individual assassin, it was useless to attempt an escape from the strong arm of the law. The details of his trial are matters of relatively little importance for the outcome of his career. Once he had been apprehended, his fate was virtually predetermined. It was as a potential insurrectionist that the Sadducees and Pilate had seized him, and it was not the custom of the Romans to institute any laborious legal procedure in connection with the condemnation of suspected Jewish revolutionists. They crucified them and their adherents in wholesale fashion and on various occasions. The Roman governor of Syria, Varus, had established a precedent when he visited Judea in the troublesome days following the death of Herod the Great. He dragged in some two thousand suspected persons from the territory round Jerusalem and condemned them to death. We cannot imagine that each one of these alleged culprits was given an extended trial, first in the Sanhedrin, since they were of course Jews, and then in some court that Varus himself might conduct. Indeed, more summary treatment was meted out to political offenders.[1]

[1] It is futile to attempt a reconciliation between the gospel stories of Jesus' trial and the legal processes of the Sanhedrin as

JESUS—A NEW BIOGRAPHY

In the eyes of the Romans, Jesus was a political menace. As between him and Barabbas, very likely Pilate would have regarded the former a less dangerous person, because he had fewer followers. On the other hand, it is not probable that Pilate would have executed Jesus had the Jewish court, the Sanhedrin, offered any serious objections. Jesus was not a sufficiently dangerous person to make it practicable for the Roman procurator to offend Jewish sensibilities. But Jesus had no friends in the Sanhedrin, either among the Sadducees or the Pharisees. A critical discussion regarding the process of the trial

---

detailed in the tractate of the Mishnah on this subject. This treatise is available in an excellent recent English translation by H. Danby (*Tractate Sanhedrin* [London, 1919]), who thinks that the Jewish criminal procedure here described is not that which was in vogue before 70 A.D. but is a projection into the past of ideas current among Jewish scholars at the end of the second century. Doubtless there is truth in this view, but it does not follow that "we may assume the historical truth of the details given in the Gospels" (p. x). The Christian writers in the last quarter of the first century were not free from the temptation, or the necessity, of creative description in recounting the story of Jesus' trial. In the nature of the case the procedure before the Sanhedrin would be only a preliminary hearing and the Roman court would necessarily have ultimate jurisdiction. The literature on the subject may be found in R. W. Husband's *The Prosecution of Jesus* (Princeton, 1916) and J. Juster's *Les Juifs dans l'empire romain* (Paris, 1914), II, 127–42.

has often been carried on laboriously, but it has little or no point with reference to the determination of Jesus' own fate. As described in the gospels, the whole story is colored by later Christian interests. The dominating concern of the Christian preachers in the gospel-making age was to cast the blame upon the Jews and to relieve the Gentiles of responsibility. The guilt of the Jews was magnified when Pilate was made to order the execution against his will. In the original situation, certainly the Procurator acted freely and probably with full satisfaction to himself. He saw in Jesus a potential revolutionist whose removal would be a warning to all future agitators. The Jews also were satisfied, both the Sadducees and the Pharisees—the former because Jesus was thought dangerous to the peace and the latter because he seemed a menace to correct procedure in the observance of Jewish religious rites. There was no protest when Pilate ordered the execution of Jesus.

CHAPTER VII

THE RELIGION JESUS LIVED

IN THE course of his career Jesus had impressed friends and foes alike with the dynamic quality of his personality. They readily believed him capable of accomplishing great things for good or for evil. Almost at sight he was generously heroized by his disciples and bitterly denounced by his opponents. By their very attitudes toward him the people with whom he came in contact bore witness to the arresting character of his living.

The religious life of an ordinary individual is not easy to fathom, much less is one able successfully to plumb the depths of a prophet's soul. His sense of seizure by God and his feeling of absolute surrender to the omnipotent will make possible for him ranges of experience unattainable by common mortals. His emotions never remain long on the dead level of perfect equilibrium. One day an Elijah appears boldly triumph-

[326]

THE RELIGION JESUS LIVED

ing over the prophets of Baal, and the next day in despair he prays that God may relieve him of the burden of living.[1] Amos, Hosea, Isaiah, Jeremiah, Ezekiel, all are men of violent moods.

Since childhood the scriptural portrayal of the prophetic experience had been familiar to Jesus, and from the' hour of his baptism the prophet's sense of divine impulsion had been his immediate possession. He too knew the heights and depths of emotion—the ecstasy of a transfiguration moment and the dark shadows of a Gethsemane—that were the portion of one dominated by a will not his own. It is not surprising that his relatives should have thought him "out of his mind," or that men today should raise questions regarding his sanity.[2]

As a means of understanding a religious personality, psychology is a wholly modern instrument. It was quite unknown in the time of Jesus. The standards of valuation used by his contemporaries were of an entirely different sort. Instead of arriving at an estimate of his character by scrutinizing his inner spiritual struggles, both his disciples and his enemies expressed their

[1] I Kings 18:36–40; 19:1–4.

[2] This question is handled, very sanely, by W. E. Bundy in *The Psychic Health of Jesus* (New York, 1922).

[327]

appraisals in the language of external relationships. Those who were most appreciative of his work saw in him one who stood uniquely high in the favor of God, while those who were most gravely apprehensive accused him of collusion with the Evil One.

I

For admiring followers, a worthy judgment about Jesus was of far greater conscious importance than any attempt to appreciate his own personal piety. Not the religion of Jesus, but a proper estimate of him as the object of his disciples' devotion was of chief concern. The quality of his personal living was not completely lost from view, and might on occasion be cited as a model for imitation; but oftener it was elevated to a height which no Christian might hope to reach, or to which he might even think it improper to aspire. Disciples were not to forget that Jesus had lived religiously—even sinlessly—but they commonly sought credentials for him in formal displays of his authority, or in his self-assertions of dignity, rather than within the inner sanctuary of his personal experience. "What think ye of Christ?" was for them the theme of supreme interest.

Much was made of fidelity to Jesus and his

cause. This attitude was thought to be in complete harmony with his well-remembered demands that men should bring their living into rigid conformity with the divine will. The service of God, to which Jesus had called his hearers, was identical for the first generation of Christian missionaries with the service of the risen Christ to which they were summoning the men of their generation. It seemed clear to them that Jesus had demanded this allegiance, in return for which they might expect him to reward them on the day of judgment (Matt. 10:32; Mark 8:38; Luke 9:26; 12:8). They would be safe at that precarious moment, since, as disciples of Jesus, they had been willing to incur the hatred of all men for his "name's sake" (Matt. 10:22; 24:9; Mark 13:13; Luke 21:17). The exhortation to be "worthy of me" constituted the great summons to heroic conduct. Separation from kindred, the distresses of persecution, and even martyrdom were in order for the sake of him and his gospel (Matt. 10:37–39; 16:24 f.; Mark 8:34 f.; Luke 9:23 f.; 14:25–27).

While it was remembered that Jesus had lived humbly, enduring the severest afflictions, imitation of his exemplary self-sacrifice was not in itself an ultimate goal for the disciples in after

years. To them his own brief earthly existence
had been only a prelude to his exaltation at
God's right hand—or, indeed, a mere interlude
between his relinquishment and resumption of
authority in heaven. Similarly, they sought to
keep themselves humble after the model of their
Master, that they might be entitled to share his
triumph in the coming Kingdom. The present
struggle, while a valuable discipline in perfection, was no real end in itself. The consummation of religious values was to come catastroph-
ically when one stood in the presence of the judge
on the last great day. At that time those who
had remained loyal to Jesus in their previous
missionary labors would enter into his promised
reward. Since fidelity to him was now the crucial test of a disciple's religion, it seemed entirely
proper to assume that Jesus himself had commanded this attitude.

In a religion where he had been made an object of adoration second only to God, the problem of worthily appraising Jesus necessarily received a great deal of attention. It was felt highly desirable to provide him with honorific titles
indicative of one or another aspect of his official
status. In so far as account was taken of his
personal religion, it too was assigned to an un-

paralleled realm of experience. Presumably he had been fully aware of possessing an authority and discharging a function which never had and never could come within the range of a disciple's own self-consciousness. As a matter of fact, probably Christians did draw generously upon their own experiences for patterns by which to visualize the religious life of their revered teacher. But this imagery had to be liberally retouched before it could suitably be applied to the favored Son of God, the apocalyptic Son of Man, or the pre-existent incarnate Logos.

Various early Christian preachers undertook the task of describing, in their several ways, the state of mind that had befitted one in Jesus' high station. They were uniformly of the opinion that during his lifetime he had aimed so to conduct himself as to demonstrate by word and deed his right to official recognition. Throughout the whole range of gospel tradition, from the earliest to the latest strata in the records, Jesus was invested with a unique authority. Never before had any prophet in Israel expressed such wisdom or exhibited so full a measure of divine approval. Not only were his injunctions assumed to be superior to those of all previous Jewish teachers, but at his word of command the very power of Satan had been broken. In the temptation incident, this mighty champion of evil had been thwarted by the ready replies of the newly designated Son of God (Matt. 4: 1–11; Luke 4:1–13). On the occasion of his first public miracle an unclean spirit had been terrified into confessing that the new teacher was the "Holy One of God" (Mark 1:24). When he spoke he filled his hearers with astonishment (Mark 1:22). His audiences marveled at the words of grace that fell from his lips (Luke 4:22). Sometimes he explicitly affirmed that his commands transcended the teachings of the most revered ancestors of the Jews (Matt. 5:21–43). One evangelist reported that at twelve years of age Jesus had amazed the learned men of Jerusalem by his wisdom (Luke 2:47). On another occasion a Roman officer had testified that no such words as those uttered by Jesus had ever before been spoken by any man (John 7:46).

The mind of Jesus was displayed still more authoritatively when he declared himself qualified to forgive men's sins, a prerogative commonly supposed to belong only to God (Mark 2:5–12). Because confident of his right to the title "Son of Man," he not only assumed authority to forgive sins, thus representing God on

[332]

earth, but he also felt empowered to declare himself superior to that most sacred Jewish institution, the holy Sabbath (Mark 2:28). When demons, because they too belonged to the sphere of the supernatural, cried out in terror, acknowledging him to be the Son of God, he commanded them not to disclose this secret as yet known only in the higher regions where he and they normally dwelt (Mark 3:11 f.). Moving upon this high plane of self-interpretation, he was represented as believing that God had selected him to fulfill the messianic expectations of the Hebrew race.

If the New Testament writers have read the experience of Jesus aright, he carried about within his breast, from the day of his baptism, a conviction that he was the individual chosen by God to establish the Kingdom, as preached by himself and earlier by John the Baptist. Only gradually had this truth dawned upon the disciples, but the moment of its apprehension marked a real climax in their own career (Mark 8:27–30). Yet if this earthly Jesus was the one appointed to officiate in the rôle of the apocalyptic Messiah soon to come in the glory of the Father accompanied by the holy angels (Mark 8:38), he must first find his way to heaven. Would he be snatched up, Enoch-like, when the crucial hour

[333]

for the Kingdom's inauguration arrived? According to the Synoptic records, all through the period of Jesus' lifetime the disciples remained very much in the dark regarding the way in which this necessary transition was to be effected. But no uncertainty is permitted in the mind of Jesus. It is assumed that he was fully aware of his approaching crucifixion, to be followed immediately by his triumphant resurrection (Mark 8:31–33).

Especially during the closing days of his earthly career Jesus had seemed fortified by the certainty that he was destined to become the apocalyptic Son of Man. Temporarily he was to be betrayed into the hands of sinners (Mark 14:41), but ultimate victory was assured. He calmly faced arrest and unflinchingly withstood his accusers buoyed up by the conviction that he was the Messiah, the Son of the Blessed. He boldly forecast his future vindication on the day when he would be seen sitting in powerful estate at God's right hand whence he would descend victoriously to earth to execute judgment and reward the righteous (Mark 14:62). Already he had taken the disciples into his confidence, telling them of impending disaster when the temple would be thrown down, as all nature agonized in travail bringing to birth the new Golden Age. He had assured them that their own generation would not pass away before this forecast of events had been fulfilled. But of the exact day and hour he confessed that he was himself unaware. The Father alone possessed this knowledge (Mark 13:3–32).

At other times Jesus is reported to have declared his absolute oneness of knowledge with the Father. There is a notable paragraph common to Matthew and Luke in which Jesus is said to have affirmed that he, and he alone among men, had been intrusted with the fulness of divine wisdom (Matt. 11:25–27; Luke 10:21 f.). Others could have a knowledge of the Father only as it might be mediated by the Son. Nowhere else in the Synoptic Gospels is this note of self-assurance on the part of Jesus sounded so clearly, but in the Fourth Gospel it is characteristic of his perpetual state of mind. Here he displays a divine wisdom carried over from his earlier existence in heaven with the Father. This memory of heavenly knowledge was an ever present possession of his religious consciousness. Even John the Baptist had declared to his followers that Jesus would tell them all things that he had seen and heard before his incarnation.

Having been sent to earth to speak the words of God among men, he was the one into whose hands the Father had delivered all things. If John possessed this information regarding Jesus, how much more thoroughly aware of his own superior knowledge must Jesus himself have been! (John 3:31–36). It occasions no surprise to hear him declare outright that he had descended to earth for the purpose of living a life strictly in accord with the dictates of heaven (John 6:38).

The Fourth Gospel is especially rich in its disclosures of Jesus' self-interpretation. He informed his hearers that they must be reborn in order to qualify for membership in the Kingdom. But he had needed to experience no such transformation, since from the beginning he was the only-begotten Son of God. By virtue of his original constitution he had always been one with the Father. He and God worked together in perfect unison, and men were to pay their respects to this relationship by honoring the Son even as they honored the Father (John 5:23). The words spoken by Jesus were not the result of any religious meditation and striving within the arena of his personal experience, but were ready-made commandments which had been intrusted to him by God, who had sent him forth from heaven that he might become the light of the world and the bread of life (John 12:44–50).

Not only the words of Jesus but also the wonderful acts that he is reported to have performed are an index to the different evangelists' conception of his state of mind. A very unusual measure of religious assurance must be assumed for one who issues orders to the winds and the waves to be calm, or steps out fearlessly upon the surface of the Sea of Galilee. He who could think his word of blessing sufficient to cause a small quantity of bread and fish to become instantly an adequate supply of food for several thousand people must have enjoyed a correspondingly unique self-confidence. Even those performances that seemed to the ancients less spectacular, such as the healing of diseases and the driving out of demons from people possessed, were not within the power of one whose religious life was of an entirely ordinary sort. The feeling of authority which Jesus must have possessed in order to work even the simplest miracles reported in the gospels sets him far above the average of religious men in his own generation.

It is quite true that when the gospels were written the healing of diseases and the exorcizing of demons were activities carried on with a measure of success by Christians themselves. Confident individuals did on occasion successfully call upon the name of the risen Jesus to effect cures, but the sense of assurance possessed by these healers was not immediate. They cured by the mediating power of Jesus' name. Not so with his mighty works. He moved across the stage with sure and certain step, confident that there was resident in his own person virtue to heal all manner of disease. In fact he did not hesitate to enter the chamber of death, or the very tomb itself, to summon spirits back to their former bodily habitations. Everywhere throughout the gospels one is led to believe that confidence in his ability to perform miracles was an intrinsic element in the religious experience of Jesus. Instances are noted where he deliberately refrained from exercising his powers, as when Satan invited him to leap down from a high point of the temple, or when his enemies asked a sign from heaven; but there is no intimation that the evangelists entertained any tremors of doubt about his personal ability to produce the miracle demanded. The immediate conditions, not his lack of native power, restrained his action.

The gospel picture of the religion lived by Jesus bears numerous evidences of heroic coloring on the part of his later followers. They were intent upon raising the respect of their contemporaries to the greatest possible pitch of admiration for the founder of the new religion. It was not their purpose to depict his own spiritual history, except as the story might serve to make him seem a more worthy object of devotion. Incidents in his career and words from his lips were selected and interpreted with a view to stimulating confidence in one or another phase of his official dignity. It was assumed that he had regularly conducted himself in accordance with the interest in his official character that was now so essential a phase of the Christian enterprise. Reported acts and sayings might incidentally shed much light on the hero's own religious living, but the narrators rarely failed to provide their story with a setting designed to stimulate the faith of believers. The mind of reverent disciples had been made the mind of the Master.

From a very early date the Christian movement had included within itself both the religion of Jesus and the religion about Jesus, both the Jesus of history and the Christ of dogma. While one readily draws a sharp distinction in thought between these two figures, historically the actual line of separation is exceedingly difficult to fix.

[339]

JESUS—A NEW BIOGRAPHY

The Jesus of history became the Christ of faith so soon after his death, if indeed the process of elevation had not set in prior to the crucifixion, that it is no easy task to determine just what elements in the new religion belonged within the realm of Jesus' personal experience and what features were later contributed by his disciples who after his post-resurrection appearances made him increasingly the object of their own adoration. It was pertinent to their situation as advocates of a new cause to stress particularly Jesus' displays of divine authority and his claims to official dignity. Since these were items of vital interest to Christians in the gospel-making age, it was readily believed that they had held a similarly prominent place in the personal interest and experience of Jesus. Was this a correct assumption? In the distinctive setting where he had actually lived, had miracle-display and messianic self-interpretation claimed from him and his close friends the same measure of attention that was given them by his later disciples on the mission fields during the decades in which the gospels arose?

THE RELIGION JESUS LIVED

II

Within first-century Christianity itself there were differences of opinion regarding the question of how far Jesus, in his own sphere of activity, had performed miracles. At an early date a distinction had been made between "things done" and "things said."[1] Sometimes interest centered quite exclusively in words of Jesus. A fragment of Christian preaching preserved in the third chapter of Acts (3:22–26) is an illustration in point. Here it is simply Jesus the prophet, with his forceful religious message, whom the speaker admonishes his hearers to heed. God's promise to the Jews to raise up from their own number a prophet like Moses had now been fulfilled in the activity of Jesus. Everything said by him had been spoken in accordance with the divine plan to provide the chosen people of God a final message of instruction, the rejection of

[1] When messengers from John came to ask for Jesus' credentials they were instructed, according to Matthew (11:4), to go tell their master what they "hear and see"; or, according to Luke (7:22), what they "saw and heard." Also in Luke 24:19 Jesus was said to have been "a prophet powerful in deed and word," and this entire gospel was later called by its author a record of what Jesus began "to do and to teach" (Acts 1:1). In Mark 6:30 it is said that the disciples when reporting their activities to Jesus also distinguished between what they *did* and what they *taught*.

[341]

which would mean sure disaster. All the prophets of old had forecast the coming of this new teacher in fulfilment of the covenant made with Abraham. Jesus had been God's especially chosen servant sent to Abraham's descendants to bring them a blessing by preaching repentance.

In this representation Jesus is significant because he had delivered a message of warning designed to augment righteousness in Israel. Responding to his summons, the nation would be ready to receive him when he should descend from his present exalted station in heaven to complete his saving-work. While formerly on earth he had been the prophet-like teacher whose words, if heeded, would produce among the Jews cleansing from sin and a consequent state of righteousness fitting them for membership in the new régime to be established with Jesus' return. The Christian missionaries who entertained this view of their master's earlier activity were themselves convinced that the most effective way to bring about repentance and remission of sins among their hearers was to reproduce the message of the great teacher.

Certain groups of early disciples had developed a distinct interest in recalling evidences of Jesus' prophetic activity. In response to this desire, collections of his sayings, embodying chiefly his ideals for religious living, had been assembled and ultimately given written form. From this type of tradition, now accessible in the non-Marcan sources taken up into Matthew and Luke, and even in the Marcan parables, a reader learns little or nothing about any miracles wrought by Jesus. (See above pp. 30–33.) Indeed, Christians of this disposition were prone to look askance at the tendencies of certain of their brethren to magnify the story of his mighty works. They took pains to note that at the time of his temptation he had deliberately rejected any appeal to the miraculous. Probably it was a Christian of this same circle who recalled that on a certain occasion Jesus had admonished his disciples not to be over joyful in the fact that demons were subject unto them in his name, but to prize more highly the less spectacular assurance that their own names were written in heaven (Luke 10:17–20).

Other Christians, however, found greater delight in rehearsing accounts of Jesus' deeds as a means of inspiring in their hearers admiration for his personality. He was thought especially worthy of reverence because of the miraculous displays that had been made in connection with

his career. God had anointed him with the Holy
Spirit at the time of his baptism, thus equipping
him to go about performing healings and exor-
cisms. Thereby he demonstrated that during
his lifetime he had been endowed in unusual
measure with power from above. Nor had these
evidences of God's favor ceased even with the
crucifixion. The resurrection had followed. Then
Jesus, showing himself again to his followers,
commissioned them to bear testimony to what
they had seen, and to announce that he was the
one whom God had chosen to sit in judgment
upon the world in the last great day. Through
the evidence thus presented, and substantiated
by their reading of ancient prophecy, Christian
preachers called upon their audiences to repent
and believe on Jesus. Such is the epitome of one
distinct type of sermon also preserved in the
composite Book of Acts (10:36–43).

For Christians of this temper the essence of
the new religion was not so much the cultivation
of the moral and spiritual precepts enunciated
by Jesus, as it was a suitable admiration for his
power and prestige. He was less a prophetic reformer and more conspicuously an heroic redeemer. His excellence was manifested most
truly in what he had done. Therefore it was

thought especially desirable to stress displays of
the miraculous exhibited in his career—his possession of the Holy Spirit, his power over demons,
his superiority to all the forces of nature, his
healings, his resurrection from the dead, his later
appearances to the disciples, and his ascent to
heaven. This distinctively heroic interest comes
into prominence particularly in the Gospel of
Mark. (See above pp. 10 ff.)

These two types of religious interest—we
may call one the didactic and the other the heroic—were both capable of flourishing within a
Jewish environment. Neither is to be summarily
dismissed as impossible in the Palestinian setting
where Jesus had lived. Jewish religion had its
great teachers, but it also had its mighty heroes.
Undoubtedly Moses was chiefly esteemed because he had mediated the divine instructions revealed in the Law, yet his miraculous performances were not forgotten.[1] Among the prophets,
Elijah and Elisha had been unprecedented won-
der-workers. True, the great preaching prophets
had not been famous miracle mongers, but they
were truly miraculous personalities because
uniquely equipped by God. It was assumed that
Isaiah had power to perform signs, an ability

[1] See P. Volz, *Der Geist Gottes* (Tübingen, 1910), p. 86.

[345]

which King Ahaz dared not put to the test (Isa.
7:11). One tradition, in fact, reported that in
the days of Hezekiah, Isaiah had actually caused
the shadow on the king's dial to move backward
ten steps (II Kings 20:7–11; Isa. 38:1–8). In
Palestinian circles undoubtedly miracles were
regarded an appropriate attestation of divine
authority which any messenger of God might be
expected to display should occasion demand.
Yet among Jews the memory of an ancient worthy's message was thought much more significant for religion than any recollection of his
marvelous deeds. The didactic interest far out-
weighed the heroic.

Among Gentiles, on the other hand, miraculous displays connected with the person and
work of a hero were most highly esteemed. Frequently he was accredited by stories of supernatural generation.[1] Human parenthood on the
mother's side guaranteed his sympathy with
men, while his divine paternity insured ability
to transcend all human limitations of conduct.
Many popular gentile divinities, whom the
Christian preacher perforce declared inferior to
his Lord Jesus Christ, were widely famed for
their miraculous powers. They were believed to

[1] See above p. 170.

[346]

protect their devotees in times of distress, to give knowledge of coming events, to heal all manner of diseases, and even to revive the dead. Not only had they performed wonders while on earth, but now from their position of power in the domain of the gods they continued to succor their disciples in the crises of life, thus proving by their marvelous deeds that they were worthy of the allegiance of mankind.

Hosts of people in the gentile world revered gods who had been, and still were, abundant in mighty works.[1] But of all marvelous displays, the healing of diseases was most highly esteemed. Among the Greeks, Asklepios was widely famed for therapeutic activity. His father, Apollo, had no mean reputation as a divine physician,[2] but he was far surpassed by his more human son. The chief sanctuary of Asklepios, the "holy Epidauros," a few miles southeast of Corinth, at-

---

[1] See R. Lembert, *Der Wunderglaube bei Römern und Griechen* (Augsburg, 1905); R. Reitzenstein, *Hellenistische Wundererzählungen* (Leipzig, 1906); O. Weinreich, *Antike Heilungswunder* (Giessen, 1909); W. F. Cobb, *Spiritual Healing* (London, 1914); W. A. Jayne, *The Healing Gods of Ancient Civilizations* (New Haven, 1925).

[2] Among the Romans also, Apollo retained this reputation; G. Wissowa, *Religion und Kultus der Römer*, 2. Aufl. (München, 1912), p. 294.

tracted invalids from all about the Mediterranean world. Although the worship of this divinity was established at various places by his wandering devotees, and his healing grace was experienced wherever his name became known, his original sanctuary at Epidauros remained the most frequented of all ancient sanatoriums for afflicted humanity. Especially in Roman times, people came thither for treatment from all quarters of the Empire.

The miracles of healing performed at the shrine of Asklepios were of many varieties. Blindness, lameness, and paralysis were very common maladies to receive successful treatment. Grateful suppliants left behind abundant evidences of their appreciation in the form of crutches, canes, and votive offerings, not to mention the more substantial expressions of their gratitude necessary for the maintenance of the institution. If too ill to visit Epidauros, one might send prayers for help, or a friend might come to seek information from the deity. The cures were effected in a variety of ways. Sometimes while the patient slept at night in the temple, the god would appear and heal. Or the sick person in a vision might receive instructions which when followed resulted in a cure. In other cases a priest or physician connected with the temple served as a medium for the healing potency of the divinity. An air of sanctity pervaded the place, even though there were many human agencies evident in the operation of the institution. On entering the vestibule of the temple, a visitor was greeted by the admonition: "Only he who is pure may cross the threshold of the fragrant temple, but no one is pure who is not holy in thought."

Popular as Asklepios was, he was not the only revered divine physician among the Greeks and Romans. In times of pestilence Bacchus too came "with healing steps over the slopes of Parnassus." Devotees were attached to him on account of his revealing oracles, and especially for the healing visions which he disclosed in dreams. Likewise the great mother-goddess, Demeter, was not unmindful of the sufferings of mortals. It was said that once by placing her mouth to that of a boy who was at the point of death she had restored him to life. But of all the Greek and Roman gods or heroes who ministered to afflicted bodies, Asklepios remained the chief. There were many grateful convalescents ready to declare him to be "the one who leads and controls all things, the savior of the whole world and

guardian of mortals." Two centuries after
Christianity had been bidding for the allegiance
of Gentiles, people were still reporting that they
had frequently seen Asklepios "healing and doing good and foretelling the future."[1]

Deities from Asia and Egypt, whose worship
had already become popular all about the Mediterranean by the beginning of Christian times,
were often also widely reputed healers. The Asi-
atic Serapis was so highly regarded that his assistance is said to have been sought when Alexander the Great was overtaken by fatal illness.
Subsequently, when Serapis had traveled to
Egypt, his sanctuary at Canobus was held in
great veneration. Many important personages
journeyed thither that they might sleep in the

[1] Origen *Cels.*, iii. 24. In early Christian art the resemblance
between pictures of Christ and Asklepios are often striking. The
latter was also reputed to have saved many persons from death
by stretching out his hand to them when threatened by storms
at sea. An inscription of the year 212 A.D. refers to "the sacred
assembly of the Savior Asklepios" (F. Poland, *Geschichte des
griechischen Vereinswesens* [Leipzig, 1909], pp. 99 f.). For further
particulars about this cult, so important for an understanding of
the ancient world's interest in religious healing, one may consult
Alice Walton, *The Cult of Asklepios* (Boston, 1894); R. C. Caton,
The Temple and Ritual of Asklepios at Epidauros and Athens
(London, 1900); and the articles "Asklepios" and "Epidauros" in
Pauly-Wissowa, *Realencyclopädie der classischen Altertumswissen-
schaft.*

temple in the hope of securing restoration to health. In the opinion of those who bore testimony to this god's ability to heal, it is apparent that his sanctuary was no mean rival to that of Asklepios at Epidauros.

Still older than Serapis, and even more famous as a restorer of health, was the great Egyptian goddess, Isis. By the first century B.C. she was well known among the Romans for her curative power exercised at all of her numerous temples. Tradition affirmed that while on earth she had been exceedingly skilful in the treatment of disease, and that now from her position of authority with the gods she took great delight in continuing these kindly activities. Many persons whom the physicians had pronounced incurable testified that she had restored them to perfect health. Votive displays in her temples bore ample witness to the faith of her disciples in the effectiveness of her cures. Under her influence cripples cast away their crutches, and blind people received back their sight; and she was believed to have power also to raise the dead.

In the gentile world where Christians were now preaching, it was widely believed that miraculous healings were one of the chief functions of a religion. It need not surprise us, therefore,

to find that the representatives of Christianity
on gentile soil claim for themselves this power in
the name of their Master. Paul reminds the
Corinthians that God himself has decreed that
the new religion should include in its operations
miracles and gifts of healings (I Cor. 12:28).
Again, in his appeal to the Galatians to recognize the superiority of Christianity over Judaism, he cites the performance of miracles
through endowment by the Holy Spirit as
Christianity's distinguishing and superior credential (Gal. 3:5). When arguing with the Corinthians in defense of his apostleship, he asserts
that he did not in the least fall behind the very
chiefest apostles, for he too had been empowered
to display the signs of an apostle through the
working of miracles (II Cor. 12:12). As early as
the time of Paul, Christianity was meeting its
gentile rivals on their own ground and offering to
the people of the time a new religion with full
supernatural equipment. Its advocates responded to this call of their age by portraying their
exalted Christ as the great physician and by
themselves healing in his name.

At the outset it was only through the power
of the risen Christ that Christians claimed ability to perform miracles. At least Paul gives no in-

timation that he had heard of any such displays in connection with the earthly career of Jesus, which on the contrary had been marked by traits of lowliness and great humility. But in reward for this submission, Jesus after his death had been elevated to a position of authority in heaven; and henceforth at the mention of his name every knee would bow, whether in heaven, on earth, or under the earth (Phil. 2:9 f.). He was now all powerful throughout the whole universe of angels, men, and demons. Every Christian missionary could confidently repeat the slogan ascribed in Acts to Peter on the occasion of healing the lame man, and declare unequivocally that in the name of Jesus Christ of Nazareth, whom God had raised from the dead, there was salvation superior to that available through trust in any other divinity, whether it be Asklepios, Serapis, Isis, or any one of all the multitude of gods to whom the sick had formerly been in the habit of appealing for relief.

By the time the Gospel of Mark had come into existence, the prerogatives of the risen Christ had been generously conferred by the evangelist upon the earthly Jesus. The Holy Spirit, which had empowered disciples to perform wonders in the days of Paul, had been bestowed upon Jesus himself at the time of his baptism; and immediately he entered upon a miracle-working career. His first duty was to meet in private and triumph over Satan, and his first public act was an encounter in a synagogue with a man afflicted by an evil spirit. Jesus cast out the demon and then went immediately to Peter's home where he cured a case of violent fever. On the same evening all the sick of the town and those possessed by demons were brought to him to receive healing. Such was the first day's work with which he had opened his public ministry.

In their present form all four gospels show great fondness for miracle narratives attesting the superiority of the new religion and its founder. Even books like Mark and John, though containing no allusions to Jesus' supernatural birth, freely accorded him full authority to perform miracles from the very beginning of his public activity. With perfect ease he transcended the ordinary course of nature, whether by turning water into wine, by multiplying loaves and fishes, by stilling a storm, or by walking on the surface of a lake.[1] On three occasions he revived the

[1] Of so-called "nature-miracles," the various gospels report eight incidents: (1) Stilling a storm, Mark 4:35-41; Matt. 8:18-

[354]

THE RELIGION JESUS LIVED

dead.[1] But his most numerous performances consisted in the closely kindred activities of healing the sick and expelling demons. These were the typical mighty works that Christians themselves, in their efforts to compete with the popular healing cults of their age, were called upon to effect by appeal to the powerful name of the risen Christ. Naturally, when recounting the story of his career on earth, they dwelt more and more upon his own success in this form of activity. At his word or touch demons had fled away, fevers had ceased, leprosy had been cured, para-

27; Luke 8:22–25. (2) Feeding five thousand, Mark 6:30–44; Matt. 14:13–21; Luke 9:10–17; John 6:1–14. (3) Walking on water, Mark 6:48–52; Matt. 14:25–33; John 6:16–21. (4) Feeding four thousand, Mark 8:1–9; Matt. 15:32–38. (5) Withering a fig tree, Mark 11:12–14; Matt. 21:18 f. (6) Locating a coin in the mouth of a fish, Matt. 17:24–27. (7) Effecting an abnormal draught of fish, Luke 5:1–11; John 21:1–14. (8) Changing water to wine, John 2:1–11. Undoubtedly Nos. 2 and 4 are variants of the same original story repeated among different congregations in connection with the celebration of the Lord's Supper (see above p. 107). Nos. 1 and 3 also show a common motif and probably are duplicates. The story of the fig tree may have started as a parable (cf. Luke 13:6–9), and perhaps No. 6 was at first also a figure of speech. In the early days of gospel tradition, evidently the disposition to dwell upon this type of miracle was not strong.

[1] (1) Jairus' daughter, Mark 5:38–42; Matt. 9:23–25; Luke 8:51–55. (2) The widow's son, Luke 7:11–17. (3) Lazarus, John 11:35–53.

[355]

lytics had walked, the withered hand had been restored, blind eyes had been opened, deafness had disappeared, the tongue of the dumb had been loosed, the epileptic had become normal, the victim of dropsy had been healed, hemorrhage had been stopped, the hunchback had been made straight, and even invalids for whom others presented solicitations were immediately restored to health.[1]

The garish display of the miraculous, with which the several gospel writers overlaid the story of Jesus' life, answered admirably to the demands of the gentile mission field where Christianity was now struggling for recognition against rival faiths that claimed to be media of divine healing. Appropriate as this picture is

---

[1] Specific instances of exorcism are: (1) A man in the synagogue, Mark 1:21-28; Luke 4:31-37. (2) The Gerasene (or Gadarene) demons, Mark 5:1-20; Matt. 8:28-34; Luke 8:26-39. (3) A demon causing speechlessness, Matt. 9:32 f.; Luke 11:14 (in Matt. 12:22 the demon has caused both blindness and dumbness). (4) The daughter of the Syrophoenician woman, Mark 7:24-30; Matt. 15:21-28. (5) The epileptic boy, Mark 9:14-29; Matt. 17:14-21; Luke 9:37-43.

Healings without reference to demons are: (1) A fever, Mark 1:29-34; Matt. 8:14-17; Luke 4:38-41. (2) A leper, Mark 1:38-45; Matt. 8:2-4; Luke 5:12-16. (3) A paralytic, Mark 2:1-12; Matt. 9:1-8; Luke 5:17-26. (4) A withered hand, Mark 3:1-6; Matt. 12:9-14; Luke 6:6-11. (5) A case of hemorrhage, Mark

for a gentile audience, it ill accords with the realities of that Palestinian Jewish setting where
Jesus had actually lived and preached. A continuous series of marvelous deeds, such as are
spread upon the pages of the gospels, finds no
suitable place in the manner of life becoming a
preacher of reform in Israel.

Confident that he stood high in the favor of
heaven because divinely summoned to his task,
Jesus could readily have believed that God
might work wonders through him—when God
willed so to work. Also, Jesus' associates could
be counted upon to make the same assumption,
in case they granted the validity of his prophetic
call. In that age supernaturalism was a common-

5:25–34; Matt. 9:20–22; Luke 8:43–45. (6) A deaf and dumb
man, Mark 7:31–37 (in Matt. 15:30 the man is "lame, blind,
dumb, maimed"). (7) A blind man of Bethsaida, Mark 8:22–26.
(8) Blind Bartimaeus, Mark 10:46–52; Luke 18:35–43 (in the
parallel of Matt. 20:29–34 there are *two* blind men, and in Matt.
9:27–30 a very similar story is again told). (9) A centurian's
servant, Matt. 8:5–13; Luke 7:1–10. (10) A stooped woman, Luke
13:10–17. (11) A man with dropsy, Luke 14:1–6. (12) Ten lepers,
Luke 17:11–19. (13) A nobleman's son, John 4:46–54. (14) A
lame man at the pool of Bethesda, John 5:1–18. (15) A man born
blind, John 9:1–7. (16) Miscellaneous healings (and some exor-
cisms), Mark 1:34; 3:10 f.; Matt. 4:23; 8:16; 9:35; 14:14; 15:30
(see No. 6 above); 19:2; 21:14; Luke 4:40 f.; 7:21; John 2:23;3:2;
6:2, 14; 7:31; 10:38; 11:47; 12:37; 20:30.

ly accepted mode of thought no less prevalent among Jews than among Gentiles. But for Jews it was the power of their God, more than the prestige of the hero, that was on display. Probably Jesus believed that he, like the Jewish exorcists of the day, could cure the sick or triumph over the most aggravated cases of demon-possession by appeal to the power of Jehovah.[1] This was the righteous man's prerogative. It meant that God was with him in especial measure, but not that he himself was constitutionally different

[1] Matt. 12:27 f.; Luke 11:19 f. Jewish leaders were properly watchful of the exorcist, who might be tempted to adopt from his gentile instructors the name of one or another heathen divinity for use in a formula of adjuration. Such an act could hardly be construed otherwise than as an infringement of a Jew's allegiance to his own God and a violation of the Deuteronomic injunction against magic (Deut. 18:9–14), the charge to which some early Christians seem to have laid themselves open when they proposed to heal in the name of their glorified Jesus (Acts 4:7–10, 18, 29 f.; cf. Mark 9:38; Matt. 7:22; Luke 10:17; Acts 16:16–18; 19:13; Phil. 2:10). But to operate through "the Power"—or whatever circumlocution may have been used by Jesus (Luke 11:20)—would have rendered the exorcist guiltless provided he avoided the danger of blasphemy that would have resulted from actual use of the divine name. Rabbis issued warnings against either whispering the name of a strange divinity to effect a cure or pronouncing the sacred name of their own God with its proper letters (*Sanhedrin* X, 1. The parallel in Tosephta XII, 9 also condemns the acts of spitting in connection with a healing, which recalls Mark 7:33; 8:23). Yet there were successful Jewish exorcists even within

from others or was in any sense entitled to the worshipful reverence of his fellows. The Deity, not the miracle-worker, was the real hero.

However firmly convinced Jesus may have been that he was the chosen instrument of heaven, the work to which he had been summoned was primarily didactic. His career had its heroic moments, but they were never free from the shadows of threatening tragedy. A life of continuous miracle-display, moving serenely above the accidents and anxieties to which common

Palestine in the time of Jesus, particularly among the Essenes, and outside of Palestine the Christian healers met some of their sharpest competition from Jewish operators (Acts 19:13-16). It is not improbable that this Jewish rivalry on gentile soil may have stimulated more than one Christian missionary to elaborate the story of Jesus' success in casting out demons during his own public career. The Talmudic stories about the miracle-working abilities of the rabbis would, even if known to any of the gospel writers, have offered them less occasion for anxiety. In the case, for example, of Hanina ben Dosa, a contemporary of the Synoptic writers and one of the most highly reputed miracle-performers of the time, the rabbi was not conspicuously a self-sufficient hero but was more passively the ideal righteous man and thus a suitable medium for the display of the divine glory. When the words of his prayer over the sick came fluently he was confident of a favorable answer, but on another occasion he might find himself halting in speech and thus know that his request was not to be granted (*Berakoth* V, 5). God, not Hanina, was master of the situation and was the real agent in effecting the miracle.

mortals are heir, was not his daily routine. He dwelt closer to the realities of experience as known to the men of his time. He shared their feelings of storm and stress and rose to greater heights of assurance only as he answered more unreservedly the summons of God to greater loyalty in personal religious living.

III

From the moment of entrance upon his public career Jesus had possessed an overmastering conviction that his life had been linked with Deity in new bonds of experience and obligation. God had made special choice of him and had uniquely equipped him to deliver a message to the children of Israel. But to what extent this religious conviction impelled Jesus to attempt self-classification is another matter. Subsequently the disciples, viewing the earlier events in the light of their later experiences, believed that he had attained to a sense of divine sonship that meant identification of himself with the one whom God had promised to raise up in Israel to accomplish the deliverance of his people. In other words, Jesus accepted the appellation "Son" as an equivalent for the title of Messiah. In that event, an awareness of his official function would have been a dominating factor in the personal religious experience of Jesus from the moment of his baptism.

The term "son" would have served very well to express for Jesus his feeling of new status as the chosen spokesman of God. But it is far less probable that such terminology, if actually used, would have had a messianic connotation either for him or for his immediate associates. All Israelites were familiarly known as "sons of God," while an especially devout or favored individual, like a wise man or a king, was specifically a "son." There was no incongruity in the Talmudic tradition that the heavenly voice had designated a first-century rabbi, famed for his piety and wisdom, "my son Hanina."[1] Not until the end of the first century A.D., and then only in one of the apocalyptic books, does the expression "Son" appear as the synonym for "Messiah," a usage exactly parallel to that of the gospels.[2] Among the contemporaries of Jesus, any individual upon whom God's favor was felt to rest in unusual measure had ample precedent for enter-

---

[1] *Berakoth* 17b. It is noteworthy that Hanina, although standing thus high in the favor of God, is said to have been content to subsist week by week on a meager supply of locusts.

[2] See the citations in Strack and Billerbeck, *op. cit.*, III, 15–21.

taining the conviction that he in particular was a "son." The epithet implied exceptional equipment for duty or special commission for service. But it could hardly have occurred to any one, much less could it have been a generally recognized interpretation, that the designation was an official messianic label. That identification was an achievement of later Christian messianism and of the still later rival Jewish apocalypticism of IV Ezra.[1]

For "Son of Man" the case is somewhat different. Since Jesus, like John the Baptist, summoned his hearers to repentance in preparation for the eschatological Kingdom, his followers in later times easily convinced themselves that he had not only predicted the coming of the Son of Man visioned in the apocalpyses of Daniel and

[1] IV Ezra 7:28 f.; 13:32, 37, 52; 14:9. If the present text of I Enoch 105:2 is original, the Messiah had already been called "my Son" in the second century B.C., but this is a solitary occurrence and its genuineness is not above suspicion (see G. Dalman, *Die Worte Jesu* [Leipzig, 1898], I, 221). Elsewhere in this apocalypse the Messiah is commonly "Son of Man." It was entirely appropriate that he should have been called "Son of God" at this time, but as the king referred to in Ps. 2:7 is called "my Son" by God on the day of anointing for office, or the righteous man in Wisdom of Solomon 2:18 is "son of God"; but this designation of itself would not suffice to differentiate the Messiah from other sons who stood high in the favor of Deity.

Enoch, but that he had identified himself with this histrionic figure.[1] If Jesus had employed this self-designation with anything like the frequency implied in the gospels, and in the contexts there indicated, it would seem to have meant for him a deliberate affirmation of his messiahship. In that event this official self-appraisal would have to be accepted as a fundamental item in the content of his personal religious experience.

All four New Testament gospels permit Jesus, with almost astounding persistence, to call himself "Son of Man."[2] Also, they restrict the term to Jesus' own vocabulary. But they allow him to employ it in such varied contexts that

---

[1] Dan. 7:13; I Enoch, chaps. 46–71.

[2] In Matthew, thirty times; in Luke, twenty-five times; in Mark, fourteen times; in John, eleven (or twelve) times. This usage is all the more arresting since Acts 7:56 is the only other occurrence of the phrase in the New Testament. The passages have often been analytically tabulated, e.g., by S. R. Driver in the article "Son of Man" in J. Hastings' *A Dictionary of the Bible* (New York, 1903), IV, 579 ff.; and more recently by F. J. Foakes Jackson and K. Lake in *The Beginnings of Christianity* (New York, 1920), I, 375 ff.; and G. Dupont, *Le Fils de L'Homme* (Paris, 1926), pp. 104 f. Whether Jesus styled himself "Son of Man," and if so in what sense, is one of the most baffling problems that in recent years has confronted students. At the beginning of the present century it seemed to many scholars the most perplexing and at the same time the fundamental issue for a correct understanding of

they bear no clear and united testimony to his exact meaning. The gospel of John comes nearest to attaining consistency, but quite severs the phrase from its older apocalyptic connections.[1] The Synoptic usage varies between settings that stress apocalyptic associations of power or dignity, and those in which suffering and humility seem to be characteristics of one who would qualify as Son of Man. But on the whole the eschatological emphasis predominates throughout the first three gospels.

Among the Christian communities represented by the gospel tradition there was a pronounced fondness for "Son of Man" upon the lips of Jesus. Like "Verily I say unto you," and other turns of speech with a liturgical or sacro-

---

Jesus. So H. Monnier, *La Mission historique de Jesus* (Paris, 1906), p. 66; E. F. Scott, *The Kingdom and the Messiah* (New York, 1911), p. 188; H. J. Holtzmann, *Neutestamentliche Theologie,* 2. Aufl. (Tübingen, 1911), I, 313. This problem called forth numerous discussions during the nineties of the last, and the first decade of the present, century. Recently it has been canvassed afresh by G. Dupont (*op. cit.*), which may be consulted for the literature of the subject. See also "A Symposium on Eschatology," by different writers, in the *Journal of Biblical Literature*, XLI (1922), and N. Schmidt, "Recent Study of the term 'Son of Man,'" *ibid.*, XLV (1926), 326-49.

[1] John 1:51; 3:13 f.; 6:27, 53, 62; 8:28; 9:35; 12:23, 34; 13:31.

sanct flavor,[1] the expression was never uttered by anyone else, not even by the demons, whose superior knowledge had led to their immediate recognition that Jesus was Son of God. Of itself "Son of Man" has no natural meaning, nor do the contexts in which it occurs always make clear its significance. This very air of mystery was not unwelcome to the ancients, although it might easily betray a later interpreter of the gospels into assuming that their authors were mechanically reproducing from earlier tradition an inherited locution so ancient that even to them it had become an enigma. On the contrary, a comparative examination of the records readily reveals the fact that the several evangelists were not controlled simply by "sources," but used the term "Son of Man" because fond of it on their own account. They thus entitled Jesus because they delighted to do so, whether they found the phrase in their sources or employed it in sentences of their own composition. Here again the mind of the disciple and the mind of the master were readily made to coincide.[2]

[1] See above, p. 244, n. 1.

[2] An examination of the gospels shows that the evangelists did not derive the title in a mechanical way from documentary (or oral) sources. For example, no one of the occurrences in the Fourth Gospel follows any close Synoptic parallel, and verbal dependence

[365]

JESUS—A NEW BIOGRAPHY

It was far easier for Christians in the latter half of the first century to designate Jesus "Son of Man" than it would have been for him

---

upon any other early source is quite improbable. In Matthew and Luke the title stands, not only in sections taken from common sources, but also in material peculiar to each evangelist where dependence upon any primitive tradition is sometimes very doubtful.

In Matthew, with only one exception, all of the Marcan occurrences are reproduced (Matt. 9:6; 12:8; 16:27; 17:9, 12, 22; 20:18, 28; 24:30; 26:24 [*bis*], 45, 64). Instead of Mark's statement that the Son of Man must suffer (8:31), Matt. 16:21 says that "Jesus" began to show his disciples that "he" must suffer. But Matt. 16:13 contains "Son of Man" where it does not stand in Mark's parallel, probably taking it from Mark 8:31, so that Matthew virtually reproduces every Marcan occurrence. In using non-Marcan source material, Matthew and Luke agree seven times (Matt. 8:20; 11:19; 12:32, 40; 24:27, 37, 44; Luke 9:58; 7:34; 12:10; 11:30; 17:24, 26; 12:40). Twice Matthew has the personal pronoun where Luke has "Son of Man" (Matt. 5:11; Luke 6:22; Matt. 10:32; Luke 12:8). One might think Luke to be secondary here, since Matthew so uniformly preserved the title in Mark; yet it may be urged that the third evangelist shows somewhat less fondness for the expression, having it only twenty-five times as against Matthew's thirty times, and copying only nine of Mark's fourteen instances, and so would be less apt to add it to his source here. Moreover, in Matthew the change to the pronoun may have been intended to make it perfectly plain that Jesus was speaking about himself and not about someone else. Which form is the more original cannot now be positively determined. But it is perfectly evident, in general, that Matthew's custom was to preserve "Son of Man" as found in the sources. And this is not all. This evangelist is manifestly inclined to use the title on his own account. In one

THE RELIGION JESUS LIVED

in his own lifetime so to style himself. In the
Aramaic speech of his native land, and with the
scriptural background of Ezekiel, the Psalms

---

instance where the source seems to be non-Marcan (Matt. 24:39;
Luke 17:27), "Son of Man" stands in Matthew only; yet here we
cannot say positively whether Matthew or Luke is the more
original. But in five instances (Matt. 16:13, 28; 19:28; 24:30a;
26:2) the use of the title is not supported by the Marcan parallels;
and since Luke agrees with Mark at these points, probably the first
evangelist is personally responsible for the additions. In four more
passages the term appears in material peculiar to Matthew (10:23;
13:37, 41; 25:31) and is not likely to have come from an early
source. Therefore we have no reason to suppose that this evangelist slavishly copied "Son of Man" from earlier documents. It did
stand in his sources, but he also used it on his own account, assuming, so far as we have any intimation in the narrative, that
the term would be perfectly intelligible to all Christian readers.

The Lucan data yield similar results. "Son of Man" is reproduced from Mark nine times (5:24; 6:5; 9:22, 26, 44; 18:31;
21:27; 22:22, 69). While it thus appears that five of Mark's passages (9:9, 12; 10:45; 14:21b, 41) are omitted, it will be seen upon
closer observation that these omissions cannot be charged to any
bias against the mere title. Sometimes the whole Marcan paragraph has been left out; at other times only a verse is omitted, or
its phraseology is freely recast either to meet some editorial interest or under the influence of a non-Marcan source. In general
Luke copies Mark's "Son of Man," but in no blind and slavish
fashion; and twice the term is introduced into Mark's narrative,
perhaps on the third evangelist's own initiative (Luke 22:48;
24:7). As noted above, when Matthew and Luke vary in their
use of non-Marcan material, the original reading of the source
must remain largely a matter of conjecture; but seven parallels
between Matthew and Luke show the existence of non-Marcan

[367]

and Daniel, if not also the Similitudes of Enoch, at his disposal, Jesus might readily have employed this collocation of words. The Semitic

---

source material in which "Son of Man" seems to have been as characteristic as it was in Mark. If we were entirely dependent upon Matthew and Luke for a knowledge of the Marcan usage, only eight instances could be fixed upon with approximate certainty (2:10, 28; 8:38; 9:31; 10:33; 13:26; 14:21a, 62). So we may fairly infer that non-Marcan tradition employed the term with greater frequency than the gospels now attest. Of the remaining five instances in sections peculiar to Luke (17:22, 30; 18:8; 19:10; 21:36), it is not possible to affirm with absolute certainty that they were or were not derived from a source. "Son of Man" seems to be as much an integral part of the original in Luke 17:22, 30, as in Luke 17:24, 26, which chance to be attested in another setting in Matthew (24:27, 37). It may be a mere accident that Matthew fails to attest also verses 22 and 30 of Luke; at such times absence from Matthew is not a sufficient criterion for determining the limits of a source. There is still less to guide us in judging of the origin of the remaining passages. Luke 19:10 may be an echo from the previous paragraph in Mark (10:45), but of course if the third evangelist was capable of independently inserting "Son of Man" into the Marcan narrative we must allow him the same freedom in dealing with other sources. Taken altogether, the Lucan usage is of the same free and natural type as the Matthean.

While the term "Son of Man" is especially characteristic of the sources used by both the first and the third evangelists, it does not appear to have been for them either an incomprehensible or a foreign term. They alike employ it only in words of Jesus, but this is not done unwittingly, nor is the term forced upon them by the mechanical use of documents. It is part of the current religious vocabulary in the Christian communities of the day for each of the four evangelists.

tongue, whether Hebrew or Aramaic, framed the expression "son of man" as easily as English says "mankind" (literally, "man's child") or German *Menschenkind*—and with the same generic meaning. But, of course, no one in his right mind goes about calling himself "the mankind," "the human race." The assumption that Jesus had put himself forward as the idealized epitome of humanity was a happy discovery of later theologians, but it is without historical justification.

If the new preacher from Nazareth used the expression "son of man," either it was in an impersonal sense, meaning mankind in general, humanity, or else he appropriated a technical term already in vogue. Perhaps the phrase had become conventionalized on the basis of its occurrence in Daniel to describe the new Israel, a figure "like unto a son of man," and its more specific titular usage in I Enoch to designate that individual existing in the form of man whom God had selected to establish the new order. Both John the Baptist and Jesus, if familiar with the relevant passages in I Enoch, might have spoken of the coming of the Son of Man in connection with the day of judgment and the inauguration of the new age. Nevertheless this

[369]

terminology cannot have been widely current, for even the majority of the apocalyptists among Jesus' contemporaries looked directly to God, rather than to any intermediary heavenly being, for the establishment of the Kingdom. Yet "Son of Man" if used in this setting would have been a perfectly intelligible expression.

Even had Jesus been sufficiently familiar with the imagery of Daniel and I Enoch, to speak of the Son of Man in connection with the institution of the Kingdom, we are not at liberty to infer immediately that he would apply the phrase to himself. Indeed it would still be very difficult if not impossible to imagine that he could have so designated himself. The Son of Man in Jewish apocalyptic speculation was not to appear on earth until the day of judgment. In the meantime he resided with God in the heavens. Ancient seers had seen him there enthroned in state awaiting the moment for his triumphant descent to earth. In this imagery where would Jesus find any suggestion of likeness to himself? He had been a Galilean artisan before he became God's chosen herald of repentance, while at that very moment the apocalyptic figure called "Son of Man" was in heaven awaiting the opportunity to discharge his messianic functions. How was it possible for Jesus to imagine that the present occupant of that exalted office should be dispossessed in order that the Nazarene reformer might assume the duties of that high functionary? Under these circumstances it is altogether improbable that Jesus had ever called himself the "Son of Man."

Whether Jesus spoke of the Son of Man in the third person is also open to question. Had he connected the coming of the Kingdom with the appearing of this apocalyptic figure after the model of the picture in Daniel and I Enoch, the disciples in later times might have found it much more difficult than they did to substitute their crucified leader for this already enthroned official. Probably this particular area of their apocalyptic imagery was still nebulous at the time of Jesus' death, and hence could be the more easily recast to meet their present necessities.

In the years following Jesus' death, revised definitions of the Kingdom soon came to be the order of the day among his surviving friends. That it should be established through catastrophic intervention continued to be a favorite opinion for upwards of a century. This traditional Jewish imagery not only survived in the Christian communities, but it was reaffirmed with new fervor. Suddenly, and in the not far distant future, the end of the present evil age was expected. In the meantime missionaries were busy announcing their gospel to all the nations. They made haste with their task, since the time that remained for them to work seemed likely to be brief. The difficulties they encountered only spurred them on all the more eagerly to accomplish their mission, while their new troubles seemed to indicate with greater clearness that they were now passing through that period of deepest darkness immediately to precede the dawn.

The most important Christian alteration made in the earlier Jewish eschatological hope was the introduction of the heaven-exalted Jesus into the office of apocalyptic Messiah. Previous to his death the friends of Jesus, including some of his closest disciples, had more or less vaguely expected that he would prove to be God's chosen leader to throw off the Roman yoke. They had been ready, on the slightest provocation, to identify him with the David-like type of messianic deliverer for whom the nationalists looked to inaugurate a successful revolt. But now that he had been crucified, had triumphed over death as they firmly believed, and had been exalted to the right hand of God in heaven, he had a new rôle to play. The disciples now became consistent eschatologists. Deviating from the main line of Jewish eschatological thinking, that portrayed God himself intervening to destroy his enemies and take up his abode among his redeemed people in the new age, they espoused the tendency that had already showed itself in Daniel and I Enoch to insert an intermediary messianic agent between God and his people. But for Christians this functionary was no pre-existent angelic figure. He was none other than their own beloved teacher who had been inducted into the office of the Son of Man. It was at this point that they made their most significant alteration in the current apocalyptic hope of the Jews.

Jesus was the new messianic deliverer who would presently appear to inaugurate the new age. Jewish descriptions of the Kingdom had now to be revised in some detail to fit the new Christian imagery. But its exponents did not pretend to make the necessary changes exclusively on their own responsibility. When they reported Jesus' teaching about the Kingdom, they soon discovered seemingly clear evidences that he too had entertained the very notions now so highly prized by themselves. They sincerely admitted that during their former personal association with him they had not entertained these new convictions. But this fact was not thought to invalidate their later conclusions. They assumed that Jesus himself had held their present opinions but for some mysterious reason must temporarily have veiled his thoughts from his contemporaries. It was their duty now to draw aside the veil. Before many years had passed they were able, with complete satisfaction, to recall supposed words of his from which it seemed absolutely certain that he had designated himself "Messiah" and had predicted his future descent from heaven as apocalyptic Son of Man.

For Jesus himself to have made the specific revisions of Jewish messianic thinking that were effected by the disciples, would have been a glaring anachronism. He would have had to anticipate an extended series of events whose historical emergence belongs exclusively to the subsequent experiences of the disciples. In the light of their later concern with his crucifixion, reappearances, resurrection, heavenly exaltation, and induction into the office of Messiah, the motives which had inspired them to revise current Jew-

[374]

ish imagery are readily discerned. They had inherited from his lifetime memories of a hope that he might prove to be the deliverer of his people from the Romans. They had been powerfully impressed by his dynamic individuality during the days of personal association with him. Doubtless, also, they had distinct recollections of his own warnings regarding the impending day of judgment. Then came the shock of the crucifixion, followed by those remarkable visions of Jesus which Peter and some others experienced on different occasions.[1] Out of this confused mass of heritages, memories, and emotions, the new Christian messianic faith was born. Here cause and effect stand related in a readily comprehendable sequence, even though it may now be impossible to recover precisely every step in the psychological and historical process.

When one ascribes to Jesus the full-blown messianic beliefs of the Synoptic writers, or even of Mark, as has commonly been done by a well-known group of modern scholars, one must presuppose that Jesus had anticipated in imagination the process of thought that the disciples later accomplished only in retrospect. The series

[1] I Cor. 15:5-8 is the earliest and fullest list of appearances.

of events that led them to their convictions had
not been a part of Jesus' own life-history. To
say that he must have predicted resurrection, reappearances, and exaltation to messiahship, else
the disciples would have had no sufficient in-
centives for their later confidence, is specious
reasoning. The ultimate problem is to discover
any incentive that would have prompted him to
anticipate their later way of thinking. If he,
during the days of his public ministry, had entertained the belief that he was to be the official
apocalyptic Messiah to usher in the Kingdom,
whence had he derived this notion? What phase
of his own experience could have inspired any
such opinion? Even in the presence of threatening death the task of preparing Israel for the day
when God would deliver his people was one of
sufficient magnitude to satisfy any prophet's
ambition. The assumption that Jesus, even
when confronted by the cross, would seek to
classify himself according to a messianic cate-
gory is in reality a begging of the whole question
by reading into his mind that interest in drama-
tization and officialization so dear to the disciples in the gospel-making age.

In the period following the crucifixion the
disciples were, both historically and psychologi-

cally, far more abundantly supplied with chris-
tological stimuli than ever Jesus had been. His
hope, like that of large numbers of his contemporaries, had fixed itself on God who would himself both judge and redeem the people of his
choice. The traditional messianic figure of Judaism, essentially a glorified Davidic prince, had
quite completely faded out of Jesus' landscape,
except as zealous revolutionists of the day might
claim to have discovered him in the person of
some promising leader of an uprising against
Rome. But Jesus, along with others who leaned
hard toward apocalypticism, was more interested in God and the Kingdom than in creating
a new messianic official. God was the only Messiah they needed in the "world to come." They
awaited the revelation of his salvation, not the
advent of a new savior. It remained for Christianity to invest the figure of a new transcendental Messiah with real popularity in the person
of the risen and glorified Jesus. This development was intimately bound up with the religious
history of the disciples during the days following
the crucifixion, but it had been no part of the
personal religion of Jesus. Messianic self-interpretation had not concerned him. His energies
had been consecrated to the task of prepar-

[377]

ing his fellow-Jews for membership in the
Kingdom.[1]

IV

Lively interest in official self-appraisal had
been quite foreign to the genius of Jesus' personal religion, and the performance of a miracle
of healing or exorcism by appeal to divine power
had been only incidental to his life of absolute
devotion to the will of God. No true prophet
was ever an adorable hero to himself, however
ardently he might be admired by his disciples.
He was God's man and had no time or taste for
vaunting self-esteem. Self-abasement was the
only garment that he wore with becoming grace,
although as spokesman for God he possessed a
self-assurance that knew no limitations save
those set by the decrees of heaven.

The outstanding feature of Jesus' religion
was the prophet's characteristic awareness of the
presence of God. Jesus did not formulate his experience in a philosophical dogma, as a Stoic
might have done, by affirming that in God he
lived, moved, and had his being; but he drew a
full measure of satisfaction from the conscious-

[1] This opinion has been stated somewhat more briefly in my
paper on "the Alleged Messianic Consciousness of Jesus," *Journal
of Biblical Literature*, XLVI (1927), 1–19.

ness of God's immediate concern for everything connected with his life. The relation was vividly real and personal. While this experience of fellowship was in the nature of privilege, at the same time it aroused a keen sense of obligation. To know God in any such intimate fashion meant not only a consciousness of his presence but also a knowledge of his holiness and his displeasure with the ordinary conduct of humanity. The sensitive soul that was dominated by the will of the Almighty inevitably reflected in its own life the feelings which God himself was supposed to entertain toward mankind. Jesus was aware, not simply of the existence and character of God; he felt the very emotions of the Deity throbbing through his own soul.

The religion that Jesus lived, like that of any true Israelite of his age, rested upon a thoroughgoing supernaturalism. One's personal experiences with Satan and his demonic kindred were taken to be just as real as one's experiences with God. The evil powers that preyed upon mortals were everywhere in evidence producing misfortunes, sickness, and death. Jesus would have men follow his example and declare themselves wholly on the side of God in the great struggle for deliverance from Satan. From the moment of baptism Jesus had possessed a sense of complete release from the power of demons. But the fact that he no longer feared Satan, because he now felt himself to be wholly under the control of God, only heightened his sensitiveness to the presence in the life about him of demonic forces in full operation.

In the great struggle raging at the moment between the powers of good and evil, Jesus was acutely conscious of taking sides with God and humanity. He stood wholly on the side of the good, and yet he remained in close contact with the present evil world. To live religiously was to be an ardent participant in the conflict. This interpretation of one's duty meant a life of high emotional tension. At one moment feeling might be inspired by joyous trust in the love and power of the Almighty to protect the righteous, or at another moment it might burst out in flaming indignation against sinners. Just as the prophets of old, representing a righteous God in the presence of a sinful people, were irresistibly driven to condemn the wickedness of their day, so Jesus felt impelled by heaven to utter his protest against all unrighteousness. Like ancient preachers, he had been called and equipped by God for this task. It was his duty, as it had been theirs, to root out wickedness wherever it might be found. When the emotion of disapproval welled up in his soul, he pronounced his verdict of condemnation irrespective of caste or custom. He could upbraid a religious leader, or hurl defiance at a Herod, or violently denounce conduct that seemed to him a desecration of the sacred precincts of the temple.

Inspired prophets never hesitated to act precipitously. Cool calculation of any results that might be expected to follow a particular line of conduct, and the weighing of advantages or disadvantages to issue from the same, was never characteristic of their procedure. They acted on impulse, on divine impulsion from within their own being, which for them was identical with a pure conscience. Never for a moment could they entertain the thought of a compromise with this inner voice. Its promptings were absolute imperatives. Having acted as God's men should act, the consequences were left to take care of themselves. Results that ordinary men might call calamities were, from the prophetic point of view, mere incidents of minor import in God's ordering of history. Whether a course of action led the individual to a crown or to a cross was of slight moment in comparison with making cer-

[381]

tain that everything had been done in conformity with the will of heaven. A reformer less thoroughly dominated than Jesus was by a sense of the divine call, might have been more moderate, more calculating, and more worldly wise, as ordinary judgments go, in his dealings with the religious and political authorities of his day. But this never could have been Jesus' way of living.

In the course of his religious career various types of experience beat upon the sensitive soul of Jesus. In spite of his knowledge that older prophets had experienced disappointment in the pursuit of their task, undoubtedly at the beginning of his career he felt hopeful of success. Each new prophet was entitled to believe that at last the moment had arrived when God's messenger would be heeded. But Jesus, like his predecessors, encountered sad disappointments. One could not pass from emotions of high hope to those of defeat or despair, through the course of days filled with conscientious endeavor, without the experience leaving some very pronounced scars upon the soul. To be convinced that the message was not man's own creation, but was verily God's summons, only made its rejection all the more amazing. In this fluctuation of emotions, the prophet had his moments of discouragement and anxiety, whose vividness was only heightened by the fact that at the next instant he might reverse the experience by rising to the very crest of assurance in the power of God. God might lift him up to the dome of heaven, or might let him sink to the bottom of the abyss, according to the divine good pleasure. In distress of mind Jesus might agonize in prayer through a night in Gethsemane, or when racked by pain on the cross might seem to despair of the divine protection. But such moments of emotional depression were the normal counterpart of those other moments of assurance—a baptismal or a transfiguration incident—experienced from time to time in the course of his career.

Although continually aware of the overshadowing presence of the Almighty, Jesus was not unappreciative of the opportunities open to the individual spirit for the cultivation through its own efforts of worthy religious living. Whether he would have said that in his own personal career he had first made choice of God or that God had first made choice of him, certainly he never minimized the importance for religion of his own conscious attitude toward Deity. The extent and manner of his personal devotions, through prayer or other forms of worship, have been all too generally lost from view in the present Christian records. Disciples who were chiefly engaged in the task of persuading their fellows to revere the Christ of faith were not prone to lay stress upon any memories of Jesus' own devotional life. They told of significant occasions when he had engaged in prayer, but the number is all too few. When they reported his visits to the synagogues they were interested in providing an opportunity to display his authority as teacher or miracle-worker, and any concern with worshipful activity on his own part dropped largely out of sight. Likewise, his visits to the temple seemed to the evangelists to have been designed for purposes of self-assertion rather than for personal religious satisfaction. That Jesus would go up to the temple, celebrate the feasts, and partake of the Passover meal, as religious acts for the benefit of his own soul, represents a side of his career that the later disciples were scarcely able to appreciate.

At the very core of his religion was Jesus' feeling of personal relation to God, the Heavenly Father. He knew God, as other Israelites did, to be the God of the universe, the God of history, and the God of his chosen people. He knew him, not only through the manifestations of his will in the Scriptures and in the religious institutions of Judaism, but above all through that experience which had come to him at the beginning of his public career. With peculiar vividness at that moment the Deity became a new personal factor in the religious life of Jesus as an individual. In this relationship he was a God of righteousness and of love, for whose service Jesus forsook family, home, and trade to pursue the prophetic task.

There is still another focus about which the religious experience of Jesus revolved. This was his sense of obligation to his fellow-men. If he felt himself completely consecrated to the Deity, it was to the end that God might use him in the service of humanity. To effect a larger measure of righteous living among men was the task to which every prophet was summoned. It would be an unwarranted modernizing of his thinking to say that Jesus felt himself to be supremely a servant of humanity, but no appreciation of him is adequate if it fails to recognize his willingness to spend and be spent without reserve for the good of his fellow-men. This self-giving attitude was an essential aspect of his religion, although he himself might have defined it simply as a phase of his duty toward God. It was God's

[385]

will that men should be helped in the attainment of righteousness, and Jesus found keen personal satisfaction in giving himself unreservedly to this cause.

The prophet lived in a relation to God that was essentially a mystical experience. But it was not the type of mysticism that evaporated in an orgy of emotions. There was a wealth of feeling in the prophetic experience, but it was of the sort that gave to life a mighty ethical and spiritual drive. Jesus did not lose himself in God, as though the emotion were an end in itself. On the contrary, the divine seizure was for the sake of increasing righteousness in the world and contributing to human welfare. Its end was to be the establishment of the Kingdom. Yet Jesus was no maker of programs, no framer of agenda to be acted on by individuals or assemblies through all time to come. Nor was he a creator of moral or religious credenda once for all delivered to his followers. His religion struck its roots more deeply into the life of the soul—a soul that enjoyed perpetual communion with God its Father. Opinions and deeds, to be of value, must be the expressions of a pure heart. Make the tree itself good and the fruits thereof would be of proper quality.

THE RELIGION JESUS LIVED

For Jesus, who felt himself wholly in the grip of the Almighty, religion was essentially an experiential affair rooted in the spiritual impulses of the inner life. Deeds were performed and words were spoken out of the abundance of the heart. He who urged others to scrutinize their motives and sanctify their aspirations, was himself a living example of the individual whose piety springs forth spontaneously from the depths of his being.

CHAPTER VIII
THE RELIGION JESUS TAUGHT

JESUS thought himself an approved spokesman for God, but not a traditional Jewish
pedagogue. Although he was a vigorous
preacher, who delivered a forceful message,
teaching in the professional sense was not his
chosen task. To represent him after the model
of a Shammai, a Hillel, or a Gamaliel is to misin-
terpret his distinctive type of activity; while to
style him "rabbi" is quite misleading. Even had
this honorable designation been current in the
Judaism of the time, undoubtedly Jesus would
have repudiated any application of the title to
himself. Only with reserve may one call Jesus
"teacher," and when he is called "preacher" the
prophetic character of his utterances have always to be borne in mind.[1]

[1] "Teacher" (διδάσκαλος) had come to be a recognized title for
Jesus within those Christian circles represented by the gospel
writers, though sometimes they strained after a more archaic form
of expression. This is true particularly of the Fourth Gospel, where

[388]

THE RELIGION JESUS TAUGHT

The characteristics that had most forcibly impressed the close friends of Jesus had been the dynamic quality of his personality and his prophet-like abandon to the cause of God. His words were the expression of emotions and convictions forged out of tremendously vital personal experiences. The prophet was entitled to speak with authority, for he believed himself to

---

ῥαββεί is introduced eight times (1:38, 49; 3:2, 26; 4:31; 6:25; 9:2; 11:8). There is a similar inclination in Mark (9:5; 10:51; 11:21; 14:45), although διδάσκαλος is commonly used as the title for Jesus in this gospel. In Luke ῥαββεί never appears, and in Matthew also the Marcan ῥαββεί is changed to κύριε (Mark 9:5; 10:51), or is omitted (Mark 11:21). Only once is it retained (Mark 14:45; Matt. 26:25, 49). But the most conspicuous occurrence of ῥαββεί in Matthew is in a paragraph enlarging upon the Marcan account of Jesus' controversy with the Pharisees who are said to like the honorable title ῥαββεί which the disciples are to avoid among themselves since "one is your διδάσκαλος" (Matt. 23:7 f.). For the author of Matthew "rabbi" is an ancient and honorable designation which Jesus alone is entitled to bear and the Greek equivalent of which is διδάσκαλος. The designation has a formal and official connotation, elevating Jesus to a position of unique dignity in relation to the "brethren." Thus the evangelist has pushed back into Jesus' lifetime a professional title that was now especially significant for Christians carrying on missionary work in rivalry with contemporary Jewish teachers called "rabbis," and it was assumed that this terminology had already been current among Jews of Palestine in Jesus' own day. But the assumption was unwarranted. Neither Shammai nor Hillel, the two most noted teachers at the beginning of the Christian Era, nor any one of

[389]

be not simply the creator of a new message, but
the medium through whom God was declaring
anew his will to man. One could not easily forget
the words of a prophet. His impassioned utterances challenged attention, whether they awakened the admiration or inspired the hatred of his
hearers. It goes without saying that the message
of Jesus would be remembered. As a matter of

their contemporaries, was called "rabbi." The first teacher to be
distinguished by a title was Hillel's son (or grandson) Gamaliel,
an older contemporary of Paul (Acts 5:34; 22:3), who was designated "rabban," as were certain other pupils of Hillel. In the next
generation the customary form of title became "rabbi," although
Hillel's descendant Gamaliel III, who belongs to the first half of
the third century, still received the title "rabban." But his more
distinguished father Jehudah ha-Nasi was known simply as "rabbi," often without mention of his name. The great religious leader
who reorganized Jewish life at Jabneh after the destruction of the
temple by the Romans in 70 A.D. was a "rabban" but his disciples
were "rabbis," according to *Aboth* II, 10: "Rabban Johanan ben
Zakkai had five disciples, namely, Rabbi Eli'ezer ben Horqenos,
Rabbi Jehoshua 'ben Hananja', Rabbi Jose ha-Kohen, Rabbi
Sime'on ben Nathan'el, and Rabbi El'azar ben 'Arach." On the
contrary, Hanina ben Dosa, a distinguished contemporary of
Johanan ben Zakkai, was called "rabbi." In practice the transition
was effected gradually, but "rabbi" as an official title for the religious teacher did not come into vogue among the Jews until the
latter part of the first century A.D. It was not current in the time of
Jesus and was not a title by which he is likely to have been addressed either by disciples or by outsiders. See also H. L. Strack,
Einleitung in Talmud und Midrasch (5. Aufl., München, 1921), p.
120, n. 1.

fact, ultimately it came to constitute one of the most highly prized heritages left by him to posterity.

I

The initial stages in the process of remembering and recording the teaching of Jesus can only be conjectured. Those who had been deeply impressed by his prophetic enthusiasm and the vigor of his personality might not have been primarily interested in gathering and preserving the content of his message. Admirers who had been induced by his picturesque activity to hope that he was God's chosen leader to deliver Israel from bondage to the Romans had been quite ready to heroize him even during his lifetime. Although the crucifixion must have temporarily dampened their ardor, the resurrection appearances offered a new stimulus to their hopes. While it was no longer possible to assign Jesus the duties of a prospective Davidic Messiah who would lead a successful revolt against Rome, his future victory could now be visualized in even more glorious fashion by using the imagery of apocalypticism. He was still the prospective deliverer who by his release from Sheol and ascent to heaven had been elevated to the dignity of the transcendental Son of Man. Suddenly and in the near future he would descend to earth clothed with divine power as God's agent to inaugurate a new messianic age.

One can hardly assume that those admirers of Jesus who now assembled to await his return would make it their first interest to codify and record in permanent form the story of their hero's teaching. For the moment at least they would be chiefly concerned to affirm his official dignity and to persuade their acquaintances that he was worthy of the faith which they now placed in him. They might, indeed, seek to recall words spoken about himself, if any such were available, that would corroborate their new views regarding his present dignity or his future program of action. They would have been eager to remember any part of his message suitable for persuading their kinsmen that he was worthy of the confidence now placed in him by his surviving admirers. But to record his words simply for the purpose of preserving a body of religious teaching that might furnish moral and spiritual guidance to the individual can hardly have been a matter of primary interest to those who were momentarily awaiting the return of Jesus in apocalyptic glory. Belief in him as a coming savior was more important than memory of a religious message that he had delivered to a previous generation.

Yet there were some surviving friends of the martyred prophet who must very early have concerned themselves with recalling things he had said, quite apart from any references to himself and his claims to official dignity. The story of "things said" had become a distinct and clearly recognized body of Christian tradition before the present gospels were composed.[1] In fact this type of tradition is one of the oldest and best accredited elements in the present records. It represents Jesus as speaking not about his claims to messianic honors, but rather about the requirements for a worthy religious life on the part of his hearers. They are exhorted to forsake their sins, to cleanse their hearts, to purify their motives, and to aim at a perfection like that which they ascribe to God himself. The Heavenly Father, and he only, is the proper object of their reverence; while a life of genuine fellowship with him should be the goal of their striving. There is not a single syllable about Jesus as a prospective Davidic prince to overthrow the rule of Rome, nor is there anything to imply that

[1] See above p. 341; also pp. 30–33 and pp. 90–94 for the distinctive character and content of this material.

he was a candidate for apocalyptic messianic honors.

It has long been a familiar fact to students of the gospels that the "Logia" source materials are singularly lacking in references to the closing scenes of Jesus' life. This body of tradition knows nothing of any words of his about the prospect of arrest, trial, crucifixion, and subsequent appearances to the disciples. It is not lacking, however, in intimations that Jesus himself had warned his hearers of impending calamity for which they should prepare by newly consecrating themselves to God. Since the great and terrible day of judgment was at hand, it behooved all Israelites to increase the quality of their righteousness. This end could be accomplished by living as Jesus had advised men to live. Until the day when God inaugurates the Kingdom, the message of the prophet is to be heralded abroad by his disciples in order that not only they who have heard him in person but all of their kinsmen may profit by his utterances and thereby be prepared for momentous events in the near future.

Were there originally two distinct groups of Jesus' surviving friends, one interested more particularly to preserve the prophet's message in order that he might continue to serve the cause of God and man, even though he had himself passed off the scene, while the other group was devoted more especially to declaring its new appreciation of the prophet's personality and its expectation of his early return in apocalyptic triumph? Some such diversity of interest among the disciples of Jesus during the years immediately following the crucifixion is easily imaginable. The group that stressed the heroic in connection with his memory was destined to dominate in the future history of the new movement, particularly when it became a missionary enterprise among Gentiles. But in Palestine the survival of a band of disciples whose chief reason for further activity would be a concern to preserve the memory of their master's message is entirely in accord with historical probability.

It was no unusual event among the Hebrew people for followers of a prophet to assume the responsibility of preserving his words to benefit their contemporaries and serve the cause of righteousness. Such disciples had no thought of officializing or deifying the founder of their movement. Their one duty was to perpetuate the message God had delivered through the prophet. In this way the memory of the older prophets had become a spiritual therapeutic for successive generations of Jews. Probably motives of essentially the same sort had prompted the members of the so-called "Zadokite" sect to continue their movement for reform. Doubtless the disciples of John the Baptist were similarly motivated in perpetuating their master's memory. That Jesus would have followers of a similar temper is entirely probable. These were men who had not shared the earlier hope of a Peter that Jesus would institute a revolution against Rome, nor had they participated in the vivid experiences that had resulted in the resurrection faith on which Peter and others now based their confidence in an early return of Jesus. These less ardent messianists would hardly have rushed up to Jerusalem on the occasion of the first Pentecost following the crucifixion. They were not aflame with the expectation, as were Peter and his associates, that at any moment Jesus might descend to the temple to set up the Kingdom in accordance with the revised eschatological hope.[1]

---

[1] That the divergent elements in Synoptic tradition can be explained only by assuming the existence of two or more "schools" or *loci* within primitive Jewish Christianity from which tradition emanated, is a conviction that has been growing in recent years. K. Lake (*The Stewardship of Faith* [New York, 1914]) thinks more account should be taken of a surviving Galilean group of disciples,

THE RELIGION JESUS TAUGHT

Whatever may have been the actual circumstances prompting certain survivors of Jesus to remember "things said" and others to rehearse "things done," by the time the Synoptic Gospels arose the two lines of interest had been liberally fused. Or, perhaps one ought rather to say, the former had been absorbed by the latter. As months and years passed without catastrophic intervention by the heavenly Christ, Christian messianists found increasing use for didactic ma-

---

not connected with the Jerusalem community (pp. 97 f.). E. Meyer (*Ursprung und Anfänge des Christentums* [Berlin, 1921], distinguishes even in Mark a *Jüngerquelle* (in fact two Jüngerquellen) and a *Zwölfquelle*, the one representing an interest in Jesus' relations with the crowds about him and the other being concerned more specifically with his relation to the limited apostolic group (I, 133–47). Adopting a similar distinction, R. Schütz (*Apostel und Jünger* [Giessen, 1921]) would make the Galilean disciples rather than the apostolic community in Jerusalem the real link between Jesus and Paul, because it was these Galilean friends of Jesus who had perpetuated his spiritual freedom from the Law. Thus true spiritual religion proceeded from Jesus through the Galilean community to Paul and Luther—an unfortunate apologetic twist to give an otherwise suggestive hypothesis (pp. 94–118). The fact that Paul has so little to say about the teaching of Jesus shows that he, like the author of Acts (see above pp. 79–81) represents the type of interest that we assume to have been characteristic of the Jerusalem group rather than of surviving disciples in Galilee. Paul and the author of Acts were concerned not with the earthly Jesus as the teacher of religion, but with the crucified hero as an object of faith.

terials. The missionary preaching now needed to enrich itself by recalling words that Jesus had spoken in summoning his hearers to a new life of holiness. Enlarging Christian communities also needed increasingly the stimulus of Jesus' mandates to discipline their own members in the way of worthy religious living. Thus memory of Jesus' message, preserving his personal religious ideals, found a permanent place in the new movement, although he had now become pre-eminently an object of reverence on the part of disciples. Henceforth Christianity was to be both the religion of Jesus and the religion about Jesus.

The accounts of Jesus' teaching that have survived in the present gospels represent a gradual accumulation of tradition within communities of believers residing in different places about the Mediterranean during the latter part of the first century. Some of these groups were composed of converted Jews, others were of gentile ancestry, while still others had a mixed membership. But since the didactic motive was notably prominent in the formation of Jewish religious tradition, while among Gentiles heroic interests were more lively, one might infer that Jesus in the capacity of teacher had at the outset be-.

longed specifically to Jewish Christianity. At least it may be confidently affirmed that the effort to recover his religious message was first made within a primitive Jewish setting.

Not only is it true that the didactic interest in religion is eminently a Jewish characteristic, but it is also apparent that at least some portions of the teaching of Jesus as recorded in our present gospels had originally circulated in the Aramaic speech of his own Palestinian environment. A Christian author of the second century informed his Greek kinsmen of a tradition to the effect that the apostle Matthew had composed the sayings of the Lord in the Hebrew tongue—probably meaning Aramaic—and that each reader interpreted them as best he could. This tradition is now unverifiable, but even today there are scholars ready to defend not only the proposition that the earliest accounts of Jesus' teaching had been composed in Aramaic, but that one or more of our present gospels had originally been written in this language. Even the Fourth Gospel has lately found zealous defenders of its complete Semitic original. Very likely there were Jewish Christians living on gentile soil who could still write in Semitic during the last half of the first century. Certainly Paul

[399]

could have done so, but apparently he never did, although he taught Gentiles Aramaic expressions like *marana tha* (I Cor. 16:22). Greek only was appropriate for missionary literature, a fact that had been recognized long before by the Jews themselves. And as for strictly Palestinian Christians, it seems quite out of the question to assume that at any period in their history they ever could have been concerned to exhibit Jesus wholly in the fashion of any one of our present gospels.

That Palestinian Christian communities, or Jewish Christians beyond Palestine, had been accustomed once upon a time to repeat teachings of Jesus in their native tongue is a proposition so self-evident as to need no demonstration, and that some of this reported tradition would ultimately assume written form may also be taken for granted. But it is not at all safe to infer that words of Jesus are reported in strictly accurate fashion just because they had been passed on from one to another individual in the Aramaic language which Jesus himself had spoken. Philology renders history only doubtful service when it is advanced to prove that an item in tradition is valid because it happened to survive in one or another language used by the human race. The problem of historicity is not so easily solved. It matters little what tongue an individual or a group employs in the defense of a favorite cause. It was quite as possible for Aramaic-speaking Christians, as for those who used Greek, to supplement or even to distort reports of Jesus' message to meet issues of immediate concern to the new communities.

Even to argue for the validity of the gospel records on the ground of genuinely Palestinian allusions might easily prove misleading. There is indeed a preponderance of Palestinian color in all of the gospels, but undoubtedly there were literary artists within gentile Christendom quite capable of visualizing scenes on Palestinian soil. They may have been Christian Jews of the Diaspora, or even gentile converts who would easily become familiar through their reading of Scripture and their acquaintance with travelers, if not through their own journeys to the country, with characteristics of Palestinian life. Even in the most remote section of the Roman world Christians found Jews all about them. Their distinctive character was well known to Gentiles. Every synagogue was a center from which missionary propaganda spread the knowledge of Jewish religious customs all around the Mediterranean. Philo and Josephus, though today the best-known Jewish apologists of their time, were not the only mediators of Hebrew culture to the world at large. Knowledge of Palestinian life in gospel times could have been had also from the memoirs of Vespasian[1] or from the captives whom Titus carried off to grace his triumphal return from Judea. It would have been hardly more difficult for a Christian preacher in Rome than for one in Jerusalem itself to visualize a controversy between Jesus and his contemporaries over such topics as Sabbath observance or the law of clean and unclean meats. Perhaps outside of Jerusalem the incident could have been more vividly depicted just because in the gentile environment the problem was more acute. The very spirit of Judaism could be successfully reproduced and used as part of the scenery in which to set instructive incidents connected with the career of Jesus.

At the same time a reader of the gospels cannot fail to be impressed with the predominance of Palestinian coloring still pervading the gospel records of Jesus' message. This is most significant when it appears only incidentally and without reference to any problem under discussion.

[1] Josephus *Life*, 358.

THE RELIGION JESUS TAUGHT

It is a well-known fact that the expansion of the Christian movement in the years following the death of Jesus went on principally among people in the cities. The scenery with which these early missionaries were most familiar must have consisted of city walls, crowded streets, houses huddled together, shops and bazaars, and other distinctive features of urban life. Even at the outset the most conspicuous group of Jesus' disciples resides in Jerusalem, and one hears little or nothing about congregations elsewhere. That there were other churches is undoubtedly a fact, but they were the less influential communities. Next to Jerusalem, Damascus seemed to Saul the persecutor to be the most important center of the new cult. It early took root at Antioch in Syria, and in the years that followed spread rapidly to all important points around the Mediterranean. During the first century when tradition about Jesus was crystallizing into the present gospel records, the new religion was eminently a city movement. It gathered its adherents chiefly from people who were wandering about from place to place in pursuit of a livelihood. Its membership was composed of artisans, traders, and slaves who could hardly have subsisted at all outside of an urban community.

[403]

On the other hand it is quite impossible to imagine that urban Christianity could have created the vivid rural color characterizing the imagery in which Jesus phrased his message. It is true that he knew city life even in Palestine. His native village had been a suburb of the great city of Sepphoris, and Jerusalem must have been vividly portrayed to the imagination of every Jewish boy. Then, too, in the course of Jesus' activity he encountered at Capernaum and elsewhere situations that were essentially urban in character. There is no incongruity about his speaking in language that had been colored by contact with city life, but this fact sets off only the more conspicuously the rural characteristics still attaching to the language in which his teaching is preserved. Scenes are laid in the wide open spaces with their rain and their sunshine, their birds of the air and their flowers of the field, that tell mankind of the love and care of God. Jesus draws his illustrations richly from the rural life about him. He talks of the husbandman and his vineyards, of the farmer following the plow, of the cattle that graze on the countryside, of the growing grain and the troublesome weeds, of seed time and harvest, of the trees and the herbs, of the herdsman caring for his flocks, of the beasts of burden, asses and camels, all of which constitute undesigned evidences of verisimilitude.

II

It is much easier to assume that in the gospel picture of Jesus as teacher, one has history in purer form than in the accompanying portrayal of him as a hero. In the capacity of teacher he was pre-eminently a Jewish figure, while the hero was more suitable to gentile tastes. But this general statement of fact might easily prompt an erroneous conclusion. Even within Jewish Christian circles, whether in Palestine or in the Dispersion, from the very first certainly there were pragmatic influences at work calling for interpretation, revision, and supplementation of the teaching of Jesus. Neither use of the Aramaic speech, nor correct information on Palestinian physiography, nor even an accurate preservation of the varying scenery amid which Jesus had carried on his activity, insured a Christian preacher against transforming the message of his master into a word of authority that would bear specifically upon the immediate problem of the missionary's own day. Although Jesus remained still a teacher, he now spoke a message suited to the ear of the later Christian congregation, or de-

[405]

signed to stimulate outsiders to ally themselves with the new cause.

Gentiles also were capable of prizing the work of a teacher, notwithstanding their natural disposition toward the heroic aspect of religion. The earliest gentile converts to Christianity sometimes were individuals already familiar with the Jewish Scriptures as read in the synagogue services which they had been accustomed to attend. The didactic side of Judaism had made a strong appeal to many persons of this class, and thus the way had been prepared for an appreciation of Jesus in the rôle of teacher to take a place beside Moses and the prophets. Even had Gentiles been unacquainted with Judaism, they would not have been utterly unprepared for this procedure. The popularizing of Greek philosophy, particularly in the propaganda of the Stoics, had accustomed the Mediterranean world at large to seek wisdom from the ancients. Many Greeks were quite as ready to look for guidance to the teachings of Socrates or the words of a contemporary Stoic preacher, as were the Jews to draw upon Moses and their rabbis. Christians were not the first to ask Gentiles to prize the words of a teacher; nor may we assume that the missionaries, when addressing gentile audiences, remained uninfluenced by the temptation to make Jesus speak in the cadence of a contemporary Greek philosopher.

In both Jewish and gentile Christian circles there was the prevailing desire to have Jesus utter words of authority upon the issues of the hour. The preachers felt assured that his prevision must have comprehended the many new problems with which they were now confronted. They hopefully sought words of his relating to the organization of the community, the propriety and the methods of missionary propaganda, and every other new issue of moment. Since the main motive for rehearsing the message of Jesus was the propagation of the new cause now sacred to his memory, it inevitably followed that the selection of material, its arrangement, and its interpretation as worked out from time to time by different preachers and authors, should ultimately portray contemporary interests quite as fully as it preserved traditional elements of genuine historical value. If Jesus were to be a thoroughly efficient teacher for the people of a later day, his message had necessarily to be modernized.

Our gospels, it has been seen, are the result of an endeavor to make Christianity at home among Gentiles during the latter half of the first century. On a superficial reading it might seem a puzzling fact that Jesus is reported in so many divergent, if not indeed contradictory, moods. But in reality it is not astonishing that the complexity of Christianity should have been reflected in the words that Jesus was reported to have spoken. One preacher, because he himself would restrict his missionary activities to a Jewish circle, believed that Jesus had ordered the disciples to go neither into gentile territory nor to any city of the Samaritans (Matt. 10:5, 23). But another missionary with a broader outlook was equally convinced that Jesus had sponsored gentile Christianity and had commanded his followers to make disciples of all the nations (Matt. 28:19). These different attitudes sometimes filtered into the same gospel when later authors gathered up from floating tradition the fragmentary materials available for their new compositions. Thus it happens that in our present records we find, perhaps in about equal ratio, teachings of Jesus that are appropriate to his own immediate environment along with pronouncements of his upon subjects that first came to light in the latter half of the first century of Christianity's growth.

THE RELIGION JESUS TAUGHT

Not only the content of Jesus' message but the portrait of him as teacher was fashioned in accordance with Christianity's new needs. As the new religious movement standardized its didactic activities, Jesus approached more nearly to the figure of the rabbi and became less and less the spontaneous prophet of reform. Christendom institutionalised him. Gradually he lost those characteristics of dynamic personality that had operated so conspicuously during his own lifetime to win him friends and to stir up enemies. Now as the founder of Christianity he was the author of its new law, a second Moses, differing from the older lawgiver not in pedagogic technique but in heightened authority as a consequence of the official stamp of divine approval which God had placed upon him at the beginning of his career. He was also represented as a conventional seer who not only fulfilled all the predictions that had been made by the ancients but who himself had foretold the future with a more unerring vision than had been possessed by any of his predecessors. He was also painted as a sage whose words were more pregnant with wisdom than any that Solomon had ever uttered. After the model of Judaism the new religion now presented its founder in the

rôle of lawgiver, seer, and sage, but more excellent than any who had ever before appeared
among men.

In the process of transmission, the form of
Jesus' teaching was also extensively institutionalized. When leaders of the new Christian society
discoursed before their audiences in formal style
on the subjects most pertinent to the activities
of the community, it seemed fitting that Jesus
should be exhibited as the exemplary sermonizer
on topics of first-rate importance to these later
congregations. Now it was easily conceivable
that he should have preached sermons, and there
was a distinct disposition to gather up the fragmentary remains of his remembered sayings into
topical groupings to form longer discourses. For
each of the New Testament evangelists Jesus
had become an ideal sermonizer. The growth of
the Sermon on the Mount is an interesting illustration in point. From a discourse of less than
thirty verses, as reported in Luke, it has been expanded into an oration three chapters long in
Matthew. Even Mark's heroic figure ceased his
miracles long enough to deliver an open-air sermon in parables to a "very great multitude"
gathered beside the sea. On another occasion,
sitting on the Mount of Olives, Jesus discoursed

at similar length with a group of disciples on the question of the end of the world and the advent of the messianic age. The author of Luke made him a typical synagogue preacher in Nazareth at the very opening of his activity.

It was in the Gospels of Matthew and John, however, that Jesus' sermonic achievements received greatest attention. According to the former, early in the ministry of Jesus he set forth the new law of righteousness for the Christian society in the Sermon on the Mount (chaps. 5–7). Next, he delivered a discourse instructing his followers on the very practical subject of preparation for missionary work (chap. 10). Later, his address in parables, which was taken over into Matthew from Mark, was enlarged by the addition of several new examples all bearing upon the question of the nature of the present growing church (chap. 13). Again, Jesus delivered still another sermon dealing with the personal relations of disciples to one another and the regulation of life within the new religious community (chap. 18). The Christian polemic against Judaism was fortified by a discourse of Jesus in which he heaped up woes against the scribes and Pharisees (chap. 23). As in Mark and Luke, so in Matthew, Jesus delivered a

[411]

lengthy address on the subject of the end of the world and the coming of the Kingdom (chaps. 24 f.). In the Gospel of John he usually discoursed on new themes and in a more philosophical vein, but he was still the ideal sermonizer, whether it was an incident of alleged violation of the Sabbath that furnished the occasion for preaching on his own divine authority, or the assembling of an outdoor audience beside the Sea of Galilee that offered an opportunity to deliver an address on the bread of life. For each of the gospel writers Jesus was the ideal preacher whose example contemporary missionaries were striving to emulate.

Interest in standardizing other portions of Christian worship exercised a similarly hardening effect upon reported words of Jesus. He seemed to the disciples to have been not only the ideal sermonizer but also the model suppliant who had taught a proper prayer to be recited by the group when assembled for worship. It was distinctly a community prayer addressed to "Our" Father, and its opening petition expressed the hope of an early realization of the Kingdom. Even though the Christian rite of baptism was not known to have been practiced by Jesus himself, its observance in the later church was thought to be authenticated by words that he had spoken. He was discovered to have taught rules about fasting and alms-giving and to have given instructions regarding the use of the ancient Hebrew Scriptures in the new congregations. The principal religious meal of the new society was traced back to his words of formal institution: "Take, eat, this is my body. . . . . Drink ye all of it, for this is my blood of the covenant."

Before the end of the first century Christendom had extensively institutionalized the figure of Jesus the teacher. In this form of activity he had been an object of liberal manipulation effected with a view to serving pragmatic interests within the expanding life of the new society. He was no longer exhibited in the simple garb of his original prophetic career among his own kinsmen. The scenes had been shifted and he was made to wear new costumes. Parables used by him to clarify his message were tranformed into words of esoteric wisdom to be understood only by the few. Language expressive of his original independence of spirit and spontaneity of action now became new regulations for the conduct of religious life within the church where duties were to be discharged with a punctiliousness ex-

ceeding that of the scribes and Pharisees (Matt.
5:17–20). Sometimes the later Christian interpreter merely heightened an effect that had actually been intended by Jesus himself, but at
other times his original message was hidden be-
neath an artificiality and formality quite foreign to its genuine content.

To recover the message of Jesus we must return to the scenes of his own activity. Topics
that were of peculiar interest to the early Christian society in the days following his death must
give place to those matters that were of first importance among the Jews of Palestine at the
time of Jesus' public career. It is still possible,
from the gospel records and our acquaintance
with contemporary Judaism, to reconstruct with
a fair degree of certainty a picture of Jesus the
preacher in his own distinctive environment delivering his forceful utterances to those with
whom he came in contact. Happily, his words so
deeply imbedded themselves in the minds of his
followers that his message to his own generation
has been preserved with remarkable fidelity,
considering the powerful motives tending to effect the transformation of tradition within the
early church.

THE RELIGION JESUS TAUGHT

III

Today perhaps no phase of Jesus' life and work awakens keener interest than the question of what he actually taught. Formulations of his message have often been attempted and doubtless will be essayed over and over again for a long time to come. Not infrequently one is perplexed by the variety of modern reconstructions. Differences in the early Christian records themselves, and the diversified interests of Christians in the twentieth century, all combine to multiply the difficulties of the task in hand. Historical accuracy at this point is a very delicate problem.

The selection of topics under which to classify the content of Jesus' message may easily prove misleading. His disciples have ever been disposed to assume that the religious issues which seemed most important to them in their own day must have been matters upon which Jesus himself made authoritative pronouncements. Hence one is prone to classify Jesus' teaching under captions appropriate to later religious interests. Moreover, Protestantism in particular has quite generally identified true religion with correct theological indoctrination. Or, at least, the latter has been greatly stressed.

The chief task of a religious teacher is thought to be that of telling people what they ought to believe. Simply to concern one's self with moral precepts is to remain on the lower level of ethics and not to attain to the real heights of genuine religion. The latter must be fundamentally a matter of faith, of belief, of dogma. Where this conception prevails, an exposition of the teaching of Jesus takes the form of a systematic treatise in the field of theological speculation. One seeks to ascertain what Jesus taught about God, about man, about sin, about salvation, about atonement, and the like. But when we recall that Jesus lived and preached among Jews in Palestine nineteen hundred years ago, it can hardly seem appropriate to exhibit the content of his message under the characteristic chapter headings of a formal treatise on systematic theology. Its captions were not the topics that interested Jesus and his friends.

Perhaps even more seductive in modern times is the temptation to classify the teachings of Jesus according to those practical interests that are liveliest in the religion of our own time. We want to know what he taught about obligations to the church, or about civic and social duties; what he said about international relations; what

was his attitude toward war; what pronouncements he made on the problems of labor and
capital; and what his views were with respect to
duties toward God, toward men, toward our religious and political institutions, toward our own
bodies and our own spirits, and toward Jesus
himself. We would regard him as the one authoritative legislator who delivered a body of
instructions which, if not in detail at least in
germ, contains a solution for every issue that
might arise in future. Working on this presuppo-
sition, captions under which to classify the teachings of Jesus tend to parallel the chapter headings in a book on systematic ethics.

To one at all historically minded it ought to
be apparent at a glance that Jesus was neither a
dogmatic theologian nor a theoretical moralist.
He was no expounder of formal doctrine who
sought to elaborate a new system of dogma. Undoubtedly he possessed very clear religious opinions which he freely expressed, but they were so
deeply imbedded in his emotional life that they
were the subject matter of immediate affirmation rather than the theme of dialectic elaboration. Jesus also was an outstanding moral force
among the men of his generation, as he has been
all through the centuries wherever his memory

has survived. Manifestly he possessed convictions of conscience so strong that he was never in doubt as to what course of action to pursue in order to satisfy his inner demands for rectitude. Within this area of experience native impulse working from within left little or no opportunity for analytical statements of abstract principles or elaborate formulations of rules for conduct. One who would know the actual topics about which Jesus preached will not seek captions in a nineteenth-century textbook on dogmatic theology or in one on systematic ethics.

Jesus derived the subjects for stress in his teaching from his personal contacts and experiences in actual life. The religious heritages of his people and the critical conditions under which they were living in his own day were the objective data upon which he fixed attention. It was in this vital setting that he determined what for him seemed important, what insignificant. His problems were how to meet existing conditions, how to shape one's course of life in view of what might be expected in the near future, and how to make more contagious and convincing the type of conduct and the state of mind which Jesus himself had come to feel were necessary for the highest attainments in righteousness. Different individuals were differently moved by the convergence of contemporary events, but for Jesus, disciplined in the school of real life, a member of the artisan class who was one with the people of action in their common task of earning a livelihood, the present critical situation was to be met by action. Ever since the time of his contact with John the Baptist he had been convinced that divine intervention was at hand and that his own duty in the meantime was to call his contemporaries to repentance in preparation for membership in the coming Kingdom of Heaven.

Had Jesus been asked to analyze his teaching and specify therein the item of first importance in his own estimation, he might have said that formally at least it was his announcement of the imminence of the Kingdom of Heaven. What did he mean by the "Kingdom?"[1] Certainly he devoted more time to proclaiming its approach, to warning his contemporaries of the danger, and to persuading them to prepare for the event than he did to formulating a descriptive definition of its nature. In his setting perhaps no definition was needed. Everyone was familiar with the current Jewish imagery. Suddenly God would come to the rescue of his oppressed people. He

[1] See above p. 244, n. 1.

would institute judgment, not only against the Romans, but also against all sinners in Israel, and those who survived the day of testing would be rewarded by membership in the new theocratic régime.

Jesus would scarcely feel that the occasion demanded an elaborate restatement of the current eschatological hope, or a fresh defense of its validity. In earlier times it had been incumbent on advocates of eschatology to persuade Jews that the hope of salvation could properly be portrayed in this fashion, and in those days the doctrine had its needed apologists. But after it had accumulated more than a century of prestige, Jesus might well have thought it quite unnecessary to offer an argued defense of his faith. We should not expect to find him multiplying words to justify the propriety of apocalyptic expectations for the men of his generation. When adopting a type of imagery already familiar, the practical preacher needed merely to treat his theme selectively, dwelling on those features that seemed to him most vitally important at the moment.

As for the details of the apocalyptic program, it was always proper to introduce novelties or retouch older features in the picture. Yet it was not at all essential that this should be done. Anyone who announced an impending day of judgment, when God would descend from heaven to destroy the enemies of Israel and purge out sinners from among the Jews, reconstituting the righteous into a new theocratic nation, had struck the fundamental note of apocalypticism. The preacher might or might not speculate as to the day and hour when God would act. It might concern him little if at all as to whether God would appear in person or would send an angelic intermediary to inaugurate the new age. The literary representatives of eschatology often reveled in pictorial displays of apocalyptic fancy, but the prophetic reformer concentrated attention on effecting a change in the lives of people. One is not to deny eschatological thinking to Jesus on the ground that apparently he said little or nothing about times and seasons and similar details of apocalyptic imagery.

The eschatological hope was rich in the promise of rewards for the faithful. It could not have been otherwise in a new régime of heavenly bliss to be established on the initiative and by the very power of God himself. But not every apocalyptic seer indulged so freely in descriptions of the new Jerusalem as did the author of the New

Testament Book of Revelation. Nor was it inevitable that a herald of the new order should concern himself in detail with the prospective beatific state of its recipients. The expectation of reward would never be in doubt, and for those who were temperamentally disposed to dwell on the subject traditional imagery offered large satisfactions. But future rewards were not the chief phase of eschatology selected for emphasis in the preaching of Jesus. Evidently he assumed without question that every righteous individual would be suitably recompensed on the day of judgment, yet he stressed preparation rather than promise.

Jesus aimed to move his hearers to action. As a practical advocate of the eschatological hope, he issued a call to repentance. He sought immediate results in real life, and thus his mission was essentially reformatory. He made it his chief task to prepare men for entrance into the Kingdom. He was not especially concerned either to validate the eschatological hope or to elaborate its imagery. He employed indoctrination only as an aid to the motivation of conduct. He accepted without question forms of apocalyptic speculation already current and devoted his energies to the accomplishment of more vital ends. To impell his hearers to higher attainments in righteousness was his dominating ambition. Hence the features of eschatology to receive his chief attention were the threatening and the remedial.

Many earnest prophets in Israel had warned their contemporaries'of disasters ahead. However kind and long-suffering God might be, there surely would come a day of reckoning when sinners would be called to account. A holy God could not forever endure a sinful people. When the prophet's own experience and the signs of the times pointed to an early intervention of heaven to reverse the present evil course of events, the first duty that lay to the hand of a preacher was to summon his kinsmen to repentance and new consecration in preparation for the approaching day of judgment. This was the task of Jesus. The new age would break upon men suddenly, like a flash of lightning shooting across the whole expanse of the heavens in the twinkling of an eye. There would be no opportunity to perceive its gradual approach by observation and reckoning. While some were looking for premonitions in one quarter and others in another, it would overtake them quite unawares, instantly appearing in their very midst (Luke 17:22–37).

JESUS—A NEW BIOGRAPHY

It was not repentance in general, or in the abstract, that concerned the prophetic teacher, but an immediate reversal of conduct on the part of concrete individuals who must each forsake his sins and purify his heart in anticipation of the new and better day. The prophet is himself so thoroughly controlled by the verdict of his own disciplined conscience that his sensitive soul is deeply wounded by the more easy-going life of the society about him. The zeal of the older prophets had glowed with a white heat as they hurled their burning words of condemnation against princes, against priests, against the rich oppressors of the poor, and against the sinner in whatever station of life he might be found. In the name of God they threatened the nation with disaster and pronounced divine judgments upon both their political and their religious leaders. They employed every turn of speech that could be devised to impress their contemporaries with the menace of the present situation. Predictions of disaster seem to have been thought by them the most effective instrument that could be used for awakening the moral and spiritual sensibilities of their hearers.

When Jesus spoke of the Kingdom of Heaven, the fact of the present kingdom of the Romans cannot have been far from the mind of him and his hearers. No Jew of Palestine in the age of Tiberius could picture the coming Kingdom of God other than as a complete reversal of the present political status of the Hebrew people. But whether Jesus had predicted the overthrow of the Jewish nation, along with the destruction of Rome, in the same vivid manner in which the older prophets of doom had spoken against their own princes, is not at all certain. In the first place, it has to be remembered that the Jewish people no longer enjoyed political autonomy. Independence had been lost, although the nation still retained a measure of integrity under the foreign ruler. In the popular mind the present situation was not altogether unlike that which had prevailed in the period of the Exile. While Jesus certainly shared the feeling of racial solidarity that had always been characteristic of the Jews, it is equally true that their experiences in more recent years had tended to develop a keener sense of individualism even among the people within Palestine. National sin as an offense against God had been supplanted by a livelier feeling of personal responsibility. That Jesus had predicted the overthrow of the weakened and divided Jewish state, when portraying the consequences that would attend failure to repent, is entirely doubtful. After the disaster of the years 66–70 A.D. his disciples were able to look back upon history and see in the outcome of recent events a fulfilment of prophecies that Jesus was imagined to have uttered against the nation and race that had rejected him. But this method of reading his mind is open to peculiar dangers for the historian.

Jesus may, indeed, like others who disapproved the popular inclination toward revolution, have looked upon the rising zealot movement with real alarm. He himself was no messianic revolutionist. He would pay the tribute to Caesar and would turn the other cheek when subjected to violence by the authorities. Since God temporarily permitted the kingdom of Rome to exist in Palestine, he would yield unquestioning obedience to the present political régime. Undoubtedly he would have rejected any such proposal as that of Josephus to accept a Roman emperor in fulfilment of Jewish messianic hopes, and perhaps he would not have admonished his followers, as Rabbi Hananja of the next generation did,[1] to pray for the success of the Roman government since it alone kept the Jews

[1] *Aboth* III, 2.

from swallowing each other alive. But a calculating estimate of what would happen to the Jews of Palestine if the revolutionary movement should develop menacing proportions is not to be found in the message of Jesus. He would not fight Rome, yet he would not despair of Israel's deliverance. That would come in God's own good time.

The early establishment of the Kingdom of God forecast by Jesus was not to be accomplished through the rehabilitation of a Davidic prince raised to a royal throne in Jerusalem. This was essentially the aim of the contemporary messianic movement that had been inaugurated by Judas of Galilee and that continued to flame up from time to time among the Jews in Palestine until finally extinguished in Hadrian's radical suppression of the revolt of Bar Koziba. It was a quite different type of disaster that had been forecast by Jesus. He was an eschatologist, not a messianist. The agonies of the last days portrayed by him were modeled after the imagery of Jewish apocalyptic thinking. The new age could not come to birth until the death agonies of the old age had passed. But the transition was imminent. Not only the enemies of Israel, but all sinners among the Jews, would be overtaken by the judgment of the all-powerful and holy God.

Jesus, like John the Baptist, announced that the Kingdom of God was at hand. It behooved the Jewish people to make haste in accomplishing their repentance. Membership in the Kingdom could be insured only on the basis of invidual righteousness. No other credentials were worthy of a moment's consideration. Ancestry, inherited privilege, institutional prestige, formal piety, or any other external qualification was utterly worthless. The poor and lowly of the land, by a simple act of consecration and devotion to sincere spiritual living, as enjoined by Jesus, would in his opinion find themselves adequately prepared for the new order. Had his attitude been pushed to its logical conclusion with reference to the established religious institutions of the Jews, it might have meant the nullification of many of their oldest and most highly cherished customs. But Jesus made no such radical demands. In his opinion these Jewish inheritances were not necessarily a hindrance to preparation for membership in the Kingdom. They merely needed to be supplemented by a keener sensitiveness to the verdict of a prophetic conscience as an aid to the realization of a more worthy righteousness. The remedial measures proposed by him looked toward the purification and enrichment of the spiritual life, not toward the overthrow of contemporary Judaism. The advent of the Kingdom would mean the consummation of the Jewish religion, not its abolition.

IV

Pictures of impending doom were, after all, only a familiar type of homiletical technique which prophets of reform were accustomed to employ in the hope of effecting repentance. One might easily give disproportionate emphasis to the denunciatory note in a prophet's message. There is a more constructive and practical side to his work. By his vivid warnings of disaster and his violent condemnation of sinners he aimed to transform the character of his hearers. He might talk much of the future, yet at the same time he was engaged in a sincere endeavor to increase righteousness in the present. Jesus sought very earnestly to impress upon his audiences the necessity and opportunity for better living here and now. His message may be said to center in one all-important issue: How could a Jew of Palestine in the age of Tiberius be truly religious?

For every Jewish teacher the very cornerstone of right living was conformity to the will of God. This ideal was central in the message of Jesus, as it was in the teaching of the scribes and had been in the preaching of the ancient prophets. But to realize the will of God implied effort in establishing more perfect accord between the human and the divine. Both God and man participated actively in these relations. Each expected something very definite of the other. One might even say that each was obligated to the other by bonds that could not be broken. While no Jew might talk of God's duties to men as debts which the Almighty could not escape, the Jewish people lived constantly under the firm conviction that God could be implicitly depended upon to deal justly with men. Although Jesus never expounded any formal theology defining the character or attributes of God, he was never hazy as to what one had a right to expect of the Heavenly Father.

The Jews at the moment might have seemed helpless under the domination of Rome, but Jesus did not believe that they had been abandoned by the divine love and care. He took up a long familiar conception of God as father of his people, and encouraged his hearers to fall back upon it individually in their yearning for assurance of divine protection. In fact the whole range of kindly human emotions, which Jesus and his friends experienced in relation with one another, furnished the happy imagery in which he delighted to depict the attitude of God toward mankind. His love extended even to the ungodly. Apparently Jesus never imagined that love of the Heavenly Father was to be won in any other way than by simply entering freely into fellowship with the great divine parent, who was more ready to commune with his children than they were to trust him. Perhaps it would be a misleading terminology to say that Jesus *taught* these things *about* God. The real fact is that in his own living, and in the life which he encouraged his contemporaries to adopt, the belief in a loving heavenly father was most clearly and unmistakably envisaged.

While mercy, love, watchfulness, and tender care were properly to be expected of God, Jesus had other moods in which he disclosed a range of feeling reflecting a firm conviction that the Deity was capable of jealousy, anger, and even vindictiveness. God was wrathful with sinners, even though he permitted his rain to fall and his sun to shine on the good and evil alike. In the judgment day he would punish the wicked without mercy, and separate the sheep from the goats in his relentless determination to destroy sinners. These conceptions had been an integral part of the characteristic sermonic imagery of many an ancient Hebrew prophet, and however much later Christians might desire to mollify the rigorous character of this aspect of Jewish thinking, we may not without undue violence eliminate it from the actual teaching of Jesus. His friendly, loving, and companionable God of immediate daily experience was also the enthroned dignitary of Jewish history, who in his majesty and power is the implacable enemy of all sinners whom ultimately he will eternally destroy.

On its more formal side, Jesus had inherited his teaching about God from his Hebrew ancestors. But one may suspect that on its practical side the varied contacts of his own life may have played an important part in the shaping of his attitudes and feelings. His personal experiences in the home at Nazareth cannot have been without their effect. During the years of his early manhood, while supporting his widowed mother and his younger brothers and sisters, he had given generously of his energies and time for the benefit of others. And one may easily imagine contacts in the neighboring city of Sepphoris that will have heightened his appreciation of human life quite beyond the bounds of Judaism. Every experience that brought to him a broadening of sympathy and interest enlarged and enriched the character of that ideal life which he ascribed to the Deity. Because Jesus loved men and gave himself without reserve to their service he talked much of the Heavenly Father who was the embodiment of mercy, solicitude, and redeeming love for his children.

Another element in the content of Jesus' religious message pertained more particularly to the way in which it was necessary for man to live in order to secure membership in the Kingdom of God. A new age was at hand, and the treasures of the present world to which people now clung would presently be found utterly worthless. The quest for economic satisfaction, for social prestige, for dominion and power, was directed toward goals that would not endure. Even the ties of family and kindred would be dissolved in the age to come. In that day there would be no marriage, no divorce, no birth, no death, no parental obligations, and none of the lesser loyalties that marked the imperfect conditions of the present life. Family relations, civic activities, and political interests were characteristic of the kingdom of this world. In the age to come, when the will of God would be effective to control all actions from the least to the greatest, the new society would be miraculously reconstructed simply and solely around God himself.

The worthlessness of the present social order made it both fitting and desirable that man in his religious struggle should gladly renounce the material world. Its possessions, its ambitions, its pleasures, its pursuits, and its rewards were, to the thoroughly religious person, matters of indifference. He was preparing himself for life in a new age where none of these things would find any recognized valuation. Not only were they worthless in the age to come, but to engross one's self with them at the present moment constituted a dangerous hindrance to the attainment of a type of life suitable for membership in the Kingdom. It certainly would profit a man nothing if he gained this whole world and at the same time lost his own soul. Jesus insisted upon the necessity of complete freedom from bondage to the things of this world for one who would engage wholeheartedly in the pursuit of an ideal of righteousness that would fit one for life in the new age.

[434]

Yet the renunciation demanded by Jesus certainly was not of the morbid, ascetic type. He and his followers enjoyed God's sunshine, they delighted in the fields and the flowers, they saw the goodness of the Almighty displayed all about them, and they regarded it as entirely proper to live happily and joyfully at the present moment. They were not given to long-worded prayers, to periods of protracted fasting, nor to other forms of physical self-discipline. On the contrary, they so conducted themselves as to gain, whether they wished it or not, a reputation for friendliness with sinners, even with gluttons and winebibbers. They trusted implicitly to God to provide them their daily necessities. The Heavenly Father knew that men had need of these things and in his kindness had bestowed abundant temporal blessings upon his children. But when these gifts were made the chief end of existence, then the good became the enemy of the best. That which belonged to a kingdom soon to pass away should not be the dominant concern of persons preparing themselves for membership in the Kingdom of Heaven.

What, on its more positive side, was the course of conduct that Jesus prescribed for men in the interim while awaiting the catastrophic intervention of God to set up the Kingdom? The answer might be given in a single sentence. They should now exemplify the very same manner of life that would characterize them in the new age. If they were then to be as free from sin as is God himself, it should be their ideal now to be perfect as the Father in heaven is perfect. Purity was the first essential of true religion. This meant not simply rectitude in action but a still more fundamental purity of purpose and motive. Genuine righteousness was an affair of the heart. From this fountain alone would spring the waters of a worthy life, even as a good tree bore its own good fruit. No righteousness was real unless inspired by holy motives brought to fruition in conduct for the service of God and one's fellowmen.

The pure life was of necessity the active life. This was particularly true under the present conditions where Jesus was busily engaged in his task of prophetic preacher. While his sense of obligation to God was uppermost in thought, the immediate goal of his endeavor was to stimulate his hearers to make real for themselves at the moment genuine religious living. In so far as he and his associates were successful in this effort, they were virtually setting up the Kingdom in proleptic fashion. In the fellowship of Jesus and his disciples with one another and with the Heavenly Father, the Kingdom was being forced into the world before its time—it was being taken by violence (Matt. 11:12; Luke 16:16). In later times Christians found it convenient to pass more lightly over the expectation of an early end of the present world and to fix upon the ideals of Jesus for human conduct as evidence of the Kingdom's realization in his own lifetime. This procedure, although only half true to his point of view, was not a serious perversion of his message. At least he had assumed that the kind of life appropriate for himself and his disciples at the moment in the presence of their Palestinian kinsmen was essentially the same in its inward aspects as the manner of life toward which they looked forward under the new conditions of the coming Kingdom.

Within recent years some interpreters of Jesus have insisted that he offered only provisional instructions applicable simply to the brief intervening days between the wretched present and the glorious future age. To use the customary expression, he preached merely an "interim" ethics. It might seem logical that one who expected the end of the present order at an early date would have but slight concern with life in a present society and therefore would advocate ideals meant to have only temporary validity. But to assume that Jesus was of this state of mind is to lose sight of the farther goal on which his eyes were fixed. He was not supremely interested in teaching men how to accommodate themselves, even temporarily, to existing conditions. At the present moment they were preparing for membership in the society of the new day. They were already living for the future.

Membership in the Kingdom was to be on a strictly moral and spiritual basis. The present was a time for preparation, and one who did not come into genuine fellowship with God now would have no hope of happy admission into the divine presence when the Kingdom was finally established. Jesus did not advocate one type of religious living appropriate to the present as a mere preparation for the future, and portray a different type to characterize the age to come. Conditions then, it is true, would be quite different. In the new age all sin would be banished and all temptations removed. There would be no further need for repentance and strenuous endeavor in the quest for true righteousness. Perfection in all things would at last be realized.

But so far as the actual quality of the new life was concerned, expressed in terms of its attitudes, its motives, its ideals, and its sincerities, it was the same that Jesus would require now of those who strive to do the will of God. Jesus taught no "interim" ethics. He demanded a preparatory discipline in the present measured by ideals that were no whit below the standards of perfection to prevail in the coming Kingdom.

As a matter of fact, Jesus inculcated ideals that were practically impossible of literal realization in the present. Perhaps he hardly expected more than a sincere effort on the part of his hearers to strive toward the unattainable goal. Not until the more favorable conditions of living that would accompany the establishment of the Kingdom had been actually experienced could one really possess the faith that would remove a mountain, or literally love one's neighbor as one's self, or be truly perfect as God was perfect. Yet one to be accounted worthy of the Kingdom must strive now, however impossible of success the effort might be, to emulate the standards of spiritual life to be maintained in the future by all those who hoped to dwell in the very presence of Deity when the Kingdom had become a fully established fact.

Jesus had no intention of elaborating a system of ethical precepts specifically designed either temporarily or permanently for the present world-order. If later generations of disciples found that his ideals for life in the new age were in any measure applicable to a world where the old order still endured, that was their fortunate discovery. Less keen in spiritual insight than he had been, and possessed of less creative moral energy, they found it exceedingly helpful to reduce his message to a body of rules so phrased and limited as to be literally applicable to present conditions. He had allowed for no exceptions, since none would be permissible in the future state of perfection on which his attention was centered. But they were more readily satisfied to be men of the present and to seek in the past norms for the regulation of conduct. They were impelled, therefore, to make his teaching applicable to their specific problems and to restate it in such fashion as to bring it within the limits of what they might reasonably be expected to accomplish. If he were to be accepted as a practical legislator on such matters as divorce, they must supplement his outright denial of its propriety by adding the prudential phrase "except for fornication" (Matt. 5:32; 19:9). In this way Christian teachers created a new scribism that was of immense practical service to themselves and their fellows, even though its temper accorded no better with Jesus' own sense of the value of creative spiritual living than had the Pharisaic scribism of his own day.

Jesus proclaimed that the good life was the perfect life. He was no champion of either mediocrity or moderation in spiritual affairs. No limit was to be set either to the ideal or to the effort necessary for worthy religious living. One must stand ready to pluck out an eye or cut off a hand in order to attain to the Kingdom. Poverty, hunger, affliction, and persecution, when incurred in the pursuit of this high goal, were to be accounted blessings. Membership in the Kingdom was the pearl of great price to which no other possession was comparable in value. He who would do the will of God acceptably must stand ready to sacrifice all else, even life itself, in his pursuit of the heavenly treasure. And what Jesus demanded of others he himself was ready to perform. His own loyalty to the ideals that he preached carried the prophet from his carpenter's home in Nazareth to Christendom's cross on the Golgotha hill.

INDEX

Abraham, 24

Acts, 52, 65, 72, 78; as history, 81; references to Jesus, 80

Alexander Jannaeus, 202

Alexander the Great, 118, 129, 350

Alexandria, university of, 156

'Am ha-'aretz, 139, 266, 312

Amos, 327

Ananias of Damascus as advocate of Christianity, 78

Ancient biographies of Jesus, 7

Andrew, 288

Antioch, in Syria, 403

Antiochus IV, persecutions of, 231

Apocalyptic: Christian, 85; Jewish, 75, 230 ff.; of Jesus, 420 ff.

Apocalyptic prophets, Jewish, 233

Apocalypticism of John the Baptist, 239 ff.

Apocryphal gospels, 8; Bartholomew, 45; Ebionites, 45; Egyptians, 45; Hebrews, 45, 46; Peter, 45, Thomas, 45; variant materials of, 51; worth of, 71

Apollo, 347

Apollos: advocate of Christianity, 78; of Alexandria, 215

Apologetic concerning Jesus' childhood, 185

Apostles, 290

Apostles' Creed, 5

Apostolic authorship, interest in, 63

Aquila as advocate of Christianity, 78

Arabia, 116

Aramaic, 155, 399 ff., 405

Archelaus, 121, 175, 181

Aretas of Arabia, 203

Asklepios, 347 ff.; savior of world, 349

Assyrians, 117

Athens, university of, 156

Augustus, 121, 181

Bacchus, 349

Bannus, 145, 207, 265, 292

Baptism, 13, 106, 412; meaning of, to Christians, 255; meaning of, to Jesus, 256 f.; significance of, 43

Baptism of Jesus, 47 f., 75, 223, 224, 225, 344

Barabbas, 324

Bar Koziba, 427

Barnabas, 69, 82; as advocate of Christianity, 78

Beatitudes, 27

Beelzebub, 96

Bethany, 269, 270, 273, 275

Betharamatha, 204

Bethesda, pool of, 37, 41

[443]

INDEX

INDEX

Jerusalem, 20, 69, 82, 84, 125, 127, 142, 150, 204, 269, 270, 271, 274, 275, 278, 279, 298, 318, 402, 403, 404, 427; synagogue in, 131 f.

Jerusalem church, pillars of, 83

Jesus: actual itinerary of, 276 ff.; allegiance to, 329 ff.; ancient biographies of, 7; apocalyptic of, 420 ff.; appearance to James, 49, 165; appearance to Saul of Tarsus, 165; appearances of, 83; apprehension of, 322; as 'Am ha-'aretz, 198; as carpenter, 205; as controversialist, 96; as eschatologist, 427; as healer, 355 f.; as hero, 99, 345; as itinerant preacher, 267 ff.; as Messiah, 76, 333, 334, 344, 372, 373, 374; as moral force, 417; as preacher, 244; as prophet, 1, 95, 246 ff., 341 ff.; as redeemer, 344; as reformer, 145, 160, 207, 357; as reformer, methods of, 266 ff.; as savior, 165; as savior in gentile thought, 168; as sermonizer, 410 ff.; as servant of humanity, 385; as son of God, 361; as Son of Man, 363 f., 374; as teacher, 27, 33, 42, 45, 96, 99 f., 208, 359, 388 f., 405, 406, 409; attitude of followers, 295 ff.; attitude toward institutional religion, 314 ff.; attitude toward John, 242; attitude toward Pharisees, 305; attitude toward Rome, 208, 211; attitude toward supernatural, 357 ff.; attitudes toward, 110 f.; authority of, 331 ff.; baptism of, 47 f., 75, 223, 224, 225, 253, 254, 344; basis of disciples' attachment to, 294; birth and childhood, 24 ff., 54; birth of, 166; birth of, at Bethlehem, 25, birthplace, 172; bread of life, 36; brothers of, as missionaries, 190; childhood of, 161; climax of Jewish hostility to, 319; companions of, 82; complexity of reported teaching, 405 f.; conception of his mission, 375 f.; conditions at home, 190; crucifixion of, 37, 84; date of birth, 178 ff.; Davidic descent of, 163, 166; death of, 282 ff., 403; development of, 160; divine descent of, 163; divine wisdom of, 335, 336; endowment by Holy Spirit, 48; evolution of tradition concerning, 87; eschatological hopes of, 243 f., 419 ff.; family of, 189; fear of assassination, 321; form of teaching, 410 f.; founder of new religion, 3, 13, 29, 39, 45, 95; genealogy of, 24, 162; generation by Holy Spirit, 169 f.; glory of, 41; home life of, 160, 161 f., 188; hostility to scribes, 302; idea of God, 431 ff.; ideals of human conduct, 436 ff., 440 f.; incarnation of, 335; incarnation of pre-existent divinity, 39; influence of John the Baptist, 227; influence of prophets on,

INDEX

Jewish education, 156; religious content of, 192, 193 ff.; traditions of scribes, 195

Jewish elementary schools, 196

Jewish eschatology, 230 ff.

Jewish hopes for deliverance, 228

Jewish hostility to Jesus, climax of, 319

Jewish life in Palestine, 116

Jewish nation, overthrow by Rome, 233

Jewish reformers, 265

Jewish religious interest, 346

Jewish scriptures, 8

Jewish society, 126; complexity of, 129

Jews, 80, 117 ff.; interest in Jesus, 1; occupations of, 126; of the Dispersion, 112, 125, 131 ff., 215; political interest of, 157; revolutionary tendencies of, 144

Jews and Christians, antagonism between, 53

Johanninism, 215

John, 287, 288, 292

John and James, martyrdom of, 69

John, Gospel of, 34, 35 ff., 66, 183; attitude toward John the Baptist, 225; authorship of, 66, 68, 69; date of, 76; itinerary of Jesus, 273 ff.; miracles of Jesus, 354; omissions of, 34; originality of, 38, 44; portrait of Jesus, 34; religio-philosophical imagery, 70; supplements, 38; unity of, 68

John, son of Zebedee, 66, 69

John the Baptist, 24, 25 f., 35, 40, 90, 145, 161, 180, 288, 419, 428; as Elijah *redivivus*, 222; as official herald, 225 f.; attitude of Christians toward, 220, 226; disciples of, 214, 292; first Christian believer, 225; in Christian tradition, 216 ff.; influence of, on Jesus, 227; political significance of, 237, 240; preaching of, 236 f.

Jonah, 220

Joppa, 116

Jordan, 117, 120, 275

Joseph, 24, 189

Joseph, brother of Jesus, 189

Josephus, 125, 135, 156, 167, 176, 178, 191, 193, 196, 204, 209, 237, 264 n., 266, 292, 322, 402, 426

Joshua. *See* Jesus

Judah, 117, 229

Judah, brother of Jesus, 189

Judaism: Christian polemic against, 411; hostility of, 14; institutions of, 146 ff.; rival factions in, 124

Judaism and Christianity, conflict between, 302 f.

Judas of Galilee, 143, 204, 209, 228, 240, 263 n., 265, 427

Judas Iscariot, 21, 270, 292, 322

Judea, 37, 117, 175, 228, 269, 274, 277, 278, 279, 323
Judgment in later Christian tradition, 220

King of Israel, 40
Kingdom of David, 211
Kingdom of God, 12, 17, 35, 42, 43, 80, 95, 108, 118, 124, 129, 133, 134, 211, 223, 386, 422, 425, 427, 433; admission to, 36; date of, 428; mystery of, 14; preparation for, 428, 433 ff., 438 f.; revised ideas of, 371
Kingdom of Heaven, 244; meaning of, 419

Lake of Galilee, 116
Lamb of God, 40
Last Supper, 275
Law, the, 155, 345
Lazarus, 37, 275
Levites, 148
Levitical tithes, 308
Lives of Jesus, 8, 45, 64; new types of, 23
Logia, 93, 95, 162, 394
Logos, 4, 36
Lord, 2
Lord's Prayer, 27, 412
Lord's Supper, 13, 43, 106, 280; authority of, 83; relation to Passover, 284
Luke, Gospel of, 22 ff., 62, 64, 71, 74, 162, 170, 171, 227; chronology in, 180; date of,

76; itinerary of Jesus, 271 ff.; source materials, 32
Luke-Acts, authorship of, 65

Maccabeans, 229; revolution of, 118, 134
Magdala, 128
Mark, Gospel of, 10 ff., 38, 62, 64, 69, 95, 107, 190; as continuous narrative, 98; as source of Luke, 88; as source of Matthew, 89; attitude of Christians toward John the Baptist, 221 ff.; date of, 76; harmony between Jesus and John the Baptist, 222; itinerary of Jesus, 268 ff.; miracles of Jesus, 354; priority of, 74
Mark, John, 64
Martha and Mary, home of, 271
Martyrdom, 17
Mary, 24
Mary, mother of Jesus, 169
Mary of Nazareth, 26
Matthew, apostle, 399
Matthew, Gospel of, 22 ff., 74, 162, 170, 175; chronology in, 179; date of, 76; itinerary of Jesus, 270 ff.; source materials of, 32; sources of, 68
Matthew (Levi), son of Alphaeus, 66
Mesopotamia, 117
Messiah, 2, 39, 40, 42, 75, 164; attitude of John the Baptist toward, 218 ff.
Miracles, 37, 55, 96, 246 f., 274; in Gospel of John, 41; of

INDEX

apostles, 80; of Jesus, 79, 337 f., 341, 345, 354

Missionary activity of Jews, 401

Missionary enterprise, 14, 88, 278; training of disciples for, 290; widening of, 112

Missionary preaching, 398

Modern interpretation of Jesus' teaching, 416

Moses, 40, 141, 155, 156, 246, 345, 406

Mount of Olives, 269, 270, 410

Mount Tabor, 48

Nathaniel, 288

Nazareth, 1, 18, 25, 127, 133, 204, 206, 246, 268, 271, 278, 411, 441; as birthplace of Jesus, 172; Jesus' preaching in synagogue at, 29; proximity to other Galilean centers, 199 ff.; tradition concerning, 175

Nero, 17

New Testament, 5, 45, 49; canon, 59, 60

Ninevites, 220

Old Testament, 59, 154, 168, 171, 172, 200; language of, 155

Olives, Mount of, 269, 270, 410

Oral tradition, 7; in second century, 72; of scribes, 157

Palestine, 6, 7, 25, 82, 109, 116 ff., 230, 268, 405, 426; apocalyptic restoration of, in

Book of Daniel, 232; gentile influences in, 130 ff.; Jewish life in, 116; languages in, Aramaic and Hebrew, 196 f.; population of, 125; spirit of revolution in, 142; under Tiberius, 228

Palestinian society, 201

Parables, 27, 75

Paschal sacrifice, relation to Lord's Supper, 283 ff.

Passion Week, 318; importance of, in Christian tradition, 279; in Fourth Gospel, 275; in Luke, 272; in Mark, 269

Passover, 41, 125, 150, 270, 274, 275, 280, 281, 319; date of, 150; in Luke, 272 f.

Paul, 16, 65, 69, 77, 161, 167 ff., 307 n., 399; as advocate of Christianity, 78; as miracle worker, 352; eschatology of, 86; knowledge òf Jesus, 85; letters of, 63, 72; memories of Jesus, 82 f.; on miracles and healing, 351; visions of, 86 f.

Pauline church, Ephesus, 215

Pauline correspondence, value of, 85

Pauline references to Jesus, 84

Pentecost, 142, 150, 396

Perea, 120, 142, 228, 274, 277

Perushim, 308

Peter, 20, 35, 64, 82, 287, 288, 292, 396; as advocate of Christianity, 78; preaching of, 52

INDEX

Simon, brother of Jesus, 189

Social basis of tradition, 104, 106

Social experience, test of gospel tradition, 113, 115

Solomon, 147, 220

Son of God, 4, 24, 26, 38, 40, 41, 163; meaning of, 361

Son of Man, 12, 75, 391; eschatological emphasis on, 364; in Daniel, 362 f.; in Enoch, 363; in Jewish apocalyptic, 370; interpretation of, 365; meaning of, 362; meaning to Jesus, 368 ff.

Spirit: endowment by, 43, 257 ff.; endowment of Jesus by, 259; guidance of, 87

Stephen, as advocate of Christianity, 78

Stoics, 406

Supernaturalism in Jesus' thought, 357 ff., 379

Synagogue, 152 ff.; as school, 194; in Jerusalem, 131 f.

Synoptic Jesus, 35

Synoptic problem, 94

Synoptic story, 44

Syria, 82, 116, 118

Tabernacles, 150

Taricheae, 128

Tarsus, university of, 156

Tatian (175 A.D.), 9

Teacher, among Gentiles, 406

Teaching of Jesus, 54, 74, 83, 84, 100, 296, 388 ff., 418 ff.;

in Hebrews, 50; its preservation, 394 ff.

Temple at Jerusalem, 147 ff.; destruction of (70 A.D.), 74, 75, 231; prestige of, 152; services at, 148; support of, 151

Temptation of Jesus, 253, 261 ff.; real meaning of, 263 f.

Theophilus, 23, 26, 28, 81, 88

Theudas, 264 n.

Tiberius, 128, 203, 205

Tiberius Caesar, 180, 227

Titus, 402

Trachonitis, 120

Tradition: pre-Markan, 77; social basis of, 104, 106

Twelve, the, 13, 20, 35, 70, 269, 289, 291, 294

Two-source hypothesis, 94

Tyre and Sidon, 268 f.

Varus, 323

Vespasian, 402

Virgin Birth, 25 f., 170

Virgin Mary, 5

Writings, 155

Written tradition, 64, 343

Word, 36

Zadokites, 139, 207, 291, 396; ideals of, 140

Zealots, 142, 240, 426

Zebedee, sons of, 288

Zerubbabel, the Servant of Jehovah, 229